A Quick Index to Twenty Essential Questions

BUILDING TYPE BASICS FOR

places of worship

BUILDING TYPE BASICS FOR

places of worship

Stephen A. Kliment, Series Founder and Editor

NICHOLAS W. ROBERTS
Leo A Daly

WILEY

JOHN WILEY & SONS, INC.

Copyright © 2004 by John Wiley & Sons, Inc. All rights reserved

Published by John Wiley & Sons, Inc., Hoboken, New Jersey
Published simultaneously in Canada

For general information on our other products and services or for technical support, please contact our Customer Care Department within the United States at (800) 762-2974, outside the United States at (317) 572-3993 or fax (317) 572-4002.

Wiley also publishes its books in a variety of electronic formats. Some content that appears in print may not be available in electronic books.

Library of Congress Cataloging-in-Publication Data:
Roberts, Nicholas W.
  Building type basics for places of worship / by Nicholas W. Roberts.
     p. cm.—(Building type basics)
  Includes bibliographical references and index.
  ISBN 0-471-22568-1 (cloth)
  1. Religious facilities—Planning. 2. Church architecture—Designs and plans. I. Title. II. Building type basics series.
  BL580.R63 2004
  726—dc22
                                        2003027625
Printed in the United States of America
10 9 8 7 6 5 4 3 2 1

CONTENTS

CONTENTS

PREFACE

STEPHEN A. KLIMENT *Series Founder and Editor*

More than in perhaps any other building type, decision making in the design and construction of a space for worship is immensely complex, whether the space is large or small. Except for some religious denominations in which architect selection and design approvals are dictated from the top down, the architecture of worship is shaped by many groups and advisory committees and boards, each of which represents a particular focus or constituency. These groups typically include a worship committee, which watches over the design of the space itself; a music committee; a fine arts and furnishings committee; a religious education committee; a fellowship committee, which deals with support space (parish hall, meeting rooms, kitchens, etc.); a development committee, charged with raising funds; as well as an architect selection committee and a building oversight committee, which consolidates all the information and acts as the main point of contact with the design and construction team.

None of this makes the planning and execution of a place of worship a simple task for the architect, the client, the consultants, or the contractor. Moreover, the complexity must be solved to the satisfaction not only of today's congregation and clergy but also of those still to come.

Despite the challenges, however, spaces for worship are in many ways the most fulfilling to create of any building type. They provide landmark buildings for public assembly, often using expressive structures and high-quality materials. They combine a concern for ritual and ceremony with careful acoustic and lighting design, and their architecture incorporates artwork and liturgical furnishings.

Today the architecture of worship has "come to a crossroads," wrote Nancy Caver of Religious News Services in the *Washington Post* (9 May 2001). "What used to be employed as a tool to draw souls *upward* is being used increasingly as a means to draw souls *in*." While architects struggle to keep *form* in worship spaces, building committees and pastors also demand *function*, argues Caver.

That tension is the reason for this book. Demand for worship spaces has continued to climb, prompted by demographics (an increasingly aging population tends to attend services at a higher rate than other age groups). Other drivers, according to Jerry Guerra, writing in *The Zweig Letter*, include the need of religious places to provide more supporting benefits, such as recreation and counseling; immigration, which in parts of the United States such as the Northeast and Southwest is prompting a need for new construction; a shortage of clergy, which calls for larger facilities that in turn require fewer clergy; and consolidation accompanied by renovation of parishes with fewer worshipers.

Author Nicholas Roberts, whose credentials include a stint as project manager at Leo A Daly for the Roman Catholic Cathedral of Our Lady of the Angels, Los Angeles, completed in 2002, provides answers to the questions and concerns that must be resolved in those first crucial stages of a project if the remaining stages are to proceed with proper regard for quality, budget, and schedule.

Confronting in particular those matters of form, light, and sound that distinguish spaces for worship from most other types, Roberts embraces the world's major religions and the mosques, synagogues, churches, and temples in which they worship, pointing out their unique planning and design concerns.

Places of Worship, like the other volumes in the Wiley "Building Type Basics" series, is not a lavish coffee table book heavy on color photography (although readers will find some brilliant examples in the color section) but weak on usable content. Instead, it contains hands-on information that architects, engineers, consultants, and governing boards of religious denominations require in their work, especially in the critical early phases of a project. Students at schools of architecture, engineering, planning, urban design, and landscape architecture will also find this book useful, as a kind of Cliffs Notes to get a head start on an assigned studio problem.

Following the format of the other volumes in the series, *Places of Worship* is tightly organized for ease of use. The text responds to a set of twenty questions most commonly asked about a building type in the early phases of its design. The twenty questions address predesign (programming) guidelines, details of the project delivery process, design concerns unique to the building type, site planning, codes and ADA matters, energy and environmental challenges, engineering systems, lighting and acoustic pointers, signs and wayfinding, preservation and modernization issues, and cost and feasibility factors. For a listing of the twenty questions, see the inside of the front and back covers of this book. Be sure to use this list also as an index.

I hope you find this volume both helpful and inspiring.

ACKNOWLEDGMENTS

I am very grateful to those who provided the inspiration for Chapter 1: The Roman Catholic Archdiocese of Los Angeles, which selected Leo A Daly as executive architect for the Cathedral of Our Lady of the Angels; Dr. Douglas Cremer, my colleague at Woodbury University, with whom I taught a course on the nature of worship space; and Hayden Salter, with whom I gave a lecture about the sacred in contemporary architecture. Rafael Moneo's vision of the sacred in the language of modern architecture has been a continuing inspiration for this book.

Thanks to all those who contributed to this book, especially to Ellen Kuch for her research and help with the text and illustrations, Janet Stephenson and Andy Howard of Arup for coordinating the engineering chapters, Dennis Paoletti and Francis Krahe for their authoritative contributions, Marti Kyrk for his drawings, Lynn Dobson and his staff for help with Chapter 14, Christy McEvoy for her splendid contribution to Chapter 16, Nick Butcher of Davis Langdon Adamson and John Mauck of O'Connor Construction Management for their help with Chapter 19, and to Gretchen Willison for her advice on Chapter 20. Dick Vosko has been an invaluable source of help and wisdom throughout this project.

A special thanks to Stephen Kliment for his guidance and support, and to my wife, Cory Buckner, whose help and encouragement made this book possible.

Dennis Paoletti would like to acknowledge Ewart "Red" Wetherill for his passion and professionalism, exemplified in his approach to acoustical consulting on worship spaces, and William J. (Bill) Cavanaugh for his constant support and encouragement.

BUILDING TYPE BASICS FOR

places of worship

CHAPTER 1

THE SIGNIFICANCE AND QUALITIES OF WORSHIP SPACES

THE SIGNIFICANCE OF THE BUILDING PROJECT

As the nineteenth-century church architect Augustus Welby Pugin said at the height of the Oxford Movement, the design and construction of spaces for worship is the greatest building work that people can do. Religious buildings are external and visible symbols of the faith of a community. Whether a parish church by the village green, a neighborhood synagogue, or a metropolitan mosque at the hub of a great city, a worship space translates a system of belief into built form and announces to the world the existence of a religious community and its history, traditions, and aspirations.

Building a worship space is not only a construction project, it is a journey of faith. From the first discussions among members of the congregation to formulate needs, to the evaluation of different design strategies, the outreach to the community to raise funds, and the commitment of the construction crews, building a worship space is a shared experience that deepens and strengthens the sense of community and reaffirms the faith of those who contribute. For an architect, it is a responsibility that elevates the meaning of professionalism to a new plane: Worship spaces will stand as landmarks for years to come, they play a central role in the life of the community, and they are built through the sacrifice and devotion of congregants.

WORSHIP

Since earliest times, human beings have gathered together to show reverence to a supernatural or divine power. The places where this worship takes place are, as Mircea Eliade says, breaks in the homogeneity of the profane world, where believers make contact with the divine. "Here in the sacred enclosure, communication with the gods is made possible" (Eliade 1987, p. 26). Through rituals of prayer, sacrifice, offering, and praise, the faithful give thanks, seek help, and beg forgiveness for their transgressions. In the worship space, the most moving rites of passage in human life are celebrated in the presence of the divine: birth, coming of age, marriage, and the burial of the dead. Worship spaces are places of commitment, where individuals commit to a faith and join a community, where couples commit to one another, and where a family and the wider family of the church commit to the upbringing of a child.

Worship spaces also house the gathering of the faithful, reaffirming the identity of the congregation as a community of faith. The people come together for worship, teaching, and fellowship in the presence of their god. In many religions, the shape

> The greatest privilege possessed by man is to be allowed, while on earth, to contribute to the glory of God: a man who builds a church draws down a blessing on himself both for this life and for that of the world to come, and likewise imparts under God the means of every blessing to his fellow creatures
>
> *(Pugin 1841, p. 50)*

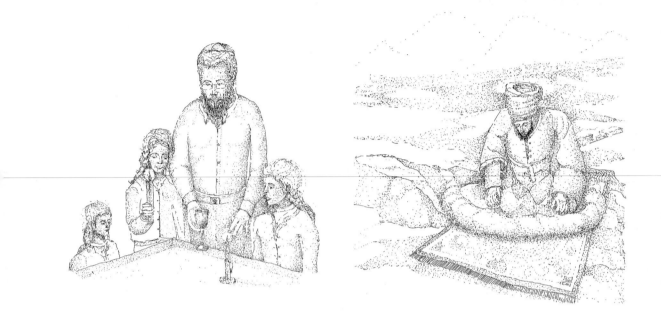

▲ Here is a sacred space defined by time and the presence of ritual objects. As the sun goes down on Friday evening, Jewish families accept the Shabbat into their homes, turning dining rooms and living rooms into sacred spaces by the lighting of candles, breaking of bread, and sharing of wine.

◥ For the Muslim, the prayer mat defines a sacred space, which does not have to be in a building; it can be on open ground or on a crowded street. The muezzin's call to prayer defines the worship space as a period in time.

of the worship space reaffirms the identity of the community gathered around a ritual focus. Members of the congregation see and hear one another in prayer and song. The Greek word for "church" is *ecclesia,* literally "those who are summoned" (*Oxford English Dictionary* 1970), and the worship space is indeed *domus ecclesiae,* the house of those who are summoned.

Worship spaces are not necessarily architectural. They may be defined by time, by ritual, or by the presence of sacred objects. For the early Christians, Jesus was present wherever two or three gathered together in his name (Matthew 18:20). Until Constantine's acceptance of Christianity in 313, when it grew from an outlaw religion to become the official religion of the Roman Empire, Christian services were frequently held in houses and even in caves. As Clement of Alexan-

dria said in the second century C.E.: "It is not a place that is called church, nor a house made of stones and earth, it is the holy assembly of those that live in righteousness" (quoted in Giles 2000, p. 34).

When Moses led the Israelites out of Egypt, their place of worship was defined by the presence of the Ark of the Covenant. Following the destruction of the second Temple by the Romans in 70 C.E. and the dispersal of Jews across the globe, the sacred spaces of Judaism were defined by the presence of the Torah and by rituals of approach and purification. It was the study of the Torah that defined communities of faith. The temple was within each faithful Jew. For the Jews, the sanctuary defined as a period of time (the Shabbat and the High Holy Days) endured, even though the sanctuary defined spatially (the Temple) was destroyed.

THE ARCHITECTURAL FEATURES OF WORSHIP SPACES
The Definition of the Sacred Precinct

The sacred space is clearly defined and set apart from the everyday by an enclosure that denotes the space as consecrated ground. The porosity of the enclosure varies from faith to faith and may be affected as much by issues of security as by religious exclusivity. For example, the inclusive Episcopal churches may have a purely symbolic enclosure, whereas some exclusive congregations such as the Church of Jesus Christ of Latter-day Saints firmly exclude nonmembers from the liturgical space.

Architecture Experienced as a Journey

The architecture of some places of worship leads the visitor on a journey or pilgrimage from the everyday world of the street to the most sacred space. The journey, sometimes made more significant by physical difficulties, emphasizes the separation from the profane world and allows time for contemplation. Architecturally, the route often leads uphill and culminates in a view back toward the point of departure. In the Christian tradition, the ritual procession from the outside world, passing the water of the font and culminating at the altar, repeats the journey that each member of the church makes, from birth, through baptism, and ultimately, to ascent into heaven.

Layering of Space

On the journey from the profane world to the most sacred space, the visitor crosses a series of thresholds that demarcate layers of space.

▲ ▼ *At the (seventeenth century, rebuilt 1945) Meiji Shrine in Tokyo, the faithful wash hands and mouth before penetrating the outer gateway, or Tori. They ascend through the outer courtyard to the second and third gateways before reaching the prayer sanctuary.*

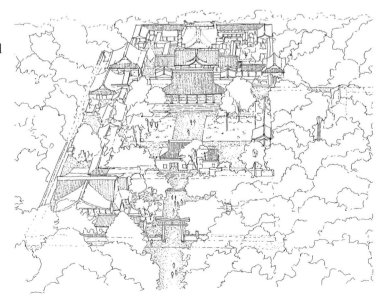

3

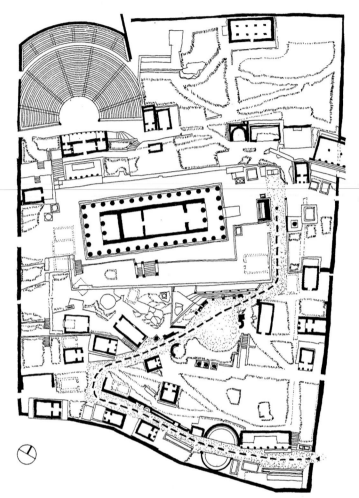

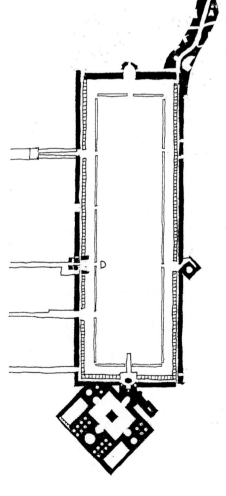

◀ For Greek pilgrims in the fifth century B.C.E., the journey to the shrine of Apollo at Delphi climbed up the foothills of Mount Parnassus toward the twin peaks of the Phaidriades, below which sits the temple of Apollo. Pilgrims passed the Castalian Spring, the site for ritual bathing, before proceeding on to the sanctuary. Inside the sanctuary enclosure, the sacred way winds up the hill, past the treasuries housing the offerings of the Greek city-states, to the altar in front of the temple of Apollo where the pilgrims have a panorama of the valley below.

▶ The Shah Mosque, Isfahan, Iran, built by Shah Abbas from 1612 to 1638, is entered from the Maidan-i-Shah, a public plaza that mediates between the profane maze of the bazaar and the sacred space of the mosque. After the visitor steps over a threshold, a 45-degree shift reorients the axis of the building toward Mecca and leads into the courtyard with a pool for ritual washing.

▶ *At Gunnar Asplund's Woodland Crematorium, 1935–1940, outside Stockholm, Sweden, the journey leads up slightly rising ground to a perpendicular axis, marked with a monumental cross. On one side is the entry to the crematorium, and on the top of rising ground opposite, a grove of trees symbolizes the souls of the departed.*

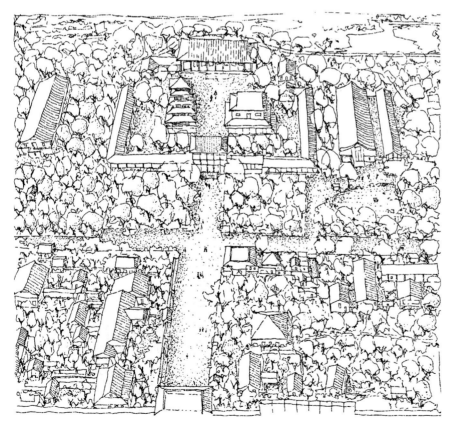

◀ *At the Temple of Horyuji, near Nara, begun in 607 C.E., one of the oldest Buddhist temples in Japan, the pilgrim walks up the long tree-lined avenue to the first portico, through a courtyard to the second gateway with a stop for ritual washing, then up the steps to the final gateway leading into the courtyard with the pagoda and prayer hall.*

▲ ▶ In twelfth-century Europe, the symbolic language of church architecture shifted from one of representation—for example, at the early Christian basilica of San Vitale, Ravenna, Italy, to an abstract language of form and light such as that in the choir of Basilique de Saint-Denis, Paris.

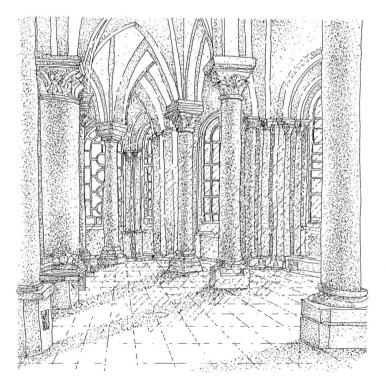

Light as Metaphor and Architectural Element

Light is used in the design of worship space as a metaphor for the Holy Spirit, for enlightenment, and for learning. Light was the Word of God that shone in the darkness (John 1:1–9). For St. Augustine, light was a metaphor for divine illumination and intellectual perception (von Simson 1988, p. 52).

For the twelfth-century medieval theologians, light was the creative principle in all things, the author of visibility, the generator of nourishment and growth, by which all things were made (von Simson 1988, p. 52).

Light is also used as an architectural device to reinforce the journey from the profane world to the most sacred space. From the relatively subdued level of light at the entry of the Cathedral of Our Lady of the Angels in Los Angeles, increasing illumination accompanies the journey toward the nave. The altar area is flooded with light from the cross window (see color plates 1, 3).

The use of natural light allows the worship space to reflect the cycles of sunrise and sunset, the movement of the sun across the sky, and the changes in the angle of the light with the time of year. East-facing windows bring in the rising sun, west-facing glass admits the warm colors of afternoon light, and the changing angles of the sunlight reflect the seasons.

At Steven Holl's St. Ignatius Church in Seattle, Washington, the use of color on the plaster baffles, coupled with colored glass, invests each of the spaces with its own color. In Holl's words, each of the liturgical spaces becomes a bottle of light (see color plate 5).

◀ As an architectural device, natural light can be used to highlight materials and colors. At the Convent of La Tourette, Eveaux, France, 1957–1960, Le Corbusier used the canons de lumiere, or light cannons, with the simple geometric forms and primary colors of the architectural concrete to create a dramatic and resonant space.

▲ For the Chumash of coastal California and travelers on the Camino Real, the cross on a hill overlooking the seventeenth-century Mission San Buenaventura communicated for miles around the presence of Father Junipero Serra's mission and its Catholic church.

▶ Familiar images of the saints frame the twelfth-century west portal of Chartres Cathedral in France.

Identified by Signs and Iconography

Places of worship are consecrated by ritual, by marking with a sign, and by the presence of sacred objects. They are denoted by the presence of religious symbols on the outside and inside of the space.

Inside the spaces, iconography, quotations from sacred texts, icons, and images communicate the message of the faith. Familiar images make the congregation feel at home regardless of their origin. In the Christian tradition, images in stained glass, tapestry, mosaic, and fresco portray the familiar figures of the history of the church. They tell the great stories of the faith and provide a catechism even for the illiterate.

The visibility of liturgical elements used in ritual, such as processional crosses, cups, seasonal banners and symbols, and particularly the holy book, confirm the sanctity of the space.

Rituals of Approach and Purification

In many faiths, rituals of approach and purification define worship spaces. For the Jews on the journey out of Egypt, the Old Testament described the prohibitions on certain unclean states and the washing, prayer, and sacrifice required for purification before approaching the tabernacle. In twenty-first-century Judaism, a ritual of prayer and the washing of hands prepare the faithful to welcome Shabbat into their homes. In Buddhist and Shinto temples, as well as in Islamic mosques, hands and mouth must be washed before approaching the sacred space.

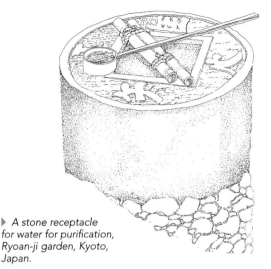

▶ A stone receptacle for water for purification, Ryoan-ji garden, Kyoto, Japan.

◀ In Islam, with its prohibition on the use of imagery, quotations from the sacred texts are executed in meticulously designed calligraphy to decorate the walls of the mosque. This geometrical pattern of tilework is based on a quotation from the Qur'an. Masjed-i-Jumi, Isfahan, Iran, thirteenth century.

▲ Detail of the stained glass windows at Chartres, France: The Anointing and The Women Finding the Sepulcher Empty, from the Passion and Resurrection window, 1150.

9

▶ *In Isfahan, Iran, the Masjid-i-Shah and the Masjid-i-Sheikh Lotfollah tower over the single-story buildings of the bazaar.*

▶▶ *At the church at Marco de Canavezes, Fornos, Oporto, Portugal, by Alvaro Siza, 1996, the scale of the door in relation to the human being unmistakably identifies this building as a place of transcendence.*

The Scale of Worship Spaces

Buildings for worship are often perceived as breaks in the homogeneity of space by their scale in relation to their surroundings. In many religious buildings, the architecture creates a landmark that affirms the identity of the faith community. Towers, domes, and spires rise out of the landscape to signify the presence of the sacred.

The scale of the building elements in relation to the human body differentiates the building from the everyday. The scale of the interior spaces, the size and weight of doors, and the exposed structural columns and beams all serve to denote the special quality of the worship space.

Sound

The reverberant sound quality created by the proportions and materials of religious buildings sets them apart from the ordinary. Sacred music, singing, chanting, the calling of the muezzin from the minaret, the ringing of bells and intoning of prayers are signifiers that characterize specific religious rituals. The change in sound quality from the cacophony of the street to the quiet garden of a *madresseh*, or the resonant silence of a baroque church, signifies entry into a sacred space.

Touch

The experience of touch identifies a sacred space: the weight of the door handle, the textures of materials on walls and seating, and the hardness of stone underfoot.

A change in temperature, such as the transition from the blazing heat of a busy city street into the cool and solitude of a church interior can also denote a sacred space.

Smell

Incense is used extensively in the Roman Catholic and Buddhist traditions as a symbol of prayers going up to the deity. In recognition of the connection between smell and memory, scented trees

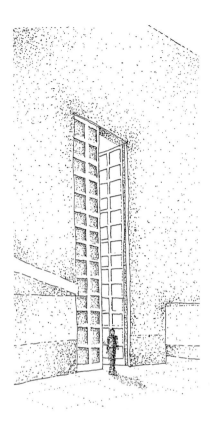

are planted in Shinto sacred compounds to identify them in the mind of the worshiper.

The Presence of Water

Water has a liturgical function in many faiths:

- It reminds Christians of their death and rebirth into the church through baptism, and it is a metaphor for Jesus Christ, the source of all life for Christians.

- Catholics use holy water to bless themselves before entering the worship space.

- In the Shinto and Buddhist faiths, worshipers wash hands and mouth before entering the worship space.

- Muslims wash hands and feet before entering the prayer hall.

- In Islam, pools of water reflect and symbolize the heavens.

The Worship Space as Image of the Cosmos

According to Mircea Eliade, the forms of all places of worship are ultimately derived from the primary experience of sacred space, the structure of the cosmos. They repeat the worshipers' myth of origin and their understanding of the structure of the universe. "For the Algonquin and Sioux, the sacred lodge, where initiations are performed, represents the universe. The roof symbolizes the dome of the sky, the floor represents the earth, the

▲ In the garden of the Madresseh Madri-i-Shah in Isfahan, Iran, the reflecting pool provides the refreshing presence of water and a reflection of the heavens.

11

▶ In this image of "Christ in the Heavenly City," from the Bible historiée of John de Papeleu (1317), note how the heavenly city is represented as a gothic cathedral with flying buttresses (von Simson 1988).

four walls the four directions of cosmic space.... The construction of the sacred lodge thus represents the cosmogony, for the lodge represents the world" (Eliade 1987, p. 46).

This cosmogony is also reflected in the archetypal form of the dwelling. For the indigenous peoples of North America and northern Asia, the dwelling itself incorporated a central post that referred to the *axis mundi,* the cosmic pillar or world tree that connects earth with heaven (Eliade 1987, p. 53). In the centralized Byzantine church, the walls represent the four horizons of the world, and a dome symbolizing the vault of heaven covers the space.

For the Christians of the Middle Ages, and in many contemporary religions, a cathedral is not merely a symbol of the presence of God but a model of the city of heaven. Its architecture reproduces the structure of the cosmos. This connection is made through mathematical ratios and primary forms in the building geometry, by the circulation route taken by the worshiper, and by the iconographic decoration.

For St. Augustine, following Pythagoras and Plato's *Timaeus,* and later for the medieval theologians, the geometry of the church reproduced the divine geometry of the cosmos, which they considered to have the same arithmetical proportions that create harmony in music. Beauty was an abstract geometrical machine, not the graphic representation of images as seen in the Romanesque church. In the Renaissance religious architecture of Alberti and Palladio we see a discipline of geometry in which musical ratios still control proportion, but man is the measure.

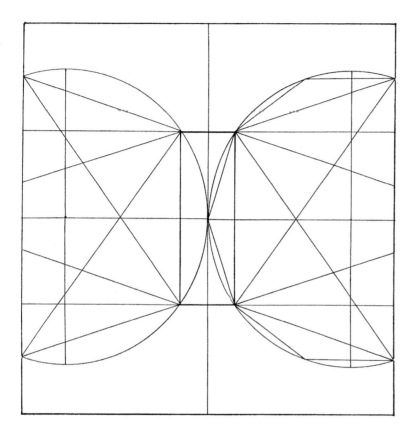

◀ *At Le Corbusier's Chapel of Notre Dame du Haut, Ronchamp, France, the geometry of the doors is an evolution of the Modulor, using pentagons that evoke the feminine and whose diagonals intersect to create the golden section of the Modulor (Evans 1995, p. 291; Le Corbusier 1957, p. 125).*

In the twentieth century, Le Corbusier's turbulent relationship with the Modulor, the proportional system he developed from the Golden Section, combined the cosmic order of the Fibonacci series and the dimensions of the human being. The use of the blue and red series in the floor paving of Notre Dame du Haut, Ronchamp, France (1950–1955), connects the transcendent geometry of the gothic cathedral and the humanist intentions of the Renaissance. Iannis Xenakis, project architect with Le Corbusier, used the Modulor as a linear series, not only to lay out the dimensions of the *ondulatoires* or window mullions at the Convent of La Tourette (1957–1960) but also to compose music (Evans 1995, p. 296).

Reference to the History of the Congregation

Rev. Richard S. Vosko reflects on the ultimate source of the sacredness of contemporary Roman Catholic churches as follows: *You cannot really build a sacred space. It becomes sacred over time—after years of celebrating Christian initiation, the Eucharist, weddings, funerals, confessions and healing. It is a space that embodies the memories and imaginations of a people. The architecture and the iconography cradle and sustain these experiences of God and that is what makes it sacred to the congregation* (Vosko 1998).

CHAPTER 2

PROJECT TEAM AND PROCESS

Building a place of worship is a journey of faith. For many reasons, it is a significant decision for the congregation:

- The building is usually built with private donations from members of the congregation and represents the religious community's largest single expenditure.

- The building expresses the congregation's worship in concrete and stone. It determines how its rituals are enacted and shapes its relationship with God, its leaders, each other, and the wider community.

- The building acts as a visible symbol of the community and its worship.

- In the case of a building renovation, the congregation must adjust to changes in a building that has become a home to generations and a landmark in the community.

THE PLAYERS

The complexity of the team for a religious project reflects the diverse functions that the building serves. In addition to the liturgy of worship, the building must often provide for the care of infants, education of children and adults, performance of sacred music, meetings of community groups, dinners, dances, weddings, and funerals.

Three groups work together to make a building: the owner, the design team, and the contractor, supported by subcontractors and consultants.

The Owner's Team

The owner generally has an advisory committee to oversee each of the functions of the institution, for example, worship, music, and child care. In addition, a building committee is formed to initiate and oversee the design and construction process.

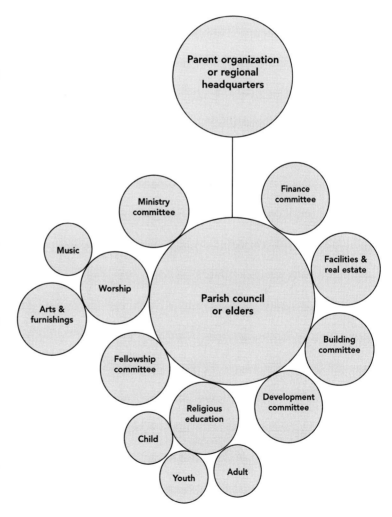

▲ Organization chart for a typical religious institution.

There are several ways of organizing a building committee:

- A relatively large building oversight committee can include representatives from the key activities within the congregation, such as liturgy, music, education, and development, or

- A core committee can manage the process but consult with the various subcommittees.

▼ Large building committee that includes representatives of other committees. In practice, a committee such as this will form an executive committee to handle day-to-day project decision making.

The exact structure will depend on the size, culture, and management style of the congregation.

Building or oversight committee

The building or oversight committee gathers and coordinates information from the advisory committees and provides a primary point of contact for the design and construction teams. For consistency, the architect and the contractor should take direction only from the building committee as the single point of responsibility.

The building committee has responsibility for setting and managing the overall project cost and schedule and balancing the project's scope and budget. During design, this committee will manage the design professionals' contracts and review requests for additional services. During construction, it reviews the contractor's schedule submittals and requests for change orders and coordinates with contractors and consultants hired directly by the owner.

The building committee is generally composed of individuals with experience in construction and development, including architects and engineers, developers, contractors, attorneys, and real estate professionals.

It typically selects one individual to act as the owner's representative, who will provide the daily contact point for the design and construction teams. This task requires a substantial commitment of time from the selected individual. If a full-time staff member or a retired member of the congregation is not available, the congregation should consider engaging a professional project manager. On larger projects this is usually essential.

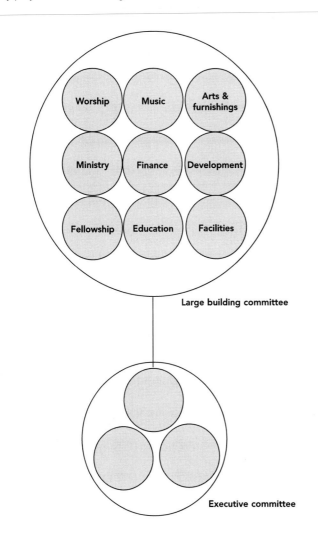

Worship · Music · Arts & furnishings

Ministry · Finance · Development

Fellowship · Education · Facilities

Large building committee

Executive committee

A professional project manager's duties include the following:

- Negotiating the design consultants' contracts
- Managing the project budgets and schedules, reviewing the design to make sure it is functional, cost-effective, and buildable
- Managing contractor bidding and selection
- Managing construction in the field, including change order negotiation, coordination of owner-furnished contracts, and advising on project closeout

Worship committee

The worship committee oversees the design of the worship space itself and coordinates with the music committee and the arts and furnishings committee. The worship committee decides on the sequence of spaces, the amount and type of seating, the layout of the seating in relation to the liturgical furnishings, the materials and finishes, and technical issues such as lighting and sound, based on the architect's and consultants' recommendations.

This committee generally includes the religious leader and other elders and may also include lead donors and senior members of the congregation.

Music committee

The music committee coordinates with the architect in regard to the size and layout of the choir, space for musicians, practice rooms, music storage, choir robing, and music staff offices. If an organ is part of the project, the music committee oversees decisions on the size and design of the instrument and frequently manages the organ builder's work. The com-

mittee also works closely with the acoustician, the audiovisual systems engineer, and the broadcast media consultant. On larger projects, an organ consultant may assist the music committee, drawing up specifications and preparing bid documents for the organ.

Arts and furnishings committee

The arts and furnishings committee, sometimes assisted by a liturgical consultant, manages the selection and design of the liturgical furnishings such as the altar, pulpit, lectern, candleholders, baptismal font, and artwork such as stained glass, murals, and tapestry. There are several ways for the committee to manage the design and fabrication process:

▼ *Small building committee consulting with other committees.*

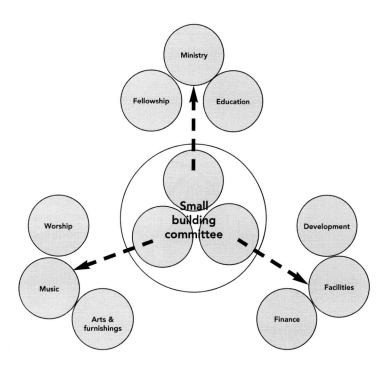

- The committee may engage a liturgical designer, who will either design the work or hire artisans to design and fabricate it.
- The architect may prepare the designs and administer the bidding and construction of the furnishings, in which case the committee oversees the architect's work.
- The committee may commission artisans to design and fabricate the work, with the architect and the committee providing design review.

If a liturgical designer is not engaged, the religious leader generally guides the arts and furnishings committee, assisted by volunteer artists and other design professionals such as furniture designers and art consultants. The architect should be a member of the arts and furnishings committee. Chapter 14 provides further details on the procurement of arts and furnishings.

Religious education committee

The religious education committee oversees the design of spaces for child care, religious education, youth programs, and adult classes. The committee is usually made up of the directors of the education programs, assisted by other members of the congregation.

Fellowship committee

The fellowship committee supervises the design and use of the parish hall, kitchens, meeting rooms, and the related public outside spaces such as patios, terraces, and amphitheaters.

Development committee

The development committee manages fund-raising, connects with potential donors, organizes events, and provides ongoing public relations information about the project to the wider community. Because most worship space construction in the United States relies on donations, a strong development committee is vital to its success.

The committee usually includes a few key donors, leaders in the community, who will provide the catalyst for the project. Well-connected and energetic fund-raising volunteers support the leaders. The committee may designate individuals or subcommittees to focus on foundations, corporate giving, and special gifts and to organize special fund-raising events. On larger projects, a full-time development manager and administrative staff reinforce the program.

One of the development committee's first tasks, in coordination with the building committee, is to set a fund-raising goal that will define the project budget. A consultant may do a feasibility study to estimate the amount of money that the community is able to raise. The consultant may also help in planning a campaign, advising on timing and the types of events to be planned, and designing and printing mailers and handouts. The architect can play an important role in the fund-raising campaign by presenting the design to groups of potential donors and conducting tours of the project site. In some cases, the architects bring in donors whom they already know.

Architect selection committee

On some projects a special committee manages the selection of the architect. The architect selection committee may include members of the congregation who are design professionals and developers who have worked with architects. On larger projects, the selection committee may include design critics and members of academia.

Other committees
Other committees, such as a real estate and finance committee, assist with the building process on the owner's team.

Small congregations
In the case of smaller congregations that do not have the network of committees previously described, the various tasks will be taken on by single individuals on the building committee or by this committee as a whole.

Liturgical consultant
Depending on the knowledge and experience of the religious leader and the amount of support provided by the parent organization, the group may hire a liturgical consultant at the beginning of the project. This consultant generally does the following:

- Helps to inform the group on current ideas about liturgy and building
- Facilitates congregational meetings and helps the group to clarify its liturgical mission
- Prepares a list of objectives for the building project
- Participates in selection of the architect and consultants
- Reviews the design as it develops and advises the congregation and the architect on liturgical planning
- Assists in the selection of artworks and furnishings and oversees their installation (see the previous section on the arts and furnishings committee)

Consultants
Other consultants on the owner's team may include:

- Project manager
- Geotechnical engineer
- Land surveyor
- Organ consultant
- Artists
- Artisans
- Environmental engineer (hazardous materials)

The Design Team
The architect, with a group of specialized consultants, heads the design team.

With an owner's team staffed largely by volunteers, architects provide leadership, facilitate decision making, and provide continuity throughout the project. It is up to the architect to keep records of decisions, issue meeting minutes, and make the volunteers feel good about what they are doing. The architect is able to see beyond the individual project and should not shrink from suggesting improvements to the institution's process and organizational structure (Beha 2001). The architect provides continuity throughout the project and his or her leadership may be necessary to keep the project on track. In addition to structural, civil, mechanical/electrical, and plumbing engineers, the architect's team routinely includes the following consultants:

- A lighting designer, who establishes the lighting levels for interior and exterior spaces, prepares a lighting design concept and lighting plans, selects fixtures, designs the lighting control and dimming systems, and aims the fixtures in the completed project. On certain projects, the lighting designer also designs theater lighting fixtures for performances and special lighting for broadcast TV.

- An acoustician and audiovisual consultant with experience in worship space design. This consultant sets criteria for room acoustics and noise control, such as reverberation time and noise criteria (NC), works with the architect and the mechanical engineer to achieve the selected criteria, reviews the contractor's submittals, and oversees the adjustment of the completed installation. This consultant may also design the sound rein-

forcement system and control booth, as well as projection systems for TV and digital images.

- A landscape architect familiar with the use of outside spaces in the liturgy and knowledgeable about the religious and historical significance of paving and plant materials can assist in the programming of the outside spaces, design the hardscape and planting areas, and select paving and plant materials.

For larger and more complex projects, the design team may also include additional consultants for the following elements:

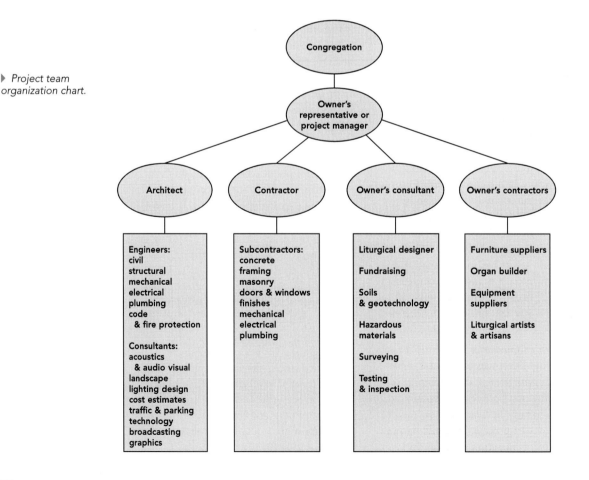

▶ Project team organization chart.

- Broadcast media design. This consultant plans locations for microphones and cameras, provides a location for electronic news gathering (ENG) teams, and designs control and editing rooms. The consultant lays out wiring and raceways, providing the infrastructure for future technology.
- Telecommunications, systems integration.
- Wayfinding, graphics, and signage.
- Fire/life-safety engineering.
- Building maintenance systems.
- Theater design and rigging.
- Security.
- Vertical transportation.
- Food service design.

THE PROCESS

Several characteristics set the building of worship spaces apart from the construction of other building types:

- The project must proceed with the approval of the entire congregation and incorporate its diverse and sometimes conflicting viewpoints. Faith communities differ in their decision-making processes, but many believe that if a vote has to be taken, somebody loses; they insist on consensus-based decision making. The result is that a vast amount of time must be devoted to listening and discussion.
- Faith communities frequently include strong differences of opinion — between progressive and conservative groups and between young and old. These must be heard and satisfied in the design process. Skillfully handled, such consideration provides an opportunity to draw members of the community closer by helping them to understand each other's viewpoint and work together. If mishandled, there is the possibility of alienating whole segments of the congregation and tearing it apart.
- Committees of volunteers, who may vary widely in experience, administrative skills, and management techniques, do most of the work of a faith community. These volunteers also have limited time and may participate for a short time only before being replaced by other volunteers. This lack of continuity places a burden on the design professionals to provide an institutional memory and to educate new committee members as they come on board.
- Building a worship space is usually undertaken once in a generation, and it is not a project in which the members will have skill and experience. Unlike a professional client such as a developer or a university, the building committees do not have a track record of managing building projects.

Keys to Success

To help navigate through the unexpected, the following characteristics are vital in the project team:

- A willingness to listen and help reconcile conflicting opinions, to make sure they are resolved early and do not surface later to disrupt the project
- An open mind toward changes in direction
- The ability to communicate ideas to people of varying levels of sophistication

- The keeping of accurate and complete records to provide a history of decision making
- A willingness to take time to explore a new idea
- A willingness to suggest ways to improve the process
- For the design team, a willingness to attend services and become familiar with the liturgy

The pastor, minister, rabbi, or imam plays a central role. The key tasks for the religious leader to perform include the following:

- Identifying members of the community with appropriate skills and persuading them to serve on committees
- Ensuring that decisions are made promptly
- Resolving conflicting opinions
- Spreading the news about the project
- Leading a fund-raising effort
- Maintaining good relations with the wider religious and civic community

A Typical Process

The following schedule outlines a typical process for the design and construction of a substantial new building. The needs assessment, programming, and master planning phases may have been completed separately, but they are included here as part of the overall project.

Committee formation

Following approval of a project by the religious institution's governing body, the first step is to establish the advisory committees that will guide the project, as discussed earlier.

The process of committee selection should address the following points:

- It is important to enfranchise groups of different ages, wealth, and race within the congregation to ensure a mandate for decision making.
- The committees must be of a manageable size. Typically, they should not exceed 20 members; 15 is ideal to provide a working group of 12.
- It is generally best for the religious leader to invite individual members of the congregation to join committees, rather than simply asking for volunteers. Those who volunteer may not represent all the constituencies (Mauck 1995, p. 14).

Design team selection

The institution then selects the professionals, beginning with the architect, the liturgical advisor (if appropriate), the professional project manager (if used), followed by the other consultants such as the land surveyor, geotechnical engineer, and hazardous materials engineer.

The selection committee should consider issuing a request for qualifications to professionals who are recommended from similar projects, from the parent religious organization, or whose work is familiar to members of the congregation. If the professionals are members of the congregation, they should be subjected to the same review procedure as outside firms.

The qualifications submittals should cover the entire proposed design team and include the following:

- A letter of interest
- Descriptions of the firms involved, including their size, ownership structure, and length of time in business
- Names of the proposed team members with their resumes

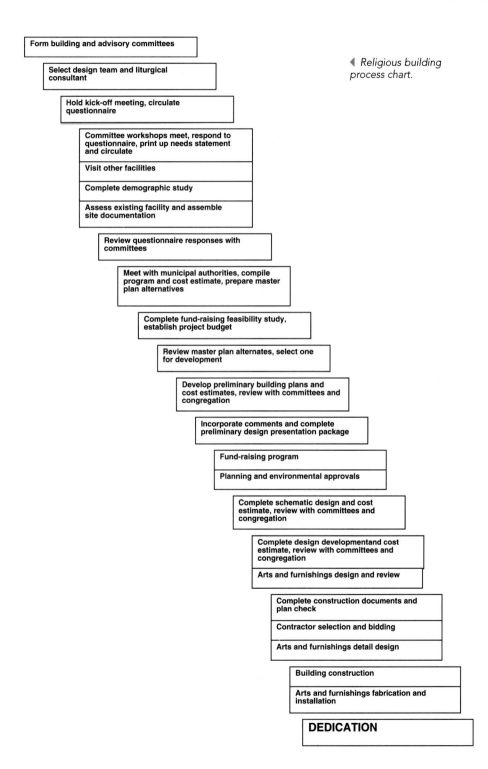

Religious building process chart.

Form building and advisory committees

Select design team and liturgical consultant

Hold kick-off meeting, circulate questionnaire

Committee workshops meet, respond to questionnaire, print up needs statement and circulate

Visit other facilities

Complete demographic study

Assess existing facility and assemble site documentation

Review questionnaire responses with committees

Meet with municipal authorities, compile program and cost estimate, prepare master plan alternatives

Complete fund-raising feasibility study, establish project budget

Review master plan alternates, select one for development

Develop preliminary building plans and cost estimates, review with committees and congregation

Incorporate comments and complete preliminary design presentation package

Fund-raising program

Planning and environmental approvals

Complete schematic design and cost estimate, review with committees and congregation

Complete design developmentand cost estimate, review with committees and congregation

Arts and furnishings design and review

Complete construction documents and plan check

Contractor selection and bidding

Arts and furnishings detail design

Building construction

Arts and furnishings fabrication and installation

DEDICATION

- Photographs and data for projects of similar scale and type completed by the team members
- A proposed organizational structure
- Client references
- The firm's Web address

The selection committee reviews the submittals, narrows the selection to three or four, requests detailed fee proposals from the finalists, and asks each to attend an interview. The requests for proposals should include all the available information about the size of the project, the program, the proposed budget, and the site. The detailed proposals should include the following:

- The proposed approach to the project, including how the professionals see themselves working with the religious institution
- Fee proposal, scope of work, services to be provided by the owner, possible additional services, and services not included
- A proposed project schedule, the number of meetings to be attended during the design phase, and the frequency of construction site visits

The congregation should approach the selection process with care to make sure it is comfortable with its choice. Communication skills and the ability to establish rapport are vital qualities in professionals. The committee should evaluate these skills as well as technical expertise and design talent. The following steps will help to complete the selection process:

- Follow up on the references provided by the professionals, but also find out about other projects not listed in their references. Speak to other institutions that have worked with them.

- Visit their offices, meet their other staff, review or visit a recently completed project, and meet the clients.
- Invite them to stay for a social occasion such as lunch or dinner.

For very large projects, it may be appropriate to have the architect finalists explore design ideas through a competition. A fee should be established in advance for participation in the competition. To avoid the complexity of establishing the program for the entire project in advance, use a simple program for the competition—for example, for a chapel or shrine—rather than the entire project.

Once these steps are completed, the congregation selects the design professionals and the owner's representative will negotiate the appropriate agreements.

Programming

During the programming phase, the team develops a detailed description of the project requirements in terms of area, dimensions, and technical elements. The phase generally begins with a meeting attended by the design professionals, the committee members, and members of the congregation. At this meeting the architect explains the process and distributes a programming questionnaire that seeks the congregation's input on the design requirements. The agenda typically includes the following:

- Opening prayer
- Introduction of the design professionals and the members of the advisory committees
- A statement of the institution's mission and vision for the project

- The history and background of the project
- An explanation by the professionals of the entire design and construction process involved in completing the project
- An explanation of the immediate tasks ahead, the schedule for their completion, and the designation of members to take responsibility for each task
- Presentation and distribution of the programming questionnaire
- Questions and comments from the congregation
- Closing prayer

A copy of one page of a typical programming questionnaire is shown on page 26.

Following the congregation meeting, the programming proceeds as follows:

- Committees meet to review their needs and respond to the programming questionnaire. If possible, these responses should include areas, room dimensions, and technical requirements for lighting, power, acoustics, and audiovisual (AV) systems.
- The building or oversight committee reviews the draft program responses to ensure that the requested building areas are broadly within the scope of the project.
- The committees review their findings at a series of workshops with the design professionals, where the designers can question the committees in detail about their requirements and obtain clarification. The architect then incorporates changes, assembles the written program, and submits it for final comment by the committees.

- At the same time, the designers and the appropriate committees should together visit similar facilities that they would like to use as models. This process helps to focus the programming and provides a series of touchstones that the design team can use for reference during future discussions. ("Do you remember how they did the entry at...?") The tour can include spaces of other denominations, and even nonreligious spaces, that possess the qualities the institution would like to embody in its new facility. The group should travel on the tour together so they can share their reactions.
- To validate the programming, the institution gathers demographic and growth projections to support their estimates of congregational growth. This research can be done by staff or outside consultants and is critical for projecting the size of the congregation and determining the needed amount of worship space seating, parking, child care, and ancillary space. The research includes reviewing historic records of congregation size to establish a growth trend, interviewing congregation members about the activities they plan to attend, and interviewing lapsed and nonmembers to see whether they might join if a new building were to be built. A study of other institutions in the region that have built or expanded their facilities may reveal a sudden growth in membership following such construction.

Using the draft program as a basis, the congregation should look at its resources and establish the project budget. This process includes a number of steps:

▶ *Programming
questionnaire sample
page. Malibu Church of
Christ, Malibu, California.
Architect: Leo A Daly.*

Malibu Church of Christ		
Questionnaire	Leo A Daly Project Number	412101

This survey is intended to provide an initial study of your assembly facility needs in order to generate a schematic design.

Worship Space Committee:

1. Your current peak attendance for a typical worship service:
   ❑ _____

2. Your proposed attendance at any typical worship service:
   ❑ _____

3. How many morning worship services do you currently run?
   ❑ _____

4. How many morning worship services do you intend to run?
   ❑ _____

5. How many people gather in front of the worship space before the service?
   ❑ _____

6. How many people attend an immersion baptism?
   ❑ _____

7. How many people gather outside for coffee after the service?
   ❑ _____

8. For what other events and activities are outdoor spaces regularly used?
   ❑ _____

9. Do you intend to provide cryrooms?
   ❑ Yes   ○ View window to assembly ○ Closed circuit TV ○ Audio only
   ❑ No

10. Do you need an interior passage to the front of the worship space from the main foyer without passing through the main assembly room?
    ❑ Yes
    ❑ No

11. How is communion served?
    ❑ At rail   ❑ In seat   ❑ Tables throughout

- Auditing and appraising unused land, buildings, and other valuables that could be sold

- Evaluating the potential for grants from the parent organization and charitable foundations

- Performing a fund-raising feasibility study to establish a target amount that could be raised in, say, five years

The architect assists the congregation to validate the program against the budget, using approximate square-foot cost estimates. At this stage the program and budget must be adjusted as necessary to bring them into line. At this stage the design team assembles data about the site. If the project is a renovation, these data will include documentation of the existing buildings. This documentation is typically provided by the owner and includes the following:

- Boundary and topographic survey
- Geotechnical report
- Aerial photographs
- Utility plans
- Plans of existing buildings (if a renovation)
- Hazardous materials survey (if a renovation)

The architect assembles, from the municipal agencies, copies of the existing entitlements and the planning and zoning requirements.

Master planning and conceptual design

Using the draft program document and the site data, the architect, assisted by the liturgical consultant, first develops alternate site layouts for review with the congregation. The selection of a preferred alternative should be determined by discussion and consensus rather than by voting.

Next, the architect develops preliminary plans of the worship space and the ancillary spaces for review by the worship committee. A liturgical consultant, if part of the team, is closely involved at this stage. There may be several alternatives to study and several reviews of the plans as they develop. Then the architect and the design team present the project to a meeting of the entire congregation for comment.

At the same time, the architect prepares an estimate of probable construction cost to present with the conceptual plans.

Finally, the architect incorporates comments from the congregation into the design and prepares colored floor plans, one or two three-dimensional renderings, and perhaps a study model. These presentation materials are used to support the fund-raising effort and to obtain planning and zoning approval from the municipality.

Schematic design

Once sufficient funds are in place, the architect begins preparing the schematic design documents based on the approved conceptual design. The schematic design shows the layout of the building components in plan and elevation and schematically defines the structural and heating, ventilating, and air-conditioning (HVAC) systems.

Regular meetings are held with the committees during the schematic design phase to review the design as it develops. All the advisory groups are asked for their comments on the size and disposition of the program spaces in the design. Not only does such consultation reduce the danger of costly additions later, it also helps to give all those involved a stake in the project.

The design team now clearly spells out the scope of services it has contracted to perform (Beha 2001). To avoid confusion, team members should explain to the congregation their responsibilities under their agreement. Issues that may be unclear include the design or supervision of the fabrication of liturgical furnishings, geotechnical or hazardous materials surveys, and how many meetings the architect expects to attend during design and construction.

The design team prepares a detailed cost estimate at the end of the schematic design, including contingencies, and recommends any adjustments to the project

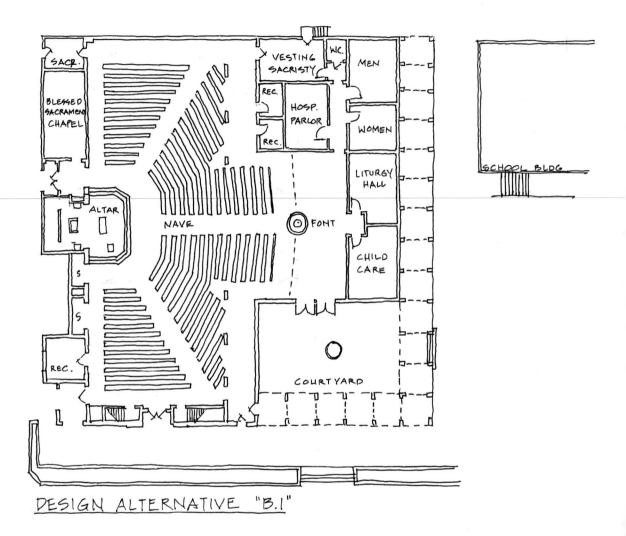

Labels within the floor plan: SACR., BLESSED SACRAMENT CHAPEL, VESTING SACRISTY, W.C., MEN, REC., HOSP. PARLOR, WOMEN, REC., ALTAR, LITURGY HALL, NAVE, FONT, CHILD CARE, S, S, REC., COURTYARD, SCHOOL BLDG

DESIGN ALTERNATIVE "B.I"

▲ Preliminary worship space floor plan, Holy Trinity Church, San Pedro, California. Architect: Leo A Daly.

budget. The worship space budget should include three contingencies:

- A design contingency, which covers unforeseen cost increases due to the detailed development of the design, including changes required by the municipal agencies during design. This contingency is typically 10 percent of the construction cost at schematic design stage and falls to

zero once the contractor is on board and the building permit is obtained.

- A construction change order contingency, which covers added costs during construction caused by any of the following:

  - Unforeseen soils and geotechnical conditions
  - Unforeseen conditions of existing building structure or utilities

- Unanticipated municipal requirements
- Errors and omissions in the contract documents
- Design changes by the owner

This contingency should be 10 percent for new construction and 20 percent for renovation.

- A furniture, fixtures, and equipment (FF&E) contingency, which is carried in the FF&E budget to cover unforeseen changes and cost increases in the FF&E items; generally 10 percent of the FF&E budget.

Design development

In the design development phase, the design team prepares large-scale drawings and outline specifications that define the project in detail. The committees review design elements, such as interior and exterior materials, finishes and colors, built-in cabinets and counters, landscape and paving materials, lighting design, and electrical power and audiovisual requirements. Meanwhile, the artisans and craftspeople preparing the owner-supplied furnishings and artwork begin their design efforts. The architect participates in the selection of the artisans and works with them to coordinate the space, structural, and utility requirements for the liturgical furnishings and artwork. Chapter 14 describes the process in more detail.

The design team's skill in communicating its design intent to the committees is crucial at this stage, to avoid surprises and expensive changes during construction. Large-scale models, perspective drawings, computer-generated renderings and fly-throughs, full-size mockups of critical elements such as the font, altar, ark, bimah, or mihrab, and large samples

of proposed materials are well worth the cost and effort involved. Critical dimensions, such as the size of the sanctuary, the music area, and the aisleways, can be mocked-up inexpensively with furniture and plywood.

A further construction cost estimate update at the end of design development checks the construction cost against the budget.

Construction documents

The design team prepares plans and specifications to describe the project in detail for construction and coordinates carefully with the artisans and craftspeople supplying the furnishings and artwork. At this stage, details of the structural loads, the attachment points, and the precise electrical, HVAC, and communications requirements for the owner-furnished items must be incorporated in the contract documents.

If the project is a remodel of an existing building, the institution may plan for temporary facilities during construction. Alternatively, the schedule of services is revised to take into account phased construction, which takes certain areas out of service for renovation while keeping the building in use.

Municipal plan approval

When the construction documents are 80 percent complete, the architect submits them for approval by the local building and fire departments. The details of required approvals are described in Chapter 5.

Project delivery

The contractor takes the final step in the development of the design by preparing detailed documents such as shop

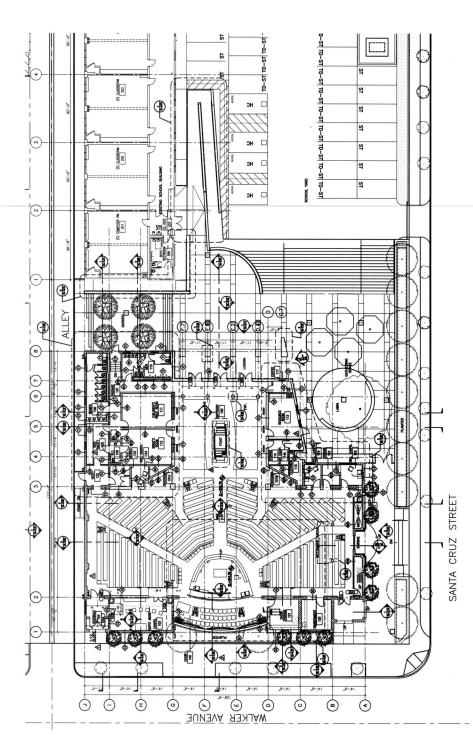

▲ Construction documents
worship space floor plan, Holy
Trinity Church, San Pedro,
California. Architect: Leo A Daly.

drawings, layout plans, and formwork drawings that give precise directions to the team in the field. The contractor also supervises the work of the trades and takes responsibility for cost and schedule management.

Generally, the institution may seek advice from its parent organization in selecting a project delivery method and developing a list of potential contractors. There are several options:

- *The design/bid/build method.* Once the design team has obtained plan approval from municipal agencies, the contractor selection process begins with an invitation to selected firms to submit lump-sum bids and construct the project. The advantage of this method is the low bid price. The disadvantages are that there may be disputes over the intent of the construction documents, that the contractor may sacrifice quality to meet the bid price, and that there is little opportunity to accelerate construction, for example by starting foundation construction before the construction documents for the whole building are complete.

- *The guaranteed maximum price (GMP) method.* This allows the contractor to become a member of the team early in the process, typically after the schematic design phase. The contractor selection process is similar to the process for architect selection, except that the contractor's fee proposal will cover the contractor's home office overhead and profit.

The contractor prepares a GMP when the construction documents are approximately 70 percent complete. The owner and design team have the ability to collaboratively manage the cost and quality of each building component as the design develops. The disadvantage is a slightly higher first cost than with a lump-sum bid.

A further advantage of the GMP process on large projects is that the construction can be accelerated using a fast-track method. Foundations and building construction can be under way while the details of the interior fit-out and finishes are still in design.

The keys to a successful GMP contract are as follows:

- Selecting a contractor familiar with the GMP process, who understands the specific needs of worship spaces
- Ensuring that the design team's pricing package used to prepare the GMP is complete
- Having all parties review the GMP carefully for omissions
- Including appropriate budget contingencies

However, if a fast-track method is used on large projects, the design team must provide a full-time presence in the field. Completion of the design documents should be done in close collaboration with the contractor's staff in the field.

- *The design/build method.* With this method, the owner contracts with a design/build team, including architects, engineers, and contractors, to provide a building of a certain specification for a fixed price. The process can be a single phase, in which the design/build team is selected on the basis of a conceptual design and rendering to be provided for a stipulated price, or a two-phase process called design/design/build. In this second process, an architect is engaged to provide a schematic design and specifications, which the owner bids out to design/build teams who provide lump-sum proposals to complete and construct the design.

The advantages of design/build are a perceived fixed price for the project and the absence of change orders. The disadvantages are the lack of direct contract between owner and architect and the resulting difficulty in controlling the design and quality of the project. This disadvantage is somewhat overcome in the design/design/build method.

Contractor selection

Depending on the delivery method, the contractor may be selected during the design phase or at the completion of the construction documents. In either case, this is one of the most critical factors for the success of the project. The first phase is the development of a short list of suitable firms with experience in religious building projects of similar scale and type:

- Seek the advice of the institution's parent organization, which may have a list of approved contractors.

- Ask other religious institutions in the neighborhood with recent building projects.

- If possible, choose firms that have a stake in the local community.

- If prospective contractors are members of the congregation, subject them to the same scrutiny as outside firms.

The procedure for requesting and reviewing qualifications, proposals, and references is similar to that described earlier for design team selection. The following

additional steps should be included in the selection of a contractor:

- Make sure all considered firms are licensed, bonded, and insured. Request details of their bonding capacity and workers' compensation claims history.

- Obtain references for and interview all team members, including principal, project manager, project engineer, and superintendent.

- Consider developing and using a list of preapproved subcontractors for key trades that may be critical to the design and the construction schedule. These may include concrete, masonry, stonework, finish carpentry and millwork, and HVAC subcontractors. Alternatively, include language in the bid documents specifying the qualifications and experience required of these key subcontractors and requiring submittance of written statements of qualification with the bid.

Construction

Building construction is the phase of the project in which the congregation's dreams become reality, but it is a venture fraught with unknowns.

Key concerns in the construction phase are to:

- Ensure that there is a single, clear line of command from the owner to the contractor. The owner must make certain that all directions to the contractor go through one owner's representative. Failure to observe this rule can result in members of different committees giving conflicting directions to the contractor. At best, this causes confusion; at worst, an unscrupulous contractor can exploit the situation to justify delays and added cost.

- Establish adequate change order contingencies. Appropriate contingencies are recommended in the preceding section on schematic design.
- Realize that there will be change orders, and put in place an experienced team whose members are available to resolve them and track project expenditures against the budget.
- Minimize the number of design changes during construction, which are almost always costly and time-consuming. If the design team has done its job of communicating the design intent to the owner, then there should be a minimum of surprises. The following procedure will help to streamline the process:
    - The design team should prepare sketches that convey the intent of the change, along with an estimate of any additional fees.
    - The contractor should provide a rough estimate of the cost and impact on the schedule.
    - With the owner's approval, the design team should issue documentation of the change.
- Keep open the channels of communication at all levels. Organize regular meetings between the owner, design team, and contractor.
- Remember that the project has a higher purpose, the building is not for the glory of humans, but for the glory of their deity. The religious leader can have a tremendous effect, inspiring the workers in the field, encouraging an atmosphere of honesty, openness, and collaboration, reminding the team of the importance of their work, recognizing extra efforts, and hosting celebrations for major festivals and project landmarks with parties and get-togethers (McCormick and Swanson 2000).

Arts and furnishings

While the contractor is completing the construction, the artists and artisans fabricate and install the furnishings and artwork. This work is critical, and supervision and coordination require full-time effort. Artists may be unfamiliar with the demands of construction, such as:

- Safety rules and union regulations
- Strict engineering requirements—for example, for structural resistance to earthquake forces
- Building code requirements—for example, those for handicap accessibility that dictate nonslip floor finishes, or fire codes that require flame-spread ratings for wall finishes

In addition, many items of liturgical furnishing call for the detailed coordination of several trades. For example, a font requires plumbing, electrical, structural, stone, and plaster work; even the ambo affects the structure and the electrical and sound systems. If the owner lacks suitable staff, the architect or contractor can provide coordination of these trades and oversee the installation of furnishings and artwork for an additional fee.

Public relations

Construction generates intense interest within the congregation and the community. The noise, dust, and traffic may also cause concern for neighbors. Signs erected at the corners of the site, including renderings, can provide information about the project, updates on the project can be provided at weekly services, and periodic meetings can supply information to the wider community.

The religious leaders should be generous with members of the print and broadcast media, inviting them to press conferences, granting interviews, and issuing press reports at important milestones. On large projects an individual should be designated to coordinate media contacts.

There may also be heavy demand for site tours. The development committee may use hard-hat tours to generate interest in the project, and friends and family members of the construction team may want to visit the site. Observing the following guidelines helps to ensure successful site tours that do not intrude on the construction process:

- Establish a single point of contact for approval of tours and coordination with the contractor. Set a fixed time for tours each week.
- Prepare a waiver form to be signed by all visitors, and provide the required safety equipment.
- For large projects, set up a display of plans and models in a visitor center, which may be in a trailer or an adjacent building, to orient visitors before going out to the site.

Dedication

As construction nears completion, the institution begins to plan the dedication ceremonies, notifying its parent organization, planning the order of the service, selecting and practicing the music, making arrangements for the event, and printing commemorative booklets.

CHAPTER 3

UNIQUE DESIGN CONCERNS

This chapter discusses the design and program factors unique to worship spaces, including churches, synagogues, mosques, and temples.

CHURCHES

In its 2000 years of existence, Christianity has developed an extraordinary breadth and variety of practice. The range of denominations includes, among others, Roman Catholic, Episcopal, Presbyterian, Methodist, Congregationalist, Baptist, Seventh-Day Adventist, the Church of Jesus Christ of Latter-day Saints (Mormon), Churches of Christ, the Religious Society of Friends (Quakers), and Unitarian Universalist. The denominations vary in their forms of liturgy, precise interpretation of Christian doctrine, and the role of their clergy, but their worship spaces, which are called churches or chapels, have common elements: a gathering space, a sanctuary with an altar and lectern or pulpit, congregational seating, a baptistery, a music area, and supporting spaces. The following sections describe the architectural elements of the worship space and their different design requirements. The referenced texts listed in the bibliography and references section discuss the belief systems and liturgical practices of the various denominations.

Recently, following the recommendations of the Second Vatican Council (1962–1965), the Roman Catholic church has dramatically changed the design of churches and cathedrals to emphasize the participation of the assembly in the ritual. These changes include the use of the vernacular language instead of Latin for the mass; the presider facing the assembly, gathered around the altar table to participate in the Eucharist; and the renewed significance of baptism, witnessed by the congregation, as an entry into the church.

Gathering Space

The journey to the gathering space begins when the visitor enters the church precinct. The walkways from the parking area and the paths that lead through the gardens and courtyards to the gathering area should be carefully designed as processional paths along which the members of the community converge to worship together (White and White 1988, p. 21). The character of this journey as part of a sacred space is further discussed in Chapters 1 and 4.

The entry to the gathering space says that all are welcome, men and women of all ages and races. It is the point at which members of the congregation greet each other and experience themselves as a community. It is the space where they meet one another before meeting God (White and White 1988, p. 21).

Inside the gathering space, the following may be provided:

- A fireplace to provide a warming welcome in cold climates

- Informal seating for older members to enjoy coffee and donuts

- Notice boards and literature racks providing information about church activities

- A table with tapes and transcripts of services and religious books available for sale

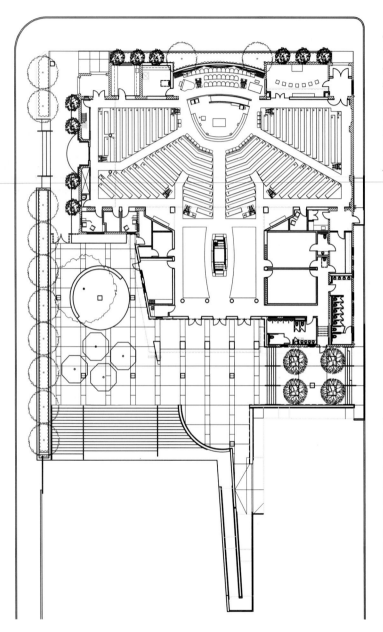

The gathering space should be large enough for members of the congregation to gather comfortably without feeling cramped. It is typically one-third of the area of the worship space, approximately 5 sq ft per worship space seat. The ceiling height should be generous enough for the space to feel inviting without being intimidating, typically 12–15 ft. Adjacent to the gathering space, the following spaces are generally provided:

- Bathrooms
- A coatroom (in cold climates)
- A small kitchen for preparing coffee and pastries
- A room for the care of infants during the service
- Bible study rooms and rooms for individual meetings and prayer
- A storage space for ushers' supplies, such as literature and offertory plates, and equipment such as walk-off mats and ropes and stanchions

An outside courtyard, partially shaded with trellis and trees, allows the congregation to gather outdoors in fine weather. A fountain with the sound of flowing water provides refreshment in hot weather, and in some churches the courtyard includes a pool for outdoor baptism. In Catholic churches the courtyard may include a special brazier to hold the Easter fire, from which a candlelit procession leads the congregation during the Easter Vigil.

For visitors to the church, the gathering space may be a point of decision, whether or not to enter the worship space and participate in the service. The entry to the worship space from the gathering space should be clear and welcoming, typically consisting of two or three pairs of 3 ft or 3½ ft doors.

▲ *Floor plan of outside gathering space showing adjacent coffee kitchen. Holy Trinity Church, San Pedro, California. Architect: Leo A Daly.*

- A special area for new members to meet and be introduced by a senior member of the church
- A table for dispensing assisted listening devices to those in need

The Sanctuary and Its Components

The ministers of the church celebrate many of the sacred rituals of the liturgy in a part of the church sometimes known as the sanctuary. This space may also be called the chancel, the altar area, or the liturgical space. The sanctuary is generally slightly apart from the main body of the church by its special design and materials and may be raised by one or two steps to improve its visibility from the seating. If steps are used, they should extend the full width of the sanctuary to give a feeling of openness and maximize its accessibility for communion, weddings, and processions.

To reaffirm that the congregation, ministers, and choir are all part of one community, gathered around the altar in worship, some liturgical designers do not distinguish between the sanctuary, nave, and choir but refer to the whole as a worship space.

The sanctuary should be large enough to accommodate the following furnishings:

- Altar
- Ambo or pulpit
- Lectern (if provided)
- Candles
- Flowers
- Crucifix or cross
- Seats for the presiding priest and/or ministers (if appropriate)

There should be adequate space in the sanctuary for the liturgical rituals to be celebrated there. These include:

- The Eucharist, Holy Communion, or Lord's Supper, in which the congregation joins in a ritual meal of celebration. Bread or wafers and wine or grape juice are blessed and distributed

▲ An outside gathering space. Note the sliding sash kitchen window for serving coffee and donuts after Sunday service. Holy Trinity Church, San Pedro, California. Architect: Leo A Daly. Photo: Erhard Pfeiffer.

to the congregation. Communion may be given:

- At the altar, in which case members of the congregation come up to the steps of the sanctuary and may receive communion standing or kneeling
- At communion stations in the seating area, where the congregation members receive communion standing
- In the seats, in which case trays of bread and cups are passed down the rows, or may have already been placed in the seat backs before the service

In some faiths, members of the congregation may take turns to approach and sit at a long table to receive communion (White and White 1988, p. 70).

Several celebrants, assisted by Eucharistic ministers, may serve the Eucharistic meal. Space is needed behind the altar for the Eucharistic prayer, in which the presiding priest raises high the bread in blessing. Adequate space is also required in front of the altar for two ministers in full vestments to pass while distributing communion.

- The Liturgy of the Word, known as morning or evening prayer, or the Liturgy of the Hours, which includes readings from the Gospels, prayers, and a sermon
- Confirmation, or laying-on of hands, for which the young members of the church kneel before the altar to be blessed by the bishop
- Weddings, for which there must be room for the bride and groom, and sometimes other members of the wedding party, to kneel before the altar to be blessed by the priest or minister
- Funerals, in which the casket is placed in front of the altar, surrounded by flowers and candles

In a cathedral, the sanctuary must be large enough to accommodate special rituals:

- The ordination of candidates to the priesthood (holy orders)
- Special services attended by large numbers of priests or ministers, who are seated in the sanctuary or behind the altar in an area called the presbyterium
- Civic and state events such as state weddings, coronations, and state funerals

In some denominations, altar, pulpit, and seating may be rearranged to provide for different worship configurations. Although the church should be seen as a symbol of permanence, this flexibility may be important as an architectural manifestation that the church is a pilgrim community, constantly on the move, that must adapt and change (Sovik 1973, p. 68). Other denominations require that the altar be fixed and dedicated in one location (National Conference of Catholic Bishops 2000b, par. 303), but different seating configurations around the altar are possible.

Although dimensions are shown for guidance, the design of individual altars and the spaces around them will vary according to the requirements of the liturgy and the preferences of the clergy. For example, some presiders may want the altar closer to the congregation for a sense of intimacy, whereas in other churches, some liturgies, such as large weddings, demand more space around the altar. The best solution is to make a mock-up of the sanctuary and the first rows of congregation seating, to try out the proposed layout and dimensions, using loose furniture to represent the altar and congregational seating.

The altar

The altar is the table for celebration of the Eucharist, Holy Communion, or the Lord's Supper. The altar is symbolically a table for the thanksgiving meal, but also an altar of sacrifice that refers to the Temple of Jerusalem and to Jesus' sacrifice on the cross. It provides a surface on which to place the elements, the bread and wine, and the book of service used in the communion. In some denominations the presiding priests also wash their hands at the altar before celebrating communion.

▶ Sanctuary Plan showing altar, ambo or pulpit, presider's chair, and critical dimensions. Holy Trinity Church, San Pedro, California.

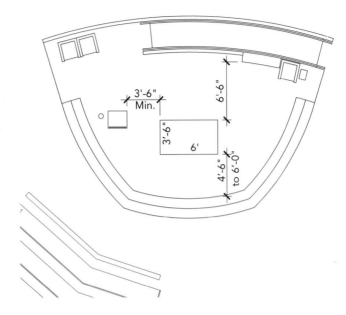

▶ Sanctuary plan showing movable lectern, communion table, and overflow seating. United Methodist Church, Charles City, Iowa; Architects: Sovik, Mathre, Madson.
1 Altar table
2 Pulpit
3 Organ and choir
4 Baptismal fountain
5 Seating for 420
6 Hall, also used as overflow seating for 180–200.

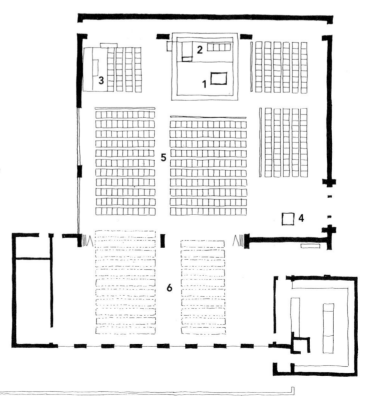

The detailed design requirements for an altar are described in Chapter 14.

Candles and flowers are usually placed on the floor on either side of the altar, and a cross or crucifix stands on the floor or hangs nearby. A table or shelf is also required close to the altar for empty pitchers and flagons of water and wine or juice, empty vessels, and offering plates and for a bowl and towel if required for handwashing. If incense is used, then a stand for the thurible, or incense holder, is required close to the altar.

Space may be provided for a special paschal candle to be carried in procession and placed adjacent to the altar during Easter services.

The pulpit, lectern, or ambo

The locations for the reading of the Gospel and preaching the sermon vary from one denomination to another. In Catholic churches, the readings from the Bible and the sermon, or homily, are given from the pulpit or ambo. The ambo also provides an opportunity to display the book of Gospels. The cantor or choir director uses a separate stand.

In the Anglican and Episcopal churches, a tradition developed for lay members of the church to read the Gospels. Because the pulpit is reserved for use by the priest, it became traditional for a separate lectern to be provided for reading of the Gospel and for the priest to preach the sermon from a pulpit on the opposite side of the church.

Ministers of Protestant and Evangelical churches sometimes prefer to move about the sanctuary during the sermon, in which case they may dispense with the pulpit for preaching but still use a lectern for the readings from the Bible.

The detailed design requirements for a pulpit or ambo are described in Chapter 14.

Celebrants' chairs

In the Catholic tradition, chairs are provided for ministers in the sanctuary, and a special chair is identified for the priest celebrant. The intention of giving the presider's chair prominence is a democratic one: When the presider is not standing, it shows that he has delegated the leadership of worship to a reader, cantor, or prayer leader (White and White 1988, p. 47). The location of the chair must show that the priest is presiding, but care should be taken that it not resemble a throne (National Conference of Catholic Bishops 2000b, p. 271). The new instruction in the *Roman Missal* reaffirms the best location at the head of the sanctuary, behind the altar, except where the tabernacle is located behind the altar or if this location would place the priest at too great a distance from the altar (National Conference of Catholic Bishops 2000b, p. 310). Many clergy, however, prefer a location closer to the congregation, often using an asymmetrical location opposite the ambo.

In a cathedral, a special chair for the bishop or archbishop, called the *cathedra*, is located in the sanctuary. The chair, which is decorated with the archbishop's coat of arms, is left vacant if the archbishop is not presiding at the service. A separate chair is provided for the priest celebrant.

In some Protestant churches, chairs are provided for the ministers in the sanctuary on either side of the altar or adjacent to the choir. In others, the leaders are seated as part of the congregation and step up from the nave seating to participate in the liturgy.

Traditionally, a church is oriented so that the sanctuary is at the east end of the church and the congregation prays toward the Holy Land. In contemporary churches the orientation is more influenced by site conditions. Chapter 4 discusses site planning in detail.

The Congregation Seating

The arrangement of the congregation seating in many churches has undergone a fundamental change in the last 40 years, relegating to history the traditional ranks of pews lined up facing the altar. Most contemporary liturgies call for the participation of the entire congregation, and many churches have rearranged the seating layout to be an architectural expression of priests, ministers, choir, and people worshiping together as one body, like a family gathered around the altar rather than an audience watching a performance. Whatever the arrangement, it is important that the whole assembly is able to participate in the liturgy by seeing and hearing the rituals performed in the sanctuary. The Eucharist is a sacrament, a ritual meal in which the whole congregation should participate.

The congregation is seated in the central area of the church known as the nave. The seating must accommodate a wide variety of functions:

- The people are generally seated during the reading of the scriptures and the sermon.

- They may stand to sing hymns and recite prayers.

- They may kneel for liturgical prayer and for private prayer before and after the service. In some churches the assembly remains seated, with people bowing their heads for prayer.

- Wafers and cups may be stored in the seat backs for communion.

- Offertory plates may be passed along, together with sign-in books.

The seating layout must be able to accommodate multiple foci:

- During the readings from the Bible and the sermon, the congregation is focused on the pulpit.

- During the Eucharist, the altar is the focus for the gathering of the congregation.

- For congregational prayers and hymn singing, the community is the focus.

- Other liturgies, such as baptisms and funerals, focus the congregation on the baptismal font for part of the service.

The circulation area around the seating is an important functional space in its own right. Many liturgies require the congregation to move about the worship space during the service, which confirms their role as active participants in the proceedings rather than passive observers. The revivalism movement discovered long ago that to move people spiritually you must move them physically (White and White 1988, p. 29). Among the activities that require movement space are the following:

- *Communion.* The congregation must be able to move freely in and out of the seating to come up to the altar or to communion stations for communion. They should not have to cross more than five seats to reach an aisle (White and White 1988, p. 27), and generous aisles, a minimum of 5 ft wide, should be provided.

- *Processions.* The layout of the seating must allow for processions such as those at the beginning and end of a service, carrying the book of service, the Gospels, a processional cross and candle; for wedding processions; and for funeral processions. Sometimes, such as on Palm Sunday or at the Easter Vigil, the whole congregation may process. These rituals generally dictate the need for a center aisle a minimum of 6 ft wide.

- *Baptism.* The congregation should be able to move to other parts of the church, such as the baptistery, for special parts of the liturgy, and gathering space should be provided around the font.

- *Communion, Offerings, and Gifts.* Ministers and ushers must also have easy access around the church, for distributing and collecting offertory plates, distributing communion if it is given in the seats, and for bringing forward the gifts of bread and wine to the altar.

All of these movement routes, including the path from the congregation seating up to the altar, must be accessible to those in wheelchairs to allow disabled persons to fully participate in the liturgy, read from the Gospels, and celebrate the Eucharist. In existing churches that have steps from the nave up to the sanctuary,

a ramp or wheelchair lift must be installed (see Chapter 5).

Critical dimensions govern the maximum effective distance from the altar to the last row of seats. Numerous studies have shown that people with normal vision can perceive the expressions on faces and comfortably communicate with raised voices for distances of up to 75 ft (Alexander 1977, p. 313). Therefore, for the congregation to participate satisfactorily in the service, the last pew should not be farther than this distance from the altar. In practice, in large churches this dimension can be increased up to 90 ft.

Seating arrangements that accomplish these objectives include the following:

The circle, with the sanctuary at one edge, is exemplified by Eero Saarinen's chapel at the Massachusetts Institute of Technology (MIT), where the sanctuary is defined by means of a lantern overhead (Hammond 1961, p. 86).

The square plan, with seating on the diagonal, is used at St. Rochus, Türnich, Germany, and at the Galvin Family

▼ *Plan, Church of the Holy Family, Oberhausen, Germany. Architect: Rudolf Schwartz.*

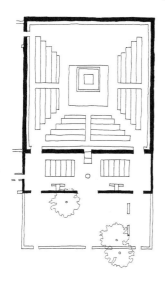

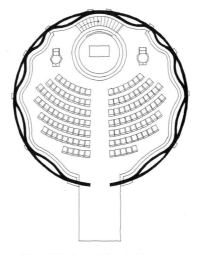

▲ *Plan, MIT chapel, Cambridge, Massachusetts. Architect: Eero Saarinen.*

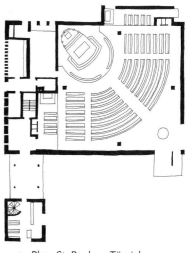

▲ *Plan, St. Rochus, Türnich, Germany. Architect: Karl Band.*

Chapel at Babson College, Wellesley, Massachusetts. This shape provides an excellent location for the sanctuary and the baptismal font within the economy of an orthogonal plan (Hammond 1961, p. 95; Crosbie 2003, p. 57).

U-shape seating can also be provided within a square plan, as at the United Methodist Church in Charles City, Iowa (Sovik, Mathre and Madson) and St. Thomas More Church in Paducah, Kentucky (Crosbie 2003, p. 96), as can "antiphonal" seating, whereby members of the assembly are seated across from one another within a square plan, as at Rudolf Schwartz's Church of the Holy Family, Oberhausen, Germany.

A fan shape is popular with many Evangelical churches, because it optimizes the efficiency of the seating layout and visibility of the sanctuary. In very large churches it is frequently used in conjunction with a gallery to provide 6000 or more seats, as at the Church of Jesus Christ of Latter-day Saints (LDS), Salt Lake City, Utah.

In large worship spaces, balconies have the advantage of bringing the congregation physically closer together and providing seating nearer to the altar. However, in churches with fewer than 2000 seats, balconies have several disadvantages:

- Those seated in the balcony are physically separated from the rest of the congregation, defeating the idea of the congregation as one body.

- An elevator must be provided for equivalent access for those in wheelchairs, unless a sloping site permits a ramp system to be used.

- Additional cost will be incurred for the two means of egress required by code.

- The space under the balcony is frequently undesirable for seating because of the feeling of enclosure. It is frequently hard to hear the organ and choir from such spaces.

The seating itself may be pews, movable chairs, a combination of the two, or theater-style fixed seating. The advantages and disadvantages of each, together with dimensions for the detailed design of seating are discussed in Chapter 14.

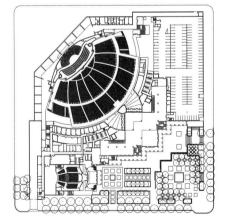

▲ Plan, Church of Jesus Christ of the Latter-day Saints, Salt Lake City, Utah. Architect: ZGF.

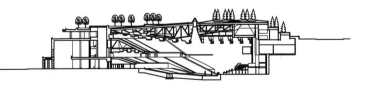

▲ Section, Church of Jesus Christ of Latter-day Saints, Salt Lake City, Utah. Architect: ZGF.

The Baptismal Font

The font is used for the ritual of Baptism, by which Christians enter into the community of the church. In the case of a full immersion, the candidates, or catechumens, enter the water dressed only in white robes, "loosening [their] hair and letting go of all fetters, leaving behind ornaments proclaiming the security of status and wealth" (Mauck 1990, p. 42).

Baptism may take various forms:

- Submersion, in which the candidate is completely submerged in the baptismal pool, as practiced by Baptists, Churches of Christ, and many Evangelical churches

- Immersion, in which the candidate is dipped three times under the water, as practiced by the Roman Catholic Church for the initiation of adults

- Affusion, in which water is poured or sprinkled over the candidate, as practiced by Presbyterians, Congregationalists, and Roman Catholics for the baptism of infants

Some churches, such as Baptist churches, Churches of Christ, and many Evangelical churches, believe that baptism should be administered only to those with the maturity to understand the profound ritual, whereas others, such as the Episcopal, Presbyterian, Congregational, and Catholic churches permit the baptism of infants.

The design and location of the font depends on the type of baptism and the role of the font in the liturgy.

- For Baptists churches, Churches of Christ, and many Evangelical churches, the font is located at the front of the church, near or in the sanctuary, in full view of the congregation. If there are candidates for baptism, the ritual is witnessed by the full congregation as part of the weekly service, emphasizing that it is the church as a community that baptizes new members into its congregation.

- In Episcopal, Presbyterian, and other Protestant churches, it may be located in a separate baptistery or to one side of the nave.

- In Roman Catholic churches built or renovated since the Second Vatican Council, the font assumes a renewed importance in the church ritual. Many liturgical designers believe the water of the font should greet the congregation as they arrive in the church. The font should be "in the way, because it is *the* way" (Stephens 2001).

▼ *The relationship between font and altar at the Cathedral of Our Lady of the Angels, Los Angeles. Design Architect: Rafael Moneo; executive architect: Leo A Daly; liturgical consultant: Rev. Richard S. Vosko. Photo: Julius Shulman and David Glomb.*

The location of the font at the entry, together with the use of similar materials for the altar and the font, emphasizes the journey of faith from entry into the church to the sacrifice of the Eucharist that takes place at the altar. Other, but less satisfactory, locations include the side of the nave and the front of the church.

Catholics also use the holy water of the font to bless themselves upon entering the church, and the presiding priest may sprinkle the water on the congregation to bless them.

There should be plenty of space around the font for the candidates, their parents, godparents, and family members, and for the congregation to gather and welcome the new member of the church. This may take the form of an open space or an area of movable seating around the font.

Detailed requirements for font design are covered in Chapter 10.

In some denominations the font also plays an important role in the funeral service and in the Rite of Dedication of a church. The casket is blessed with holy water at the entrance to the church and may lie adjacent to the font for the wake, in which case space must be provided for candles and flowers. In the Rite of Dedication of a church, the bishop blesses the water and then sprinkles the people, the walls of the church, and, finally, the altar (Mauck 1990, p. 48).

There should be bathrooms and changing rooms for men and women located adjacent to the baptismal font. The adjacent floor finishes should be durable and not slippery when wet, anticipating that in some liturgies the catechumens will emerge wet and dripping from their baptism.

▲ *Diagram showing the relationship between font and altar.*

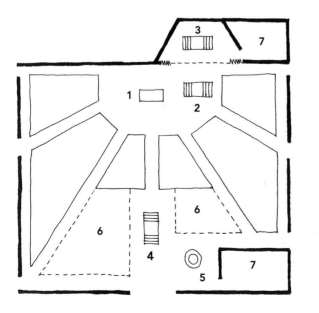

◤ *Church plan showing alternative font locations.*
1 *Altar.*
2 *The font is usually located in the sanctuary in Presbyterian and Baptist churches. It may be covered when not in use.*
3 *In Evangelical churches and the Church of Christ, the font is located in a separate baptistery, which is opened and lit for the congregation to watch during baptism.*
4 *The font at the entrance to the church is favored in current Catholic liturgy.*
5 *In Episcopalian churches the font is frequently to one side of the nave.*
6 *Sufficient space for movable seating should be provided around the font.*
7 *Bathrooms should be close by, to allow participants to change out of their wet garments after immersion.*

▲ Interior showing organ, seating for choir, elders, and congregation, Church of Jesus Christ of Latter-day Saints, Salt Lake City, Utah. Architect: ZGF. Photo: Timothy Hursley.

The Music Space

The expression of prayers and praise in music is an important part of Christian worship; it takes place in a number of different ways. There are two concepts for the role of the choir, which may apply to Catholic and Protestant churches alike.

In the first concept, the "choir" is the whole assembly of the people, singing together; if there are trained singers to support the congregation, the singers' dress and the location of their seating emphasize that they are part of the assembly. Some churches have only a quartet of singers leading the assembly, which sings unaccompanied in harmony. Musicians are part of the assembly, emerging as required to lead special musical elements in the liturgy.

To successfully accommodate this form of music, the church building must provide the following:

- *Proper acoustics.* The building acoustics must be designed to support congregational singing, by means of strong reflective surfaces that allow members of the congregation to hear the choir and one another. These requirements are discussed further in Chapter 12.

- *Choir space.* Space for the choir should be provided where choir members are part of the assembly and can support congregational singing. There are several possible locations for the choir:

  - At the side of the sanctuary, toward the front where the choir can see and respond to the cantor and celebrant in the responses and join with other musicians.

  - At the rear of the church, where the choir can support congregational singing. However, this location is unsatisfactory because the choir should be adjacent to other musical components such as the cantor, organ, piano, or musicians that have to be at the front of the assembly.

  - A balcony location at the rear of the church supports congregational singing but does not include the choir as part of the assembly.

  - Behind the altar, in which case the choir is sometimes hidden by a low screen to avoid the impression of its members being on stage and so that they do not distract from the liturgy. The screen is of such a height that the choir is hidden when seated but visible when standing.

See the floor plans on page 169.

In a second concept, a well-trained choir uses its special talents to sing psalms and sacred music and to lead the assembly in congregational hymns. In this tradition, which is characteristic of the Anglican, Episcopal, Baptist, and some Evangelical Christian churches, the choir members are robed and prominently located behind or adjacent to the altar, separate from the assembly.

Choir seating should be carefully designed to make the most of the choir's efforts.

- Movable seats are preferable, so that the number of seats can be adjusted to exactly match the number of choir members.

- The seats should be spaced 24 in. on center to allow space for robes and large music folders.

- The choir should be seated on risers to permit each of the choir members to see the director and to allow their voices to project. Risers should preferably be built-in, of substantial construction rather than portable, so that they adequately project the sound. The riser height can vary from a minimum of 8 in. to a maximum of 24 in.

- In a medium-sized choir, there should not be more than three rows of singers for optimum eye contact with the director. There may be five rows in large choirs.

Space for musical instruments should be provided adjacent to the choir space to accommodate a variety of ethnic music. These instruments may include an organ console or piano, trumpets, drums, guitars, and a set of hand bells. A location for the music director, if he or she is not leading from the keyboard, should be provided so that all the musicians have eye contact with the music director.

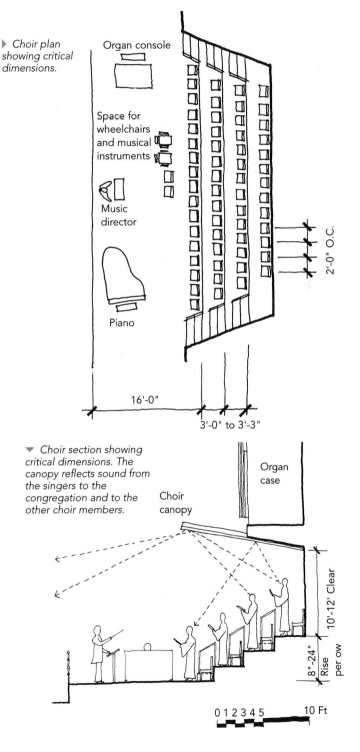

▶ Choir plan showing critical dimensions.

Organ console

Space for wheelchairs and musical instruments

Music director

Piano

2'-0" O.C.

16'-0"

3'-0" to 3'-3"

▼ Choir section showing critical dimensions. The canopy reflects sound from the singers to the congregation and to the other choir members.

Organ case

Choir canopy

10'-12' Clear

8"-24" Rise per ow

0 1 2 3 4 5   10 Ft

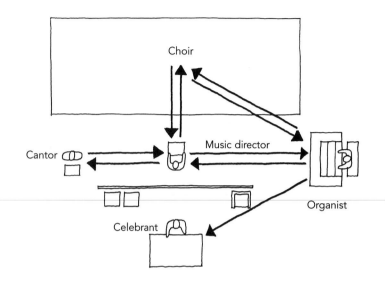

▲ Diagram showing the relationship of music director, organ console, choir, cantor, and celebrant.

The Organ

A pipe organ is the most effective instrument for accompanying congregational singing and is the preferred instrument for use in churches. A genuine pipe organ is preferable over an electronic instrument for authenticity of sound, long-term value, and durability.

From a planning standpoint, there are a number of important design considerations for locating the organ:

- The console should be close to the choir so that the organist can conduct from the keyboard.

- The pipes should be as close to the choir as possible to minimize the sound delay between the organist playing and the choir hearing the sound.

- The pipes should be located so that the sound projects well into the assembly.

The optimum layout is for the organ pipes to be mounted immediately above the choir so that the organ loft acts as a choir canopy. See Chapter 12 for recommendations on organ location. The de-

tailed design considerations for a pipe organ are discussed further in Chapter 10.

Bells

In the Christian tradition, cast bells were introduced in the West in the eighth century C.E., and their use spread widely throughout Europe in the tenth and eleventh centuries during the age of great cathedral building. Bells are used to summon the faithful to prayer, to mark the passing of the hours, to mourn the dead, to warn the community of impending danger, and to ring out in jubilation at times of collective celebration. Bells are also used in the form of carillons and in change ringing to provide music. In Eastern religions, where bells have been cast since the twelfth century B.C.E., bells are used to communicate directly with the gods. In many religions, bells are regarded as sacred objects. They are consecrated before being rung for the first time, and special prayers are spoken for their dedication.

The detailed considerations for the design and location of bell installations are described in Chapter 10.

The Reservation of the Sacrament

In Catholic churches, unused consecrated bread is kept, or reserved, for private devotion and for ministering to the sick and dying. The Sacrament should be kept locked in a tabernacle and, in accordance with the *General Instruction of the Roman Missal* (National Conference of Catholic Bishops 2000b), "The tabernacle in which the Most Blessed Sacrament is reserved [should] not be on the altar on which Mass is celebrated" (315). The location of the tabernacle should be determined "according to the judgment of the diocesan Bishop," and may be:

- Either in the sanctuary, apart from the altar of celebration, in the most suitable form and place, not excluding an old altar that is no longer used for celebration, or
- In another chapel suitable for adoration and private prayer of the faithful, and which is integrally connected with the church and conspicuous to the faithful.

New and renovated Catholic churches frequently include a Blessed Sacrament Chapel for the reserved Sacrament, which should include the following:

- A small number of pews or chairs (eight to fifteen) with kneelers.
- A pedestal or shelf for supporting the tabernacle so that it is visible to those seated in the chapel. The ciborium, or receptacle for the Sacrament, must be located at a height that is within comfortable reach of the priest.
- A sanctuary lamp hung over or adjacent to the tabernacle.

Although the chapel should be "conspicuous to the faithful," it should be acoustically separated from the main body of the church for quiet private prayer. In some churches, arrangements may be made for perpetual adoration of the Sacrament, when the Blessed Sacrament Chapel housing the Sacrament is open to the public 24 hours a day by means of a separate entrance. In this case the heating, ventilating, and security systems should be zoned to permit separate controls for the chapel.

Reconciliation

The Catholic Rite of Reconciliation or Penance, also known as confession, requires a private, soundproof room called a reconciliation chapel for meeting with a priest. Following the recommendations of the Second Vatican Council, the chapel should provide for both anonymous confession, kneeling at a fixed screen, and for a meeting, seated face to face with the priest.

In addition to the screen, grille, kneeler, and chairs, the chapel should be provided with a shelf for a Bible and appropriate iconography in the form of stained glass or artwork. Outside the door there should be two lights, one behind the name of the priest, indicating that the priest is present, and another connected to a pressure-sensitive switch in the penitent's chair and kneeler, indicating that the chapel is occupied.

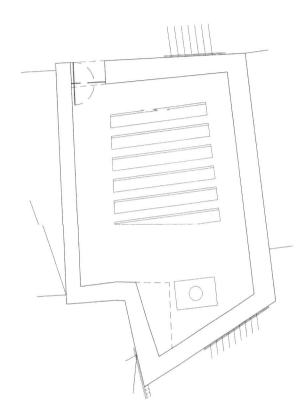

▲ *Plan of Blessed Sacrament Chapel, Cathedral of Our Lady of the Angels, Los Angeles, showing seating with kneelers, and the tabernacle on a low platform.*

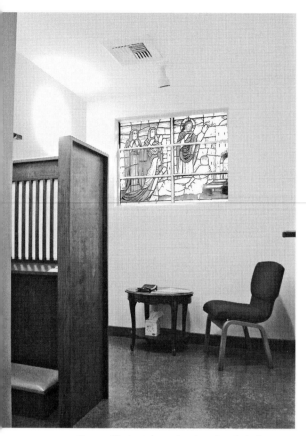

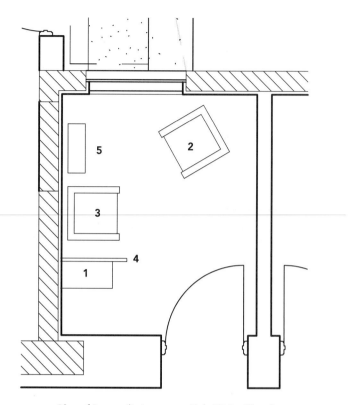

▲ Reconciliation room showing the chair that welcomes the penitent to a face-to-face meeting, and the screen for anonymous confession. Holy Trinity Church, San Pedro, California.

▲ Plan of Reconciliation room, Holy Trinity Church.
1 Kneeler for anonymous confession
2 Chair for face-to-face reconciliation
3 Priest's chair
4 Screen
5 Table for Bible and other items

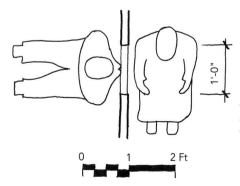

▶ Section of Reconciliation room showing critical dimensions.

◀ Plan of Reconciliation room showing critical dimensions.

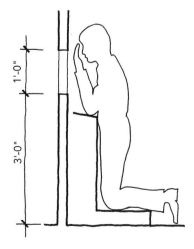

Ancillary Spaces

The following ancillary spaces are required in a church. Depending on the scale of the building, several functions may be combined into one space:

1. For denominations in which the priests are robed, a vesting sacristy should be provided, including the following:

   - Hanging wardrobes and large drawers for vestment storage

   - A large table or counter for laying out vestments

   - Drawers for the priests' personal effects

   - A reading desk and bookshelf

   - A hand sink, or adjacent bathroom

   - Space for several priests to robe

   - The controls for the church lighting and sound system (often located in this space)

   - A safe for the collection, or a money drop to a basement safe

   This space is usually approximately 10 ft × 20 ft, but the detailed requirements should be carefully reviewed with the users. It can be combined with a sacristy for sacred vessels, as described next.

2. A sacred vessels sacristy, or communion preparation room, is used for preparing, cleaning, and storing the vessels and elements used in the Eucharist. This space should provide:

   - Lockable and secure storage for the vessels used in the Eucharist

   - Storage space for glasses, cups, bowls, and plates used in communion

   - Counter space

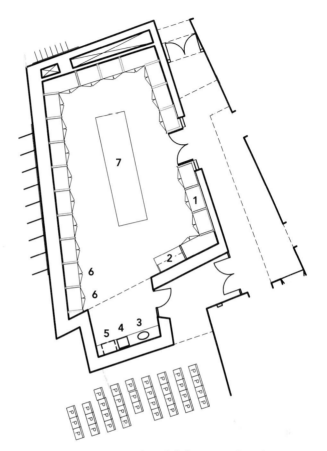

- A two-compartment sink and dishwasher

- In Catholic churches, a sacrarium, or sink draining directly to a dry well in the ground, not into the sanitary system, for disposal of holy water and washing of the vessels

This space is generally 8 ft × 10 ft, but the detailed requirements should be reviewed with the users.

3. A work sacristy, flower room, or environment room is used for storage and preparation of the flower arrangements, seasonal décor, and linens that decorate the church. It should include the following:

▲ Plan of vesting sacristy, Cathedral of Our Lady of the Angels, Los Angeles.
1 Vestment cabinets
2 Desk with bookshelf above
3 Sacrarium
4 Sink
5 Dishwasher
6 Control cabinets for sound and lighting systems
7 Vesting table

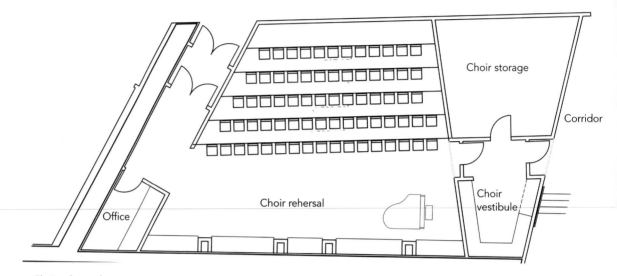

Choir storage

Corridor

Choir rehersal

Choir vestibule

Office

▲ *Choir rehearsal room. Note the double doors for soundproofing, the music director's office, and the musical instruments and music storage. In a church where the choir is robed, additional space is needed for storage and robing. Cathedral of Our Lady of the Angels, Los Angeles.*

- Cupboards for storing linens and flower vases
- A large two-compartment sink
- A work counter

This space should be approximately 8 ft × 10 ft.

4. A ministers' vesting room, similar to item (1), for the liturgical ministers and servers to store and put on their vestments.

5. Choir room. The requirements will vary according to the denomination and whether or not the choir is robed, but it may include:

- Music storage shelves
- Choir practice space (if the budget permits)
- Robe storage and robing space
- Lockers for storage of personal effects
- Musical instrument storage
- Drinking fountain
- Access to bathrooms

- Acoustic separation if used for choir practice

6. A bride's room, in which a bride and her entourage may dress and prepare for the wedding, includes the following:

- Work counter and sink
- Full-length mirror
- Access to a bathroom

7. In Presbyterian and Evangelical churches there may be rooms for private prayer and for small groups to pray together. The requirements for these spaces include:

- Acoustic isolation
- Natural light
- Dimmable artificial light
- An appropriate view, such as into a private garden

8. Some churches provide a cry room, from which parents, infants, and young children can participate in the service without the children's cries

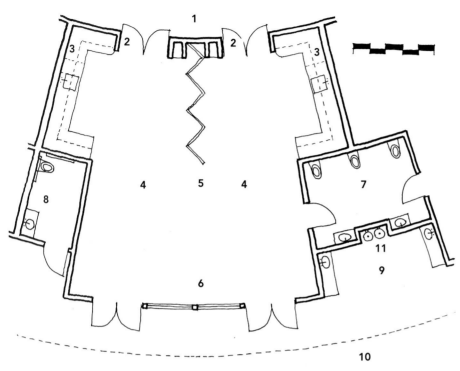

◀ Floor plan, child care room for 20 children, 840 net sq ft. The room is divisible and provided with both toddlers' and conventional bathrooms to allow it to be used for day care by two groups of children during Sunday services.

1 Access corridor for parents bringing their children to check in
2 Glass doors for observation by teachers and parents
3 Storage cabinets, sink, and dishwasher
4 Sleeping area
5 Accordion partition, allowing the space to be used by two groups during Sunday services
6 Indoor play area
7 Bathroom where teachers take children of both sexes
8 Separate girls' and boys' bathrooms for grade school children
9 Covered outside crafts area with sinks
10 Outside play area
11 Drinking fountain

disturbing the liturgy. The requirements include:

- Seating with easily cleanable finish
- Acoustic separation from the main worship space
- Sound system conveying the service
- A window overlooking the worship space; closed-circuit TV is sometimes used but not desirable
- Access to a bathroom without going through the worship space

9. A Bible study classroom, which may be used for children's worship during the service and for Bible classes before and after the service. The requirements are:

- Acoustic separation from the main worship space

- Storage cabinet for books and seasonal materials
- Appropriate room acoustics for singing and the spoken word
- This space should be approximately 30 ft × 30 ft

10. Child care spaces may range from a simple room where infants are cared for during the service to a fully developed child care facility that also serves the community during the week. Child care rooms should typically be provided with the following:

- Play area
- Nap area with space for cots
- Toy storage cabinets
- Counter, sink, and refrigerator
- Bathroom immediately adjacent

▲ *Devotional, Holy Trinity Church, San Pedro, California. Architect: Leo A Daly.*

- Counter for signing in children
- Immediate access to outside play space
- Cleanable finishes

Licensed child care facilities require a minimum area per child defined by local codes for indoor and outdoor play and additional spaces for staff offices and support.

11. Bathrooms should be provided for the worship space in accordance with local building codes (for example, a 1000-seat church requires 14 WCs for women and 7 fixtures for men). Where a vesting sacristy is provided, separate bathrooms should be provided for the priests, and separate facilities are required for child care. Separate facilities should also be provided for bride's room and for the choir if they are not adjacent to the main bathrooms.

12. Storage spaces are essential for keeping movable seating, seasonal décor, and banners. General storage space should be approximately 1.5 percent of the floor area of the church.

13. A kitchenette is often provided for preparing coffee and pastries before and after the service and for storing cups and plates. A space 6 ft × 8 ft is adequate, with a sink, refrigerator, and electrical power.

Devotionals

Catholic churches generally include several shrines or devotionals dedicated to the patron saints of the community. These may be either enclosed in separate chapels or located in niches off the nave. Each devotional includes the following:

- A shelf or pedestal supporting a statue or picture of the saint
- An offering box and candle rack
- Kneelers for private prayer

The candles can give off considerable heat and smoke. Adequate ceiling height should be provided over the candles to prevent staining of the ceiling, and air supply and exhaust should be provided to remove the heat.

Stations of the Cross

During the Lenten season, Catholics use the Stations of the Cross to symbolically reenact Jesus' journey to his crucifixion. Fourteen images, in painting or bas-relief, showing the events of the journey, are usually mounted on the nave walls, with a pew or kneeler for private prayer near each station. In some churches the entire congregation processes from station to station, in which case a generous aisle should be provided in front of the stations.

SYNAGOGUES

The synagogue is where members of the Jewish community come together for worship to affirm their commitment to enhancing Jewish life, to strengthen their bonds to Judaism, and to ensure their identity.

Design

Since the World Wars, synagogue design has shown a tendency to reject historical styles in favor of a contemporary architecture. This expression has encouraged the use of modern materials such as steel and reinforced concrete and has allowed synagogue architecture to adapt to the needs of climate and social environment.

Synagogues usually take the shape of a rectangle in plan, but may be of other shapes as well. The Jewish Law states that a synagogue should, whenever possible, face toward the Land of Israel. In the West, this means that a synagogue should be oriented with its entrance into the sanctuary on the west, and the congregation facing the east wall, which houses the sacred elements of the synagogue. The Law also declares that a synagogue should have windows along the wall that faces Israel. Many synagogue designs contain 12 windows along this wall as a symbolic reference to the twelve tribes of Israel. The Jewish Law has many references to the characteristics of a synagogue, and although it is not always exactly followed, there is often an effort to abide by it.

A synagogue reflects a triple function, as a House of Prayer, a House of Education, and a House of Assembly. These three functions act together to provide a place for worship, study, and the social activities of the Jewish community.

House of Prayer

The first function of a synagogue is to provide a place for prayer. The synagogue, unlike other places of worship, is not a house of God, where the deity dwells. Its sanctity rests in the community of believers. Although orthodox Jews believe that there was only one Temple, in Jerusalem, which was destroyed by the Romans, Reform congregations may refer to the synagogue as "temple." All synagogues contain a large worship space, or sanctuary, where the congregation meets for services. Within the sanctuary are a number of key programmatic elements.

Program elements

There are two key program elements in the sanctuary, the ark and the bema.

- The ark is a sacred shrine, recessed into the wall that faces Israel, which houses the scrolls of the Law. These scrolls are the first five books of the Hebrew Scriptures (Old Testament), called the Torah. The ark is kept closed, either by a set of double doors, a curtain, or both, and is decorated lavishly. The space in front of the ark is left open for accessibility to the scrolls. Hanging in front of the ark is a light, which always stays lit as a reminder of the Eternal Light and indicates respect for the holiness of the Torah. On each side of the ark is a plaque of the Ten Commandments, in Hebrew. At each side of the ark is a box with a seat. Typically, one side holds the seat of the rabbi and the other holds that of the cantor. A tall candleholder with seven branches is also placed near the ark (see color plate 14).

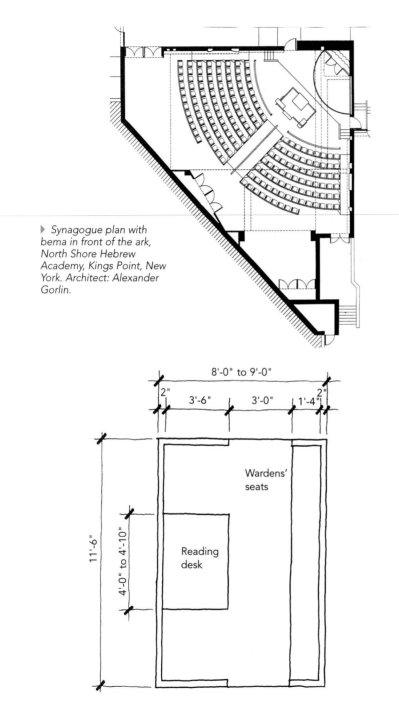

▶ *Synagogue plan with bema in front of the ark, North Shore Hebrew Academy, Kings Point, New York. Architect: Alexander Gorlin.*

8'-0" to 9'-0"

2" 3'-6" 3'-0" 1'-4" 2"

11'-6"

4'-0" to 4'-10"

Wardens' seats

Reading desk

▲ *Detailed plan of bema.*

- The bema is a raised platform from which the Torah is read and interpreted and from which services are conducted. The bema must be large enough to accommodate a reading desk and provide space around the desk for as many as five people. During services, the scrolls are taken from the ark and carried to the bema before the reading and returned afterward.

The location of the bema has moved over time. Originally, the bema was located in the center of the worship space, with the seats arranged along the three sidewalls facing inward. Then the bema was moved to the back wall in front of the ark, integrating these two features into one element. For this type of design, the seating is arranged in auditorium style, facing the direction of Israel. Today the location of the bema has returned to the center of the worship space, to emphasize the communal act of worship.

Considerations

Besides the two main program elements of a worship space, other considerations need to be addressed, such as the congregational seating and the separation of men and women.

- *Congregational seating.* Designing the congregational seating is a difficult task because of the wide range of attendance. The seating must provide for its members during usual services, as well as accommodate the large attendance on the High Holy Days. This problem is often solved with movable walls or partitions. Four types of seating are typically used: wooden pews, combination seating, upholstered individual chairs, and portable chairs. Each seat should contain a box beneath it to hold prayer books, shawls, and a book rest. The detailed design of congregational seating is discussed in Chapter 14.

- *Separation of men and women.* In some synagogues, particularly those that follow the Orthodox tradition, there is a required division between men and women. Some synagogues have separate rows for women marked by a dividing fence or balustrade, and others contain a separate gallery. The galleries are usually located on a balcony level to allow the women to hear the service without distracting the men. (See color plate 19.)

House of Education

Another function of a synagogue is to provide a place for education. Education has always played an important role in Jewish culture because the scriptures have been regarded as a complete guide to correct living. The educational role of the synagogue is to teach Hebrew, to provide an understanding of the Bible, and to transmit Jewish culture.

Program elements

Synagogues typically use classrooms for education. These classrooms may be located next to the main worship hall or in a separate wing, depending on the number of rooms. The size of the classrooms can vary according to the group size; however, a minimum requirement of 15 sq ft per child is essential. If an activity space is desired in the classroom, then the allotted space per child increases to 20–25 sq ft. Larger classrooms can act as a meeting rooms or banquet halls. Often there is a library within the educational facility.

House of Assembly

The third function of a synagogue is to provide a place for the community to gather. This gathering has always been a big part of the Jewish culture and has become more significant because of the Synagogue 2000 movement, a national project to revitalize the role of North American synagogues as sacred community centers.

Program elements

Program elements, such as a social hall and lounge, are important to the social aspects of a synagogue.

- The social hall is a large space, usually with tables and chairs that can be manipulated to serve multiple functions. If a kitchen is designed nearby, the social hall may act as a dining hall. If a stage is added, it may become a theater or lecture hall. With the chairs and tables removed, the social hall may be transformed into a dance hall or a game room. The social hall may also be used as an expansion of the worship space during the High Holy Days. The size of a social hall can vary, depending on the size of the congregation and the position and design of the tables and chairs that will be used. When folding chairs positioned in rows are requested, 7 sq ft per person should be estimated. If long tables are used, then the square footage increases to about 12 ft per person.
- The lounge also serves many purposes. It may be used after services, evening affairs, meetings, or receptions for conversation and refreshments. The location of the lounge is significant for two reasons. First, the congregation should be able to retire

to the lounge after a service is held, which suggests that it be adjacent to the worship space. Second, because tea and coffee are usually served in the lounge, it is important that it be located near the kitchen.

Considerations

Besides the spaces designed for social functions, other features accommodate the social needs of a synagogue. Because members of the congregation enjoy meeting and visiting with other members, generously sized corridors, aisles, and lobbies should accommodate social interaction. A few extra feet of space permits friends to pause and talk without obstructing the flow of other people. Social needs are also accommodated outside the synagogue with wide sidewalks and paved areas.

Other Program Elements

Synagogues include program elements that do not fall specifically within the aforementioned three divisions. These features are the foyer, the kitchen, the administrative units, and the rabbi's office.

- The foyer is the space that lies between the street entrance and the entrance to the sanctuary. This space is significant because of the orientation of the synagogue. Because the doors that lead into the sanctuary must face a specific direction, and not all sites allow for the street entrance to follow this orientation, a space is needed before entering the sanctuary to make any adjustments needed.

- Most synagogues have a kitchen; some have more than one. The size of the kitchen depends on the number of people being served. Generally, it

▼ *Synagogue plan with bema in the center, showing entry foyer with street entrance off-center from the sanctuary entrance. Congregation Orach Chaim, New York City. Renovation architect: Alexander Gorlin.*

1 *Entry at street level below*
2 *Grand stair*
3 *Upper level lobby*
4 *Sanctuary*
5 *Bema*
6 *Ark*
7 *Double-height vestibule open to below*
8 *Office*
9 *Library*
10 *Rooftop sukkah*

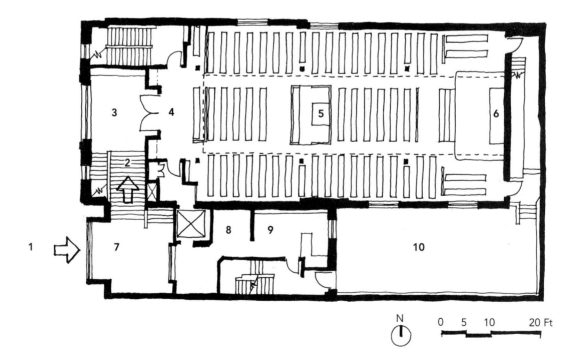

requires a larger area than a commercial kitchen for the same number of meals served, and it needs to have large areas for preparation and storage. The location of the kitchen is important because, as mentioned earlier, it needs to serve the lounge and the social hall. In Orthodox synagogues, there must be two separate kitchens, one for the preparation of dairy products and one for meat. There are also separate place settings for each food group, which suggests the need for more dishes and larger storage facilities.

- The administrative offices are usually located on the ground floor, where they are easily accessible from the main entrance. A typical administrative suite contains a main business office, an executive director's office, a mail and equipment room, and a waiting room.

- The rabbi's office, also called a study room, should be easily accessible but not too public. It must connect to the sanctuary and the administrative offices. The rabbi's office usually houses a small library. Because a rabbi does not live in the synagogue, no special arrangements are made for living quarters.

Separate Facilities

Synagogues have separate buildings for certain activities, such as funerals and purifications.

- Funerals are not permitted in synagogues, so there is a separate prayer hall at Jewish cemeteries. This hall is a covered open space with a door at each end, one for the entrance and the other for the exit.

- A *mikvah,* which is similar in design to a hydrotherapy pool, is a separate facility used for purification. In Judaism, purification is accomplished by adults through total immersion. Pools are described in detail in Chapter 10.

MOSQUES

The mosque is the principal religious building of the Islamic community. It embodies the Islamic identity through its architecture and reinforces traditional values through its symbolism. The mosque itself takes on an identity by drawing from the social, cultural, and economic factors of its surroundings.

"Although the rites of prayer are identical for all branches of Islam, there is no rigidly prescribed architectural vocabulary" (Serageldin 1996, p. 9). The ritual requirements in Islam have created only few specific formal and symbolic features of the mosque. The most important of these requirements are that a place of worship is set aside, the direction of prayer should be toward Mecca, and a series of movements should accompany the recitations of prayer. A mosque is a place where Muslims bow before God to affirm their obedience to his will, and therefore it must speak to those who use it. It should provide a spiritual experience and be seen as an anchor of identity for the community.

Site Planning

Most mosques sit on a raised platform, above street level, which allows visitors to reach the mosque by ascending a set of stairs. This gives the mosque a sense of monumentality, which is imperative for contemporary mosques, inasmuch as they tend to merge into the urban fabric.

Building Types

According to Ismail Serageldin, there are five different building types that house mosques. He characterizes these types as large state mosques, major landmark mosques, community center complexes, small local mosques, and *zawiyas* (Serageldin 1996).

- A large state mosque is a monumental structure, commissioned by governmental authorities to signify the state's commitment to Islam.

- A major landmark mosque is just as the term implies, a mosque that is designed to function as a landmark that dominates the landscape.

- A community center complex serves multiple functions. Usually, it contains libraries, educational spaces, and meeting rooms, in addition to serving as a place for prayer. Parts of a complex may also be used by the imam, the leader of the religious community, as a home for himself and his family.

- Small local mosques are located in neighborhoods or small villages. Their dimensions are modest.

- A *zawiya* is a small prayer area found in a larger complex. Usually, it receives only a designated space and therefore is not a building itself.

Plan Types

Most generally, mosque plans fall into two categories: open and closed.

- The open-plan design is a rectangular structure with a partial roof. The prayer area located under the covered section is lined with rows of columns, which create aisles that can run either laterally or longitudinally. The uncovered section can also be lateral or longitudinal.

- The closed-plan design consists of a square prayer space, defined by walls or piers at the four corners, and is usually covered by a dome. The closed-plan mosque has few, if any, internal supports.

Program Elements

Whether an open-plan or closed-plan design is used, there are basic program elements—the prayer area, mihrab, *qibla* wall, *minbar,* courtyard, ablution facilities, galleries, and minaret—that are common to all mosques.

- The prayer area is the designated space for male worshipers to pray, shoulder to shoulder, in rows facing the mihrab. Often the floor is designed to mark each row through the

▼ *Mosque site plan showing orientation toward Mecca, Islamic Cultural Center of New York City. Architect: SOM.*

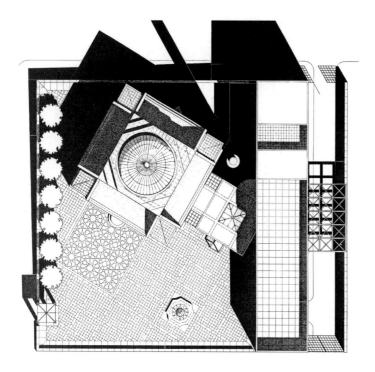

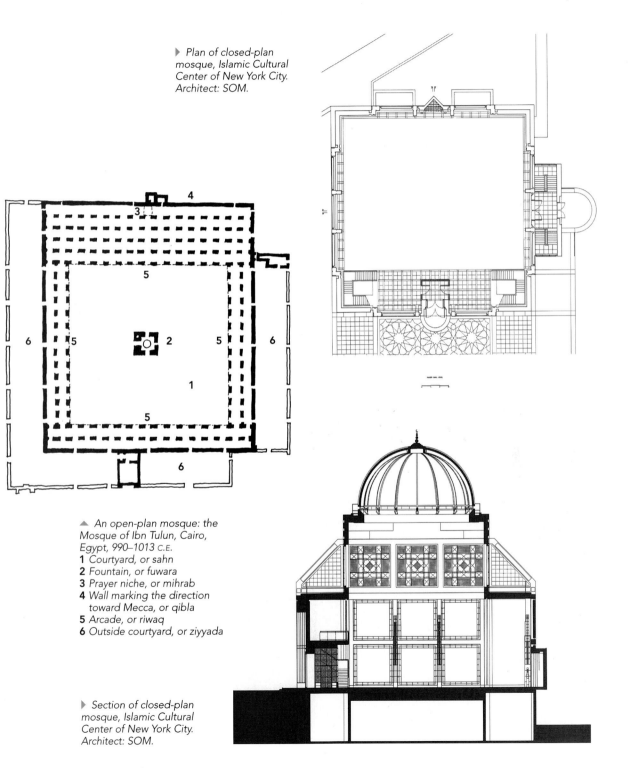

▶ Plan of closed-plan mosque, Islamic Cultural Center of New York City. Architect: SOM.

▲ An open-plan mosque: the Mosque of Ibn Tulun, Cairo, Egypt, 990–1013 C.E.
1 Courtyard, or sahn
2 Fountain, or fuwara
3 Prayer niche, or mihrab
4 Wall marking the direction toward Mecca, or qibla
5 Arcade, or riwaq
6 Outside courtyard, or ziyyada

▶ Section of closed-plan mosque, Islamic Cultural Center of New York City. Architect: SOM.

▲ Qibla *wall and gallery, Anjuman e Najmi Mosque, Irving, Texas. Oglesby Green Architects. Photo: Charles Davis Smith.*

polygons. The polygon shape is usually driven by the orientation toward Mecca.

- The orientation toward Mecca is identified in a mosque by a mihrab, or niche. The prayer leader stands in front of the mihrab when he delivers the sermon. The mihrab is located in the *qibla* wall.

- In every mosque there is one wall that differs from the rest, the *qibla* wall. The difference between this wall and the others is usually defined by its size and the mihrab. This wall indicates the direction of Mecca.

- The minbar is the pulpit used for Friday sermons and special occasions. The minbar takes the form of a miniature flight of stairs, leading to a platform at the top, from which the speaker addresses the congregation. Usually, the minbar is an enclosed structure with an entrance portal. It is located to the right of the mihrab, in front of the *qibla* wall.

- The courtyard, or *sahn,* is often used as a transitional space between the outside world and the mosque sanctuary. The courtyard provides a space for colonnades, or *riwaqs,* with one that is larger than the others, oriented toward Mecca.

- Many mosque courtyards contain a fountain or pool. This fountain can be either decorative or used for ablution. If the fountain is for decoration, there will be another source of water at the entrances of the mosque for ablution. It is here that Muslims remove their shoes and perform a ritual of ablution of the face, hands, and feet. This ritual is imperative to prevent any dirt from being carried into

use of color or pattern. The prayer area is usually of square or rectangular shape in plan, although there are many mosques that take the shape of

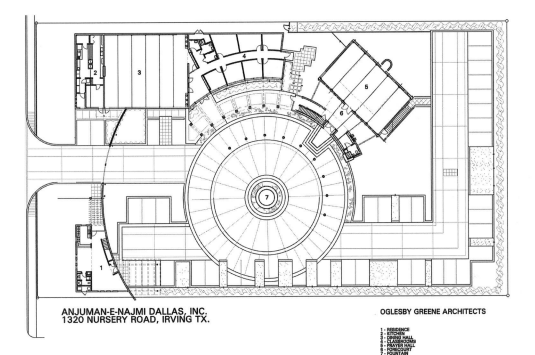

ANJUMAN-E-NAJMI DALLAS, INC.
1320 NURSERY ROAD, IRVING TX.

OGLESBY GREENE ARCHITECTS

1 - RESIDENCE
2 - KITCHEN
3 - DINING HALL
4 - CLASSROOMS
5 - PRAYER HALL
6 - FORECOURT
7 - FOUNTAIN

▲ *Plan, Anjuman e Najmi Mosque, Irving, Texas.*

▶ *Minbar, King Fahad Mosque, Culver City, California. Photo: Ellen Kuch.*

▲ *Minaret, Anjuman e Najmi Mosque, Irving, Texas. Oglesby Green Architects. Photo: Charles Davis Smith.*

lim prayer times are fixed by the sun and change daily, it becomes the job of the muezzin to call the followers to prayer.

Other Facilities

Besides the worship spaces, there are other facilities within a mosque, such as a classroom, a conference room, a library, and a shoe storage area.

- Many mosques have a classroom for teaching religion and Arabic. The size of the classroom depends on the size of the congregation. Because chairs are not typically used, but an activity space is customary, 15 sq ft per person should be provided.

- The conference room is used for meetings and lectures and is not open to the public. It is usually located on a separate level, away from the prayer area, so that it does not disrupt prayer and ritual.

- Mosques usually contain a library or an adult study room. It is typically located on the first floor, giving access to all. The books and information provided in the library are written in Arabic.

- A storage facility for shoes is necessary in every mosque. It may take the form of a separate room or simply racks aligning the walls of the mosque. In either case, it must be located at the entrance to the mosque. When a visitor enters a mosque, the shoes must be removed and the ritual of ablution followed.

Architectural Features

Mosque designs include architectural features such as gateways, domes, and *muqarnas.*

the prayer area, which is a clean, pure space. There are separate ablution facilities for men and women. These facilities are described in detail in Chapter 10.

- The galleries of a mosque are designated prayer areas for Muslim women. They allow women to join in the prayers without distracting the men or being distracted themselves. The prayer area floor space allotted to women ranges from 5 to 25 percent of the main prayer area. Many mosques have a separate entrance into the galleries for Muslim women.

- The minaret is a distinguished freestanding tower that serves dual functions. First, it is seen as a landmark, because it signifies a place of worship for Muslims. Second, the minaret is the place from which the call to daily prayer, *adhan,* is made. Because Mus-

- The gateway, or *iwan,* marks the threshold to a sacred space. It takes one from the common place of the street to the spiritual space of the mosque.
- Domes were first used in Islamic memorial buildings because of their symbolic reference to paradise. Later, they were incorporated in places of worship and soon became common architectural features in mosque architecture. A dome highlights the centrality and symmetry of the mosque and provides a visual focus for the building complex. (See color plate 21.)
- *Muqarnas* are commonly found in Islamic architecture. They resemble stalactites and are used to make the transition from square to round shapes in vaulted ceilings.

Interior and Exterior

Certain traditions are followed in designing the interior and exterior walls of a mosque. The interior walls are decorated, in a variety of styles, to signify the sanctity of the interior space. Although the interior is highly ornate, it does not include any statues, pictures, or stained glass windows, so as to avoid the dangers of idolatry. Because depicting living beings through art is not favored, many Islamic artists use geometric designs to create decoration. Aesthetic expression is also achieved through calligraphy, woodworking, and tile working. The word is one of the most powerful reminders of the existence of the God, as the Qur'an is seen as the unmodified word of God. Muslims use calligraphy to present the Qur'an, to give visibility to the word of God, and to remind themselves of their faith. (See the illustration on page 9.)

▲ Street facade of storefront mosque, Paris, France. In the newly-forming Muslim communities of Europe and North America, converted commercial buildings and residences are often used for worship.

The exterior walls of a mosque are usually left bare. The exterior is treated to blend into a non-Muslim cultural context.

Symbolism

The mosque's architectural symbolism sets it apart from other buildings and establishes its position in the community. This symbolism is primarily created by the basic elements of the dome and minarets. The use of geometry and sym-

▲ *Dome with muqarnas form the interior. Shah Mosque, Isfahan, Iran (sixteenth century).*

teachings. Temples offer a noble and dignified atmosphere to meditate and calm the mind to the accompaniment of peaceful chanting.

The temple and temple complex

Buddhist temples range in size from small temples consisting of only one building to those that are a part of larger complex. Many temple complexes that are built today are designed to act not only as places of worship, but also as social meeting places for the surrounding areas. Such a complex may include educational buildings, dormitories, and a dining hall or tea room.

Site planning

Because temples can range in size, the amount of land needed can vary from a few thousand square feet to hundreds of acres. Ideally, temples are set on their grounds to take best advantage of the views of the surrounding terrain. Where a scenic vista is not available, as in an urban temple compound, care is taken to incorporate a reminder of the natural world in the form of a garden with ponds and trees.

Paths

There are many approaches to Buddhist temple design, all of which lead the visitor on a designated path that signifies a journey toward enlightenment. The design may be that of a circumambulating path, a segmented path, or an axial path.

- The circumambulating path surrounds a central sacred space and leads the worshiper through the concentric rings around the sacred center until it is finally reached.

metry symbolize the order of the world created by God. The symmetry along the axes of the mosque creates a flow of forms and rhythms, which convey a sense of peace. The open-plan design expresses divine infinity, whereas the closed-plan design signifies divine unity. (See color plate 22.)

TEMPLES

Temples house the worship spaces of many religions. The following sections discuss Buddhist and Hindu temples.

Buddhist Temples

The numerous strands of Buddhism create many different styles of temples. Buddhist architecture of every region has its own unique character due to differing cultural and environmental factors, but overall it presents an image of beauty, strength, and stability. The temple is the main Buddhist sanctuary. It is a gathering place where followers make offerings to the Buddha and learn the Buddha's

▷ *Site plan of a large rural Buddhist temple. International Buddhist Progress Society, Hsi Lai Temple, Hacienda Heights, California.*
 1 *Gateway*
 2 *School*
 3 *Gift shop*
 4 *Bodhisattva hall*
 5 *Courtyard*
 6 *Auditorium*
 7 *Conference room*
 8 *Dining hall*
 9 *Tea room*
 10 *Main shrine*
 11 *Meditation hall*
 12 *Requiem pagoda*

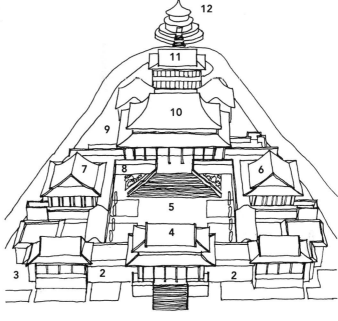

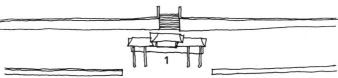

▽ *Small urban Buddhist temple. Higashi Honganji Buddhist Temple, Los Angeles.*

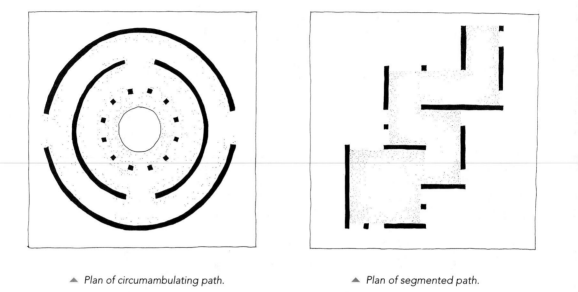

▲ Plan of circumambulating path.

▲ Plan of segmented path.

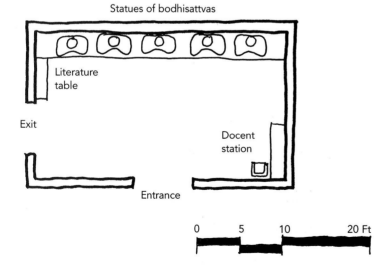

Statues of bodhisattvas

Literature table

Exit

Docent station

Entrance

0   5   10   20 Ft

▲ Plan of typical bodhisattva hall.

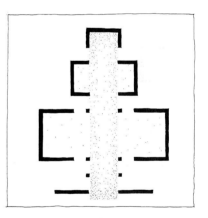

▲ Plan of axial path.

- The segmented path is a multidirectional connected series of paths that often lead through gateways and other spaces before reaching the sacred place. This is the most commonly designed path in Buddhist temple complexes.

- The axial path leads the visitor along a linear axis, with buildings arranged symmetrically on either side. The axial path is commonly found in a temple complex designed with the gate, the entrance hall, the main shrine, and the mediation hall all in line with the axis (Barrie 1996).

Program elements

Buddhist temples are usually part of a larger complex that includes program elements such as a main gate, a bodhisattva hall, a meditation hall, a courtyard, gardens, and a main shrine.

- The main gate of a temple complex establishes a clear threshold that delineates the passage from the outside world to the inside, sacred world. The main gate is reached after climbing a set of steps, which symbolizes the visitor's rising above the everyday world. These steps continue up to the bodhisattva hall.

- The decorated bodhisattva hall, consisting of statues of the Buddha or bodhisattvas, beings who help others in the quest for salvation, is the first building encountered after passing through the gateway. Followers may bow or make offerings below these statues to show respect for the Buddha or the bodhisattvas.

- The meditation hall is a quiet, bare space where devotees may go to meditate and pray and, in some temples, to attend meditation class. Some strands of Buddhism allow for kneeling pads to be placed in rows on the floor for prayer.

- The courtyard is important in the temple complex design because it allows for walking meditation. The design and elements of the courtyard differ between temples. However, the elements chosen for the design of the courtyard are specific to the form of Buddhism that is practiced in the temple. Usually, there are statues placed on the corners of the courtyard to ward off evil.

- Gardens within the temple complex, usually with running water or ponds, are rich in symbolism in the Buddhist tradition. The gardens frequently include statues that emphasize certain beliefs.

- The main shrine, where the religious services are conducted, is not only the largest and most decorative building within a temple complex, but also the most important. The elements of the main shrine are the altar, a statue or statues, instruments, kneeling pads, and offering tables with candles.

  - The altar is located along the back wall of the main shrine. Its design can range from the simple and modest to the elaborate and large scale. Most altars contain a statue or statues of the Buddha.

  - The statue or statues of the Buddha are the most prominent objects of worship. They are usually large and decorated in gold.

  - Placed to the sides of the altar are instruments, such as gongs, drums, and bells. These are used by members of the monastic community during chanting ceremonies.

- Kneeling pads may or may not be used, depending on the beliefs associated with the temple. If kneeling pads are used, they are placed on the floor of the main shrine in rows facing the altar.
- The offering tables are usually placed on the sides of the altar. On these tables are candles, which can be lit as offerings to the Buddha. Other offerings can be made to the Buddha, such as incense, flowers, lamps, soaps, fruits, tea, food, treasure, beads, and clothes.

Other facilities

A temple complex usually has many other facilities, such as a meeting room, an auditorium, an education center, a library, a gift shop, and a dining hall with a tea room, all of which are open to followers. These facilities are spaces within buildings and are not necessarily separate buildings themselves. A temple complex also houses dormitories for members of the monastic community and their separate dining hall.

- The meeting room is used for national and sometimes international meetings and lectures. It can vary in size, depending on the size of the temple and the types of meetings that are held there.
- The auditorium is equipped for lectures, performances, and Buddhist wedding ceremonies. Unlike that of a typical auditorium, the floor is level throughout, but there may be a raised platform or stage at the front.
- The education center consists of one or more classrooms where devotees study their faith and culture. Some larger temples function as a Buddhist study and research center for educational institutions nearby.
- The library houses a variety of Buddhist material and is open to all. It is usually situated next to the education center.
- A gift shop offering books, cassettes, videotapes, statues, incense, beads, meditation supplies, and artwork is usually found in the larger temples.
- The dining hall and tea room may be one space or two separate spaces. The dining hall is designed to accommodate the vast number of people who visit the temple during ceremonies. Its layout is similar to that of a buffet restaurant. If the tea room is a separate space, it is usually a small room with tables and chairs.
- The dormitories are separated from the rest of the temple complex because they are used only by the monastic community. Most dormitories are composed of individual rooms with shared bathrooms.

▼ *Plan of a typical main shrine.*

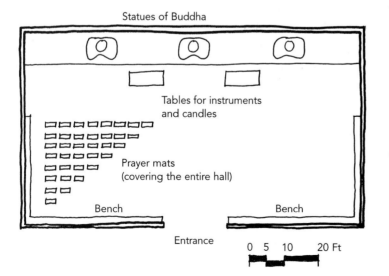

Statues of Buddha

Tables for instruments and candles

Prayer mats (covering the entire hall)

Bench   Bench

Entrance   0 5 10   20 Ft

Structure and materiality

The reverence for nature in the Buddhist faith is reflected in the structure of the sacred buildings, which are generally built of wood. Some temples, especially those in Japan, use wood for the details throughout the space, paper for screens, straw for mats, and wood shingles. The primary structure of a Buddhist temple is usually a post-and-lintel frame.

The post-and-lintel frame creates large rectilinear spaces in plan, which are often subdivided by both fixed and freestanding walls. The space between each pair of posts is called a bay. The core of the temple is usually an odd number of bays in width by at least two bays in depth. Surrounding this central core, in most structures, are peripheral sections, usually one bay wide.

Resting on the post-and-lintel skeleton is a great roof, which is usually the most arresting aspect of the exterior design. The eaves extend well beyond the sides of the building, protecting the verandas beneath. (See color plates 23 and 24.)

Proportion

To ensure harmony within a single building or between many buildings, Buddhist temples follow a system of proportional design. Building dimensions are related to one another through modules and mathematical ratios.

Hindu Temples

The Hindu temple is a central element in all aspects of everyday life in the Hindu community. To a Hindu, the temple is important not only for its religious elements but also for its cultural, social, and educational functions. All aspects of a Hindu temple focus on the goal of enlightenment and liberation through the principles of design and construction and through the elements and form of its architecture.

The Hindu temple is designed to effect contact between humans and the gods. The process by which this contact is made stems from ancient texts on Hindu ideas and beliefs, which have created complex symbolism and strict regulations that guide the form of temple architecture.

▲ *Center of Gravity Foundation Hall, Jemez Springs, New Mexico. View of entry and main shrine. Predock Frane Architects.*

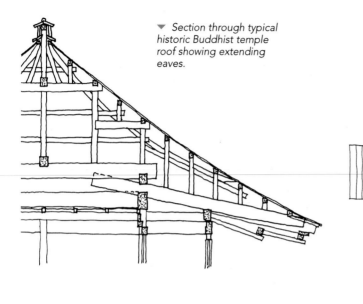

▼ Section through typical historic Buddhist temple roof showing extending eaves.

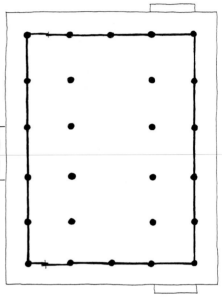

▼ Center of Gravity Foundation Hall, Jemez Springs, New Mexico. Exterior view showing extending eaves. Predock Frane Architects.

▲ Plan of temple core with peripheral sections. Raido, East Precinct, Horyuji, Japan.

Site planning and rituals

To gain full benefit for their resident deities, early temples were erected in locations where the gods dwelled or might be revealed, such as near groves, rivers, mountains, and springs. Today, many temples are built on hilltops and near rivers. However, where these natural locations are not available, water, shade, and seclusion can be used to connect the temple to nature.

The ground plan

The Hindu temple connects the world of the gods with the work of humans through its ground plan, providing a link between humankind and the universe. The ground plan "functions as a sacred geometric diagram of the essential structure of the universe" (Michell 1988). This sacred geometric diagram, or mandala, is a concentric figuration, which regulates the layout of the temple. It is based on a strict grid made up of either 64 or 81 squares. These squares are dedicated to deities. The position of the squares is in accord with the importance attached to each of the deities, with the squares in the center representing the temple deity and the outer squares depicting the gods of lower rank. It is at the center of the mandala that the sacred object, image, or symbol of the deity is placed. Because astronomy and astrology are integral to Hinduism, the orientation of the mandala and the plan of the temple follow a strict cardinal orientation.

Mathematics also plays an important role in determining the proportions of the ground plan and the temple design. "Only if the temple is constructed correctly according to a mathematical system can it be expected to function in harmony with the mathematical basis of the universe" (Mitchell 1988).

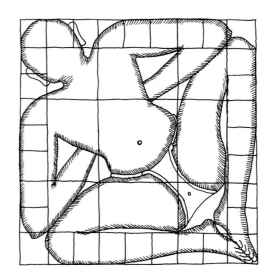

Elements and form of the architecture
Key program elements

The worshiper's movement through a Hindu temple is of great importance. The key program elements are arranged to promote the movement of the devotee from the outside toward the sanctuary through a series of enclosures, which become increasingly sacred. All of these elements are aligned along the east-west axis with their entrances facing the rising sun. The key program elements are the *ardhamandapa, mandapa,* and *garbagriha.*

- The *ardhamandapa,* or porch, acts as the entrance to the temple. It is usually on a raised platform with steps leading up to it.

- The *mandapa* is the central hall that serves as an assembly for the devotees. There may be one or more *mandapas,* which may be either attached or detached from the *ardhamandapa.*

- The *garbagriha,* literally "womb chamber," is the inner sanctuary that houses the sacred objects, images, and symbols of the deity to whom the temple is dedicated.

▲ Mandala plan used to establish the geometry of a temple sanctuary. The plan is overlaid with a figure called vastu purusha, or cosmic man, whose body determines the geometrical layout.

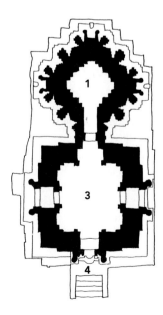

▲ ▶ *Floor plan and section
of Hindu temple aligned on
east-west axis showing
principal spaces.*
1 Garbagriha *or shrine room*
2 Sikhara *or pyramidal roof*
3 Mandapa *or pillared hall*
4 Ardhamandapa *or porch*

Traditionally, the height of the temple
is not important, although the highest
point occurs over the center of the
garbagriha. The movement upward is
both visual and symbolic, inasmuch as
it dominates the external appearance of
the temple and connects the worshiper
with the universe beyond.

Other programmatic elements
All temples have an *ardhamandapa, mandapa,* and *garbagriha,* but some include
other program elements such as educational facilities, auditoriums, courtyards, and
places for ablution. Education is of great
importance in Hinduism. In some temples
the *mandapa* is used for recitation and
singing, and larger temple complexes have
separate buildings dedicated to education.

Architectural styles

Although there are formal regulations for the design of a Hindu temple, a particular temple may have its own style, corresponding to its geographical, climatic, cultural, and historical environment. Many of the temple styles found in the United States and throughout the world were influenced by those of India. The styles of India are characterized in early documentation, which classifies three orders: the Nagura, the Dravida, and the Vesara. "These orders do not function as all-embracing stylistic categories, but indicate a general impulse to classify temples according to their typological features" (Michell 1988).

- The Nagura, or northern style, is characterized by a beehive-shaped tower, or *shikhara,* which rises in a massive conical shape. The *shikhara* is made up of layers of architectural elements such as *kapotas* and *gavaksas,* all topped by a large round element called an *amalaka.* Even though the plan is based on a square, the walls are broken up so that the tower gives the impression of being circular. Over time, the tower has been surrounded by many smaller reproductions of itself. The *shikhara* is seen as the most prominent element of the temple.

- The Dravida, or southern style, is characterized by a pyramid-shaped tower consisting of progressively smaller units as it near the top, which is capped with a dome. In southern terminology, the dome is called the *shikhara.* Elaborate gateways, or *gopurams,* are the most striking feature of the temple.

- The Vesara is a hybrid of the Nagara and Dravida styles.

Structure and materiality

Because of its physical appearance, and because its structure has relied on gravity and mass instead of spatial enclosure, Hindu temple architecture has often been called large-scale sculpture.

Even though many temples today are modeled after older temples, the materials used to build these temples have been modernized. Older temples were built with stone and brick, but temples being built today use concrete, which is molded to reproduce the curved and clustered towers typical of older temples. (See color plates 25 and 26.)

CHAPTER 4

SITE SELECTION AND PLANNING

Site planning includes site selection, planning for vehicle and pedestrian circulation, the location and arrangement of the buildings, drives, walkways, and parking lots, and preliminary selection of plant and paving materials.

SITE SELECTION
Location
If possible, the congregation should select a site that is geographically close to its population center to minimize travel distance. Survey the congregation to determine the population center.

Size and Potential for Future Expansion
The site should be large enough, or adjacent contiguous sites should be available, to accommodate the full program and anticipated future expansion, taking into account the building height and lot coverage permitted by the zoning code.

A rule of thumb for determining the area of a site area is one usable acre of land for each 120 persons attending the service for a suburban site. Calculation of the site area should take into account the required setbacks.

Visibility
The site should be sufficiently prominent to make the place of worship a landmark at the center of a community. It should play a significant role in the urban fabric.

Availability of Public Transport
The site should be within ¼ mile of bus lines and rail or subway stations, to provide access for elderly people, teenagers,

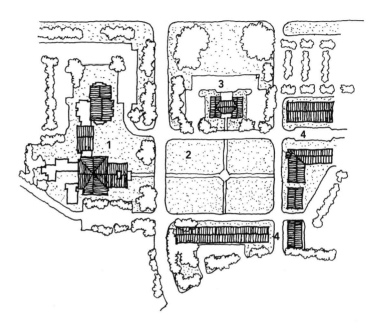

and others without cars. Otherwise, the religious organization will have to provide its own bus or carpool system to pick up members of the congregation who do not drive.

Ease of Vehicular Access
Large-capacity streets should serve the site for peak in and out traffic. The site should preferably have multiple exits onto more than one street so that cars can quickly leave the parking lot in preparation for the next service. For a worship space with more than 2000 seats, a traffic engineer should calculate their traffic flows and their impact on the surrounding streets.

Zoning and Environmental Constraints
The architect should verify the current zoning of the site. It is preferable to select a site where the construction of the wor-

▲ Site plan showing the church as the focus of a community, Mashpee Commons, Massachusetts. Planners: Duany & Plater-Zyberk.
1 Church and parish hall
2 Village green
3 Village hall
4 Retail and residential areas

ship space is permitted without a conditional use permit or zone change. Because of organized community opposition, zoning changes for worship buildings in residential areas can be lengthy and costly processes (see Chapter 5). If the site has not been previously developed, a preliminary environmental review should be conducted to ensure that construction will not have an adverse environmental impact, for example, on endangered species, historic sites, existing view corridors, or watercourses.

Adjacent Land Uses

The adjacent land uses should be compatible with the worship space and the outside gathering of the congregation and should not generate excessive noise or odor. If possible, they should be community functions, such as a school, community center, or park, that complement the worship space.

Physical Condition of the Site

The institution should conduct a preliminary physical, geotechnical, and environmental survey to make sure the following conditions are appropriate for constructing buildings, driveways, and parking lots:

- Topography: Is there adequate flat land not requiring extensive grading?

- Utilities: Are electricity, water, gas, telephone, and sanitary sewer facilities available?

- Soils, geology, and water table: Can the subsoil support the proposed project?

- What were the previous uses of the site? Are there likely to be hazardous materials buried on-site?

VEHICULAR AND PEDESTRIAN MOVEMENT
Traffic and Parking Design

Automobile parking is an essential but potentially unattractive and expensive component of most worship environments. For significant projects, especially those that require environmental review or a conditional use permit, traffic and parking are politically charged issues that require the help of a professional traffic consultant.

Municipal zoning codes generally require one parking space per 30 sq ft of seating, or three seats, measured as 18 in. of pew length. Good practice requires 1 car space per 2.5 seats. Each parking space requires 400 sq ft, including landscape and driveways, which means approximately 100 spaces per acre. Parking stall sizes vary from 9' × 20' to 8'6" × 18', and some municipalities permit the use of compact spaces. Drive aisles are generally 24 ft wide.

With the agreement of the municipality, the parking does not have to be built all at once. To accommodate the growth of the congregation:

- Part of the site can be landscaped and set aside for future parking as the congregation grows.

- Parking on-grade can be replaced with multilevel structures in the future.

Parking should be conveniently available on-site for regular services; it is generally undesirable to walk more than 500 ft from a car to the door. For special holiday services, the following can be used to provide additional parking:

- Parking agreements with neighboring shopping centers, schools, and office buildings

- Rented shuttle buses to bring the congregation from remote parking lots
- The temporary use of school playgrounds or grass playing fields

The driveway design should be based on the following criteria:

- Allow the parking lot to empty and refill in the time between the end of one service and the beginning of the next, usually 45 minutes to 1 hour.
- Assume 300 cars per hour entering or exiting from each entry lane.
- The driveway design and parking aisle layout should allow drivers to circulate easily and look for parking spaces.
- Multiple driveways exiting onto separate streets help to distribute the traffic onto the surrounding road network.

Provide a drop-off lane on the right hand side of the entrance driveway close to the worship space, with accommodation for two or three cars dropping off passengers.

Local fire departments generally require driveways to provide access for their trucks to within 150 ft of any point on the exterior building wall. Driveways are typically 24–28 ft wide, with turnarounds at dead-ends, and must be designed for full highway loading to support the axle weight of the loaded trucks and their outriggers. Perforated blocks, that allow planting material to grow through them, are acceptable if installed on a gravel base to support the truck load.

▼ Site plan showing drop-off point and parking. St. Benedict Church and Parish Center, Chandler, Arizona. Architect: Leo A Daly.

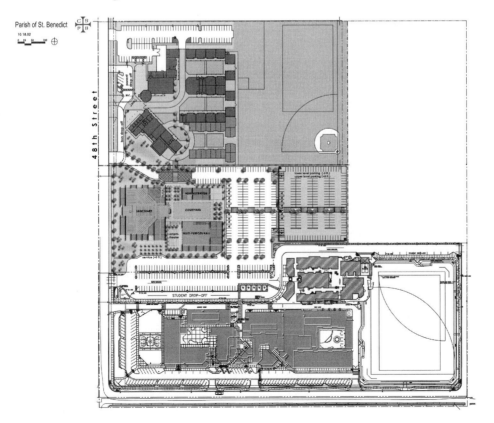

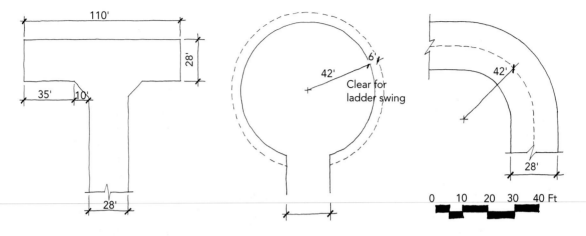

▲ Fire department driveway width and turnaround requirement.

If the program includes a fellowship hall and kitchen facilities, then a separate truck dock and trash compactor should be provided away from the public entrance. In certain climates, space should be allowed on the site for snow removal and storm water retention.

Pedestrian Movement

- Paths leading to the gathering space should be generously sized. Five feet is the minimum width that permits two people to walk abreast. Ten feet is appropriate for the main entrance to a 700-seat building, while 20 ft is appropriate for a 1600-seat space.

- The route from the parking to the gathering space should be accessible to those in wheelchairs and those who have difficulty walking, so they do not have to take a separate route:

  - Avoid the use of steps.
  - A slope should not exceed 5 percent, with a cross slope not exceeding 2 percent.
  - If ramps steeper than 5 percent are required, they should be no steeper than 8.33 percent, with handrails on both sides.

- Use paving materials, such as stone, brick, concrete or asphalt paving, or stabilized decomposed granite, that provide traction in all weather conditions but do not offer resistance to wheelchairs.

The pedestrian spaces should accommodate large crowds for religious festivals, but they should also have sufficient detail and "nooks and crannies" to feel comfortable when only a handful of visitors are present.

Promoting fellowship is an important function of most religious institutions. The design of the pedestrian spaces can support casual encounters and conversations by:

- Concentrating the flows of people into primary walkways and plazas.

- Providing comfortable places for conversation such as arbors and benches.

- Making the circulation visible, using verandas and cloisters on the outside of buildings and using open landings with overlooks at upper floors instead of internal corridors.

- Making pedestrian spaces extensions of lobbies and gathering spaces. Building entrances should open off major open spaces.

DESIGN PRINCIPLES

Once a religious community has selected the site for a new building, it generally engages an architect and, on larger projects, a traffic engineer, landscape architect, and civil engineer to prepare a master plan. This master plan accommodates the needs of the institution, taking into account a forecast of future growth, and is submitted to municipal authorities for planning and zoning approval (see Chapters 2 and 5).

The principles of planning are discussed in the following paragraphs.

Landmark

Although the buildings should be designed to harmonize with existing structures and landscape, the worship space should be a visible landmark:

- By its situation at the high point of the site, in a location clearly visible from heavily trafficked streets and public spaces.

- By the height of the building in relation to its surroundings. Verify the height limit mandated by the zoning code.

- By the use of a bell tower, minaret, spire, or dome to give added height. Such structures are generally exempt from height regulations, although some communities may object to the elevated display of religious iconography.

- On an urban site, where the front of the building is part of a continuous street facade, by identifying the worship space through the use of unique materials or elaborate decoration or detailing.

▲ The church as a landmark in a typical New England community. First Christ Church, Farmington, Connecticut.

Site Definition

The threshold between the site and the public street must be carefully considered, on the one hand to mark the site as hallowed ground, but on the other to make sure it is visible and welcoming from the street.

- On an urban site, a forecourt defined by the use of distinctive paving, landscaping, and the presence of water can invite the public. The street in front may be closed to all except emergency vehicles, enhanced by paving and trees, and shared with other civic functions.

- On a suburban site, the edge may be marked with an attractive wall or well-tended landscaping.

- A sign should clearly identify the religious building and welcome visitors.

▲ Exterior plaza, Church of Jesus Christ of Latter-day Saints Temple, Salt Lake City, Utah. Architect: ZGF. Photo: Timothy Hursley, courtesy ZGF.

▼ Site plan showing pathway marked by special paving and shaded by trees to the gathering space. St. Benedict Church, Chandler, Arizona.

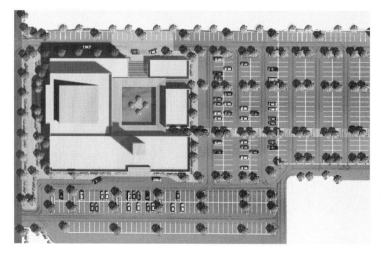

Journey to the Worship Space

The journey from the everyday world of the street to the gathering space should be carefully orchestrated.

- It may take a path leading up gently rising ground.
- A canopy can provide shade and protection from the rain
- Paving can define a walkway and separate it from the parking area.
- In hot climates the presence of water is welcoming and refreshing.

From the entry threshold, a focal point seen from a distance, partially concealed and then reappearing, draws the visitor to intermediate spaces such as courtyards or fountain areas that create a feeling of anticipation. From each space there is a glimpse of the next. The climax is a clear point of arrival at the most sacred space.

Orientation

For most Christian churches, the site layout will outweigh the need to orient the church. If possible, the church should face to the east to allow the morning sun to light the sanctuary.

Orthodox Jewish synagogues require the ark to be oriented toward Jerusalem, but for Reform congregations this is not important.

Mosques should always have the mihrab and prayer hall oriented so that the faithful pray facing Mecca.

Views

Views of nature, such as at the Wayfarer's Chapel, San Pedro, California (1949), by Lloyd Wright or the Chapel at Otaniemi, Finland (1956), by Kaija and Heikki Siren, can create a feeling of serenity and wonder. However, views from a worship space pose several challenges:

- If the view is from the front of the space, behind the ceremony, then strong frontal lighting from a clerestory or incandescent sources will be needed to avoid silhouetting the celebrants against the view.

- Any moving objects in the view, such as birds, airplanes, or distant figures, will be distracting.

- Unless the landscape covered by the view is protected, future development may spoil the vista that inspired the site plan.

- Unless the view is to the north, opening up to the view will expose the worship space to solar heat gain and glare at certain times of day.

It is generally safer to reserve the views for public areas such as gathering spaces and lobbies. Where there is potentially distracting activity around the site, such as in an urban setting, captured views into enclosed gardens can be provided.

Designing for Growth and Change

Religious institutions are dynamic. The site plan for a worship space must provide a clear organization for buildings, circulation, and open space that will maintain its coherence through phased construction and future expansion. The plan for St. Benedict Church, Chandler, Arizona, follows a courtyard form. A cloister is built first, which allows the surrounding buildings to be added as funds become available (see the illustration at left).

The design must accommodate the maturing of the site. Materials will weather, the landscape will mature, and buildings will be added and replaced over the life of the institution.

▲ Chapel at Otaniemi, Finland (1956), by Kaija and Heikki Siren. View to the outdoors from the sanctuary.

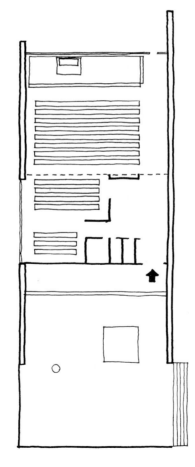

◀ Taking advantage of the view without silhouetting the celebrant. Plan showing the generous clerestory that lights the celebrant and the slender furnishings that do not obstruct the view of the cross and the landscape outside. The Chapel at Otaniemi, Finland (1956), by Kija and Heikki Siren.

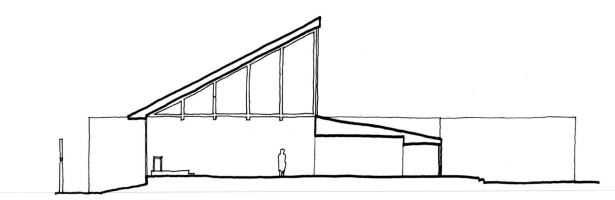

▲ *Chapel at Otaniemi, Finland (1956), by Kaija and Heikki Siren. Section.*

Design for Climate and the Seasons

Visitors will experience the site at different times of day, weather conditions, and seasons of the year. Depending on the amount of clothing worn, the temperature below which the sun is important for warming is approximately 72°F (21°C), and this is also the temperature above which air movement is desirable for cooling. The site design should use orientation, porches, breezeways, canopies, and deciduous plant materials to provide shade and cooling breezes in summer and sunlight in the gathering spaces in winter.

A computerized shadow study can show which areas of the site receive sunlight at different times of the year.

A skilful site design can celebrate the passing of the seasons:

- Using plant materials that provide color at certain times of the year.

- Providing various gathering spaces that take advantage of microclimate or landscape planting at different times of the year. Japanese temple gardens, with tea pavilions providing different focused views of the landscape for different times of the year, offer a sophisticated example.

Zoning of Functions

The site plan should zone spaces according to their functions. The main worship space, fellowship hall, and administration offices should be immediately visible upon arrival. Take care that noisy spaces such as child care rooms, loading docks, and parking lots are separated from quiet spaces such as rooms for private prayer.

Scale

The scale of the outside spaces must be appropriate to establish a comfortable sense of enclosure. This enclosure may be provided by buildings, by trees and shrubs, or even by natural features.

Humans can distinguish facial features from about 80 ft, and this is a comfortable maximum dimension for outside spaces. Buildings create a sense of enclosure if their height is one-half or one-third the width of the space. At less than one-quarter of the width, the sense of enclosure is lost (Lynch and Hack 1990, p. 194).

Building Form

The forms and arrangement of the buildings should provide an easily understood visual structure. Visitors should be able to find their way intuitively to the primary spaces—the worship space, fellowship hall, and administration offices—with minimal use of signage (see Chapter 15). Generally, the buildings will create a hierarchy of form, dominated by the worship space that gathers the institution into a comprehensible whole.

The following are the most common building forms:

- The courtyard, or cloister, characterized by a strong figurative space at the center of the composition. Buildings can grow and change around the courtyard and can extend outward along corridors from the courtyard.

- The campus plan, in which a series of buildings, walks, gardens, and parking lots are arranged on a suburban site. Landscaped walkways focused on landmarks create a structure of pedestrian movement that allows for future infill.

- The urban block plan, in which the functions of the institution are assembled into a single building, frequently of several stories, on a tight urban site.

- The street plan, which arranges the buildings along a linear path of movement. Paving, landscaping, and aligned building facades give form to the street. Buildings may be added in the future by extending the street or by building along added spur walkways.

Accommodation of Topography

The layout of buildings, driveways, and parking areas should accommodate the topography with a minimum of grading. If grading is required, then the designer should balance the cut and fill to avoid a costly import or export of soil.

Landscape, Paving, and Fencing Materials

The site plan can use plant materials to organize and enclose space, to provide a foil for architecture, and to provide shade or shelter from the weather. The design team should include a landscape architect to develop the landscape concept, advise on the plant materials and hardscape layout and selection, and oversee the installation. The plant materials selection should:

- Be appropriate to the climate zone.

- Require a level of maintenance, such as fruit collection, leaf clearing, trimming, root management, and pest control, that the institution is able to provide.

- Be appropriate to the place and the religious institution. It may include plants that are native to the region, have symbolic importance to the religious practice, or are connected with the history of the institution.

- Create an appropriate composition of form, color, and texture.

- Anticipate growth and look good in both youth and maturity. Strategies for accomplishing this include:
  - Preserving old trees on the site
  - Including some mature trees in the planting plan

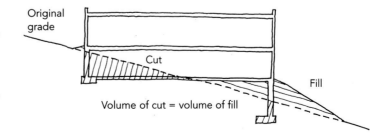

▼ *Balancing of cut and fill.*

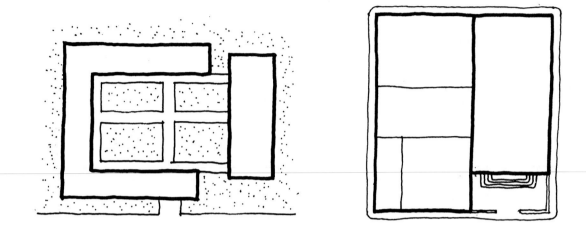

▲ Courtyard plan.

▲ Urban block plan.

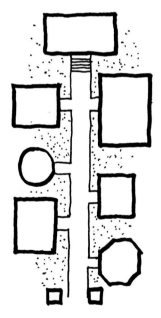

▲ Street plan.

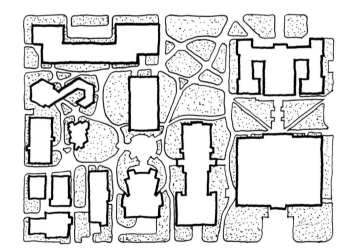

▲ Campus plan.

- Using succession planting, whereby quick-growing trees are removed as slower-growing trees mature
- Planning to thin out trees as they mature and grow in size

Site paving is one of the largest design elements that the visitor touches. Not only must it provide for functional pedestrian and wheelchair circulation (see "Pedestrian Movement," page 80), but its form and texture can lend dignity to the site and differentiate the sacred precinct from its surroundings.

Suitable materials include (in descending order of cost):

- Stone, ashlar (or random) laid
- Brick
- Ceramic pavers
- Concrete pavers
- Poured-in-place concrete, exposed or seeded aggregate, sandblasted or broom finished
- Asphalt
- Decomposed granite

Other materials such as terrazzo, ceramic tile, and wood block may be used in limited areas.

The materials used for fencing and walls have a strong impact on the quality of the site. The material should be appropriate to the region and the institution. A variety of materials are available, including, in descending order of cost:

- Fieldstone
- Brick
- Poured-in-place concrete
- Plaster on concrete block
- Adobe
- Sheet metal panels
- Woven wire
- Wood board
- Wrought iron pickets
- Plastic panels
- Wood post and rail

Chain link fencing is neither attractive nor durable. If it must be used for reasons of cost, then it may be concealed within a fast-growing hedge.

Site furniture, which includes benches, trash receptacles, light poles, and signage, has a strong impact on the visual field. The architect or landscape architect should select these items as part of a coordinated design. Too often, uncoordinated trash receptacles purchased after the project is completed mar a carefully designed site.

CHAPTER 5

PUBLIC AGENCY APPROVAL

Before beginning the design of a worship space, the design professional should perform a detailed code analysis and meet with the local officials to review the regulations affecting the project. This chapter is not intended to replace this review.

The regulations affecting worship spaces cover environmental impact; planning and zoning; building, safety, and fire regulations; energy conservation; and disabled access.

ENVIRONMENTAL IMPACT

Places of worship are often large buildings that have a significant impact on their environments. In the United States, legislation at the federal, state, and local levels controls this impact and mandates a series of approvals for large projects.

The Clean Air Act, signed into law in 1955 and amended in 1990, and the Clean Water Act, which became law in 1977, are administered by the Environmental Protection Agency (EPA). The Endangered Species Act, which became law in 1973, is administered by the Fish and Wildlife Service of the Department of the Interior.

Federal environmental regulations are enforced through legislation at the state level, which controls impacts such as air pollution, water pollution, traffic, noise, impact on viewsheds, and effects on endangered species and historic resources. At the local level, the environmental impact report (EIR) process identifies a project's significant environmental impacts, incorporates mitigation measures if they are feasible, and presents the findings for public scrutiny and decision making.

If the lead agency, which is generally the local planning department, determines that an environmental study is required, then the agency commissions an EIR prepared by a specialized consultant. The EIR describes the environmental effects of the project and outlines potential mitigation measures.

For the project to require an environmental impact study, the impacts must exceed threshold levels. There are no federal or state standards for threshold levels of impact; the definition of these thresholds is determined at a local level and depends on the sensitivity of the local community. The absence of objective standards for the thresholds means that local politics and the level of organization of neighborhood opposition have a significant effect on the lead agency's decision as to whether to require a full environmental impact report.

The lead agency makes one of three determinations: a negative declaration, in which case an EIR is not required; a mitigated negative declaration, in which case an EIR is not required but the project must incorporate certain mitigating factors; or a full EIR is required.

EIR preparation and approval can take from six months to several years, depending on the level of opposition from the community and local agencies. EIR preparation generally takes a minimum of three months, followed by a comment period and public hearings.

For religious institutions planning substantial buildings in well-organized and politicized communities, the environmental review process can cause substantial delay and additional cost. The following are particularly thorny issues for religious building projects:

- Traffic and parking: congestion on surrounding streets and intersections, and on-street parking in neighborhoods

- The effects of the building on views and the neighboring architectural context

- The effect on existing historic buildings or sites

In the last 20 years residents of existing communities have come to regard religious buildings as undesirable neighbors. This condition has developed despite the services offered to the community in education, child care, and social services. It is due primarily to three factors: the recent rapid growth in attendance and the resulting building programs, weekend traffic and on-street parking, and the weekday traffic generated by child care and nursery school facilities.

To offset local opposition, the congregation may have to mobilize support, including a traffic engineer, with experience in:

- Making presentations at to public meetings and responding to opposition by neighborhood leaders

- Analyzing the traffic generated by complex daily schedules that may include worship services, child care, adult classes, and teen social events.

The congregation may seek further support, such as by engaging land-use attorneys and public relations specialists to mount a campaign with mailers and media coverage and organize public meetings to present the project favorably to the local community.

PLANNING AND ZONING

Planning and zoning codes control land use and the form of development. Generally, such codes control permitted uses, building setbacks, height limits, lot coverage and floor area ratio, required parking, landscaping, and signage. In certain communities with very specific community plans, the planning and zoning code may also control specific architectural elements such as the shapes of roofs, porches and window openings, exterior materials, and landscape plant materials.

Frequently, religious institutions are located in areas zoned for residential use only, in which case a conditional use permit (CUP) is required to enable an institution to build. The conditional use permit describes the uses, floor area, and height of the proposed project and includes preliminary plans and elevations of the buildings, on-site parking, driveways, and landscaping. The CUP also specifies the number of seats in a worship space and even the number of pupils enrolled in a religious school.

The CUP procedure is as follows:

- The institution submits an application to the local planning department.

- The planning department advertises the application and holds a public hearing.

- The department makes a determination, which frequently contains mitigation measures to address the concerns expressed by the neighborhood.

- The codes provide for a fixed period of time to appeal the decision. Such an appeal may be made to the planning commission, to the city council, or to the county board of supervisors.

- The approval of a CUP is always subject to challenge by lawsuit.

Recent legislation has clarified the rights of religious institutions in land use entitlements. The Religious Land Use and Institutionalized Persons Act of 2000 forbids discrimination against religious institutions in development entitlements. Among other provisions, it requires that in matters of planning and zoning, "[n]o government shall impose or implement a land use regulation in a manner that treats a religious assembly or institution on less than equal terms with a nonreligious assembly or institution" (Section 2.b.1).

Early on, consult with the officials concerned to confirm the requirements, the process, and the probability of success. Planning, zoning, and traffic departments are generally keen to meet with architects to discuss new projects. See them before beginning the planning process.

BUILDING, SAFETY, AND FIRE REGULATIONS

In the United States, the Building Officials and Code Administrators (BOCA) code governs constuction in the East, while the Southern Building Code (SBC) is enforced in the South and the Uniform Building Code (UBC), with amendments added by local agencies, governs building construction in the West. The International Building Code (IBC), prepared by BOCA and the International Conference of Building Officials (ICBO), is scheduled for introduction in 2004. Building codes are moving from prescriptive to performance-based requirements, which permit greater latitude to the design professionals in conforming to the requirements.

The purpose of the building codes is to: "provide minimum standards to safeguard life, limb, health, property and public welfare by regulating and controlling the design, construction, quality of materials, use and occupancy, location and maintenance of all buildings and structures within this jurisdiction" (UBC 1997, Paragraph 101.2).

The building codes are applicable to every construction project, whether it is for a new building or a renovation. Special criteria govern additions or modifications to existing building structures to ensure that the existing buildings are not overloaded by new construction. Local agencies frequently adopt special codes to address historic buildings, which permit the maintenance of historic materials and means of construction not acceptable under current codes.

The codes control the following factors critical to worship space design:

- The allowable area and height for buildings of different types of construction and occupancy. The code specifies the fire-resistive performance of materials and types of construction, the maximum sizes of buildings, and the separation between them to prevent the spread of fire and allow access by firefighters and equipment.

- Adequate means of egress in case of emergency, which may be fire, earthquake, terrorist attack, or storm. It specifies the design requirements for the access to exit ways, the exit ways themselves, and their discharge to the public way. It also specifies openings such as doors or windows in the building exterior for access by firefighters.

- Requirements for automatic sprinkler and standpipe systems and their design, and the use of sprinklers to permit longer travel distance, to increase

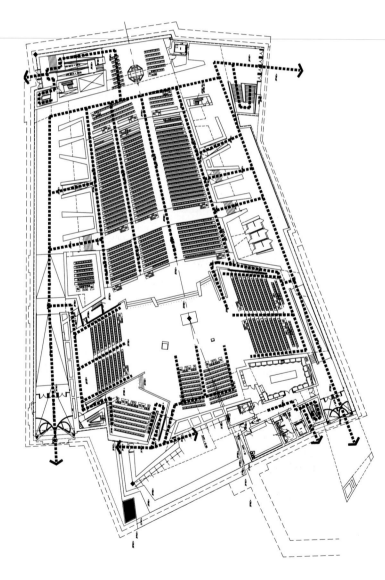

▼ Exit plan, showing exit routes marked with a dashed line. Cathedral of Our Lady of the Angels, Los Angeles. Design architect: Rafael Moneo; executive architect: Leo A Daly.

the maximum allowable building area, and as a substitute for fire-resistive construction.

- Natural light and ventilation. In the case of buildings that are naturally ventilated, and spaces for human habitation, the codes have specific requirements.

- Allowable live and dead loads, allowable material stresses, and methods of structural design analysis. The building codes detail these and other design criteria for building structures.

Special Requirements for Worship Spaces

Worship spaces are assembly occupancies, and codes closely regulate their design. Designers should pay particular attention to the following:

- The building and fire codes determine the number and distribution of exits. Spaces with an occupant load of 300 require three exits; those with 1000 require four exits. Exits must be evenly distributed around the space and sized so that at least half the occupants can exit through the main entrance. The exit ways must be enclosed by fire-rated construction until they discharge into an open yard or the public way.

- The building and fire codes determine the seating layout and the width and distribution of aisles. The number of seats that exiting occupants can traverse depends on the spacing of the seats, and aisle widths are determined by the number of occupants and the distance from the exit.

ENERGY CONSERVATION

Local codes regulate building envelope design, addressing issues such as insulation and shading, the efficiency of mechanical and electrical equipment, and the allowable energy use per square foot for climate control, lighting, and power. Chapter 6 details the contribution of energy conservation to sustainable design and describes measures the designers and builders of worship spaces can use to increase energy efficiency.

ACCESSIBILITY

The Americans with Disabilities Act (ADA) of 1990, the landmark civil rights legislation administered by the U.S. Department of Justice, prohibits discrimination on the basis of disability in employment, state and local government, public accommodations, commercial facilities, transportation, and telecommunications.

Religious institutions are exempt from the requirements of the ADA, but the UBC and state and local codes require all assembly buildings to comply with American National Standard A117.1, published by the Council of American Building Officials (CABO/ANSI A117.1). This standard provides detailed requirements for the design of accessible routes, building entrances, stairs, ramps, doors, seating, sanitary facilities, kitchens, and work areas. It also specifies how equipment such as elevators, drinking fountains, audio equipment, and alarm systems should be made accessible to persons who are disabled.

Places of worship are intended to be accessible to all members of the faith community, regardless of ability. Provisions for disabled persons should be incorporated from the beginning as an integral part of the design, so that those who use them appear to be part of the congregation and not set apart. These provisions include the following:

- Ensuring an accessible parking area and path of travel to the entrance, which includes specifying a type of paving material that provides adequate traction for wheelchairs and complying with the requirements for slopes and ramps.

- Making the stage, lectern, and pulpit accessible so that those with disabilities can participate in the liturgy with dignity. If the sanctuary area is raised, then a ramp should be incorporated into the design to provide access for wheelchair users. The pulpit or lectern should be adjustable in height to accommodate wheelchair users and standing readers.

- Ensuring an accessible path of travel to the choir loft and the organ console. This means that the choir and organ console should be placed close to the main floor, rather than in the traditional gallery in small churches where an elevator is not practical.

- Making every building entrance and exit accessible, or providing an accessible route close by so that disabled members of the congregation can accompany their able-bodied colleagues.

▼ Ambo, Cathedral of Our Lady of the Angels, Los Angeles. The levers allow the reading surface to be raised and lowered mechanically to accommodate readers standing or seated in wheelchairs.

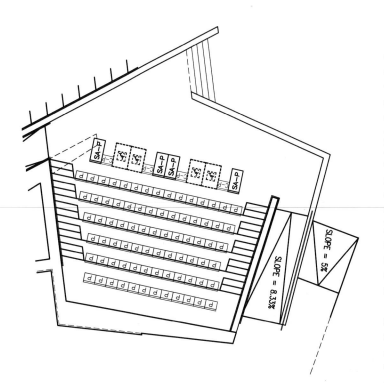

SLOPE = 8.33%

SLOPE = 5%

▲ Choir loft showing accessible seating and ramp access. Cathedral of Our Lady of the Angels, Los Angeles. The plan shows the ramps for wheelchair access to the choir, wheelchair spaces, companion seating (C-P), and seating for the semiambulant (SA-P). Design architect: Rafael Moneo; executive architect: Leo A Daly.

- Designating spaces for wheelchair seating, distributed in each seating area in locations where occupants can have a view of the celebration even when the rest of the congregation is standing ("stand-up sight lines"). This can be accomplished by locating the wheelchair spaces adjacent to aisles, where their occupants can move slightly to see down the aisles, or on slightly raised platforms. Adjacent seating should also be provided for companions. Seating for semiambulant individuals should be provided with additional width and legroom and removable armrests to facilitate entry and exit.

- Providing assisted listening devices with a sound-reinforcement system and visual warning devices (strobes) as a part of the fire alarm system for persons with hearing impairments.

Although all new construction is required to comply with the requirements of CABO/ANSI A117.1, the decision as to whether a renovated building must be completely upgraded depends on the cost of the renovation and the relative cost of providing accessibility. Municipalities have a threshold construction cost, below which upgrading is not required beyond minimal provisions. Building codes provide the possibility for building officials to waive certain requirements, based on hardship, or to accept alternative provisions. The design team has the option of appealing a decision of the building official to the agency having jurisdiction over the project.

The local department of building and safety, which administers building accessibility requirements, will check drawings concurrent with building plan check and will inspect the project before issuing a certificate of occupancy. As with all regulatory requirements, an early conference with the building officials and, if possible, with the field inspector will identify problem areas and allow the designers to resolve them.

FIRE REGULATIONS

Using national and local fire codes, municipal fire inspectors generally check the plans for life-safety issues and sign off on the completed building prior to occupancy. They are particularly concerned about the following issues:

- Layout of seating and aisles in assembly occupancies

- Layout of exit ways and exit signs

- Storage of hazardous materials

- Flammability of finishes and decorations

- Sprinkler and fire-alarm systems and standpipes

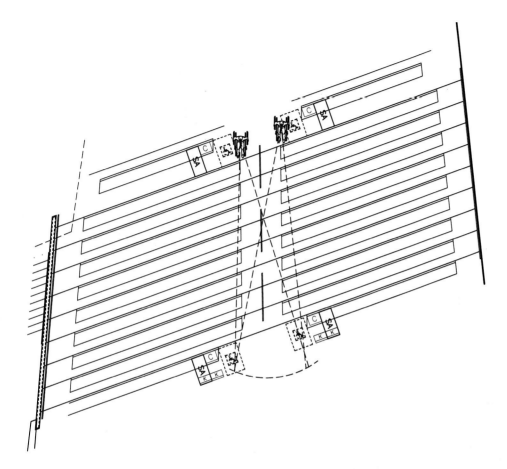

Local fire departments, which are the first to respond in case of emergency, have jurisdiction over fire truck access and fire hydrant location. The designers should consult with the local fire department early to resolve these issues that have a significant impact on site planning.

BUILDING SYSTEMS

Heating, ventilating, air-conditioning, plumbing, and electrical systems are regulated by their own codes, which are administered by the local building department. The design engineer submits design drawings for plan check review, and the specialized contractor obtains the building permit upon submittal of license and insurance documentation.

PUBLIC HEALTH

If a kitchen is provided as part of a meeting hall, the design of the kitchen and the food service equipment must comply with the local public health codes. Adequate restroom facilities and handwashing sinks must be provided for employees, and the kitchen must have easily cleanable floor, wall, and ceiling finishes. Automatic fire-protection systems and adequate make-up air are required for exhaust hoods.

▲ Seating layout, north transept, showing wheelchair spaces, semiambulant seating (SA), companion seating (C), and sight lines from wheelchair spaces when the congregation is standing. Cathedral of Our Lady of the Angels, Los Angeles. Design architect: Rafael Moneo; executive architect: Leo A Daly.

CHILD CARE

If child care facilities are provided as part of the project, they must comply with state and local regulations. Requirements for the floor area of the interior and exterior space provided for each child, the number of children per teacher, and the bathroom facilities are all closely spelled out in the regulations.

IMPLEMENTATION

The following procedure is recommended for complying with building and fire codes:

- *Preliminary conference.* While the project is in the schematic design phase, the design professionals should meet with the building and fire department officials to review the design to verify the allowable area, construction type, and exiting provisions. For larger projects that require review by other departments, such as traffic, street maintenance, and redevelopment agencies, most municipalities schedule a meeting that includes the relevant municipal departments. Some cities provide a "case manager" who helps guide the project through the multiple approvals required.

- *Plan check.* When the construction documents are approximately 80 percent complete, the architects and engineers submit the drawings for review and approval by the local building and fire departments (plan check). Depending on the workload and the size of the project, the review can take from two to six weeks. After the architects and engineers have responded to corrections, the plan checker approves and stamps the documents. Depending on the type of project de-

livery (see Chapter 2), the contractor generally picks up the building permit upon presentation of the required insurance.

- *Modifications and appeals.* The design professionals may meet a particular code requirement by providing equivalent materials or methods of construction. In this case, they submit a request for modification and pay a small review fee, and the plan check staff then reviews the request. Applicants can appeal staff decisions to the Building and Safety Board and, ultimately, to the municipal authority.

- *Field inspection.* Municipalities enforce adherence to the building codes and the approved contract documents by means of field inspections. Even though a design may be approved in the plan-checked documents, the field inspectors reserve the right to require modifications in the field to comply with the code. For example, inspectors may require added concrete reinforcement around special conditions, and fire inspectors may call for additional exit and alarm devices to deal with actual field conditions. The design professionals should include unit prices and allowances for additional devices in the bid documents to cover these additions.

The project team should maintain good relations with the field inspectors, alert them when approvals are required, and notify them about particular design concerns. Periodic "goodwill meetings" between senior members of the religious institution and city officials help to ensure good relations.

CHAPTER 6
SUSTAINABLE DESIGN

The ideas central to the concept of sustainability emerged from the new discipline of ecology and the increasingly visible impact of humans on the environment during the middle years of the twentieth century. These ideas were distilled and popularized in the seminal work, *Silent Spring,* written by Rachel Carson and published in 1963. The publication of this book is generally recognized as the start of modern environmentalism.

The concept of sustainability as a requirement and component of design for the built environment grew from these roots and has been developed since the 1960s through the efforts of governmental organizations and various individuals. In 1987, the Brundtland Commission (Brundtland 1987) proposed the following definition: "Sustainable development is development that meets the needs of the present without compromising the ability of future generations to meet their own needs." This definition was adopted by the United Nations at the Earth Summit held in Rio de Janeiro in 1992.

Sustainability is relevant to the design and planning of religious buildings because all development projects have impacts in three broad interlinked areas: the environment, society, and economics. If the impacts in each of these three areas are not balanced with each other, the development will not be sustainable over the long term. This approach is often referred to as "the triple bottom line."

Some companies choose to measure their performance using triple bottom line accounting methods, producing an-nual statements that measure their activity in all three areas, rather than with the traditional method of reporting financial indicators only.

Spaces for worship affect, and are affected by, the environment, society, and economics in ways that distinguish them from other building types. Social and environmental issues arise because the way in which people are supposed to interact with each other and with the earth is at the core of every religion that is widely practiced in the United States. The people and committees who direct and oversee design and construction for their worship space are likely to see themselves as stewards of their community and their religion; environmental and social hopes and goals will be central to their decision making. Yet most religious organizations do not benefit from a reliable revenue stream, and thus the economic constraints on the construction of places for worship are often more severe than for other building types.

▼ *Components of the "triple bottom line." Optimal solutions occur within the intersection of social, economic, and environmental impacts.*

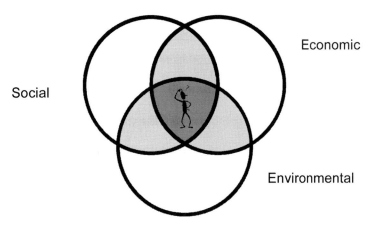

97

THE RELIGIOUS BASIS FOR SUSTAINABLE DEVELOPMENT

Many religions are practiced in the United States. The majority of people practice, or grew up practicing, one of the Western monotheistic religious traditions of Christianity, Judaism, or Islam. An increasing number of people practice Eastern religions, such as Hinduism, or follow a Buddhist spiritual path. Across these religions, importance is placed on both environmental stewardship and social stability, and this emphasis is generally derived from each religion's sacred texts.

The value of the various interactions between people and the environment varies according to the sacred texts and the particular sect, denomination, and even location of worshipers.

The economic aspect of sustainability shapes the design, construction, and operation of any place of worship in the United States because of the way funds are raised for building construction and the economic system that generates those funds through its presence in a capitalist economy. Specific economic factors are discussed in more detail in Chapters 19 and 20.

Each of the three components of the triple bottom line—environment, society, and economics—are discussed in the follow-ing sections with respect to each religion.

ENVIRONMENTAL STEWARDSHIP AND RELIGIOUS BELIEF

All major world religions developed their belief systems in the preindustrial age, when communities were more intimately allied with the earth. People generally had a closer connection to the natural rhythms of the planet and understood the relationship between overharvesting, damage, and the time required for recovery before new crops could be planted. During these times it was necessary for people to work as a community to ensure their individual survival. Community and religious leaders, such as Moses and Solomon in the Western tradition, or swamis in the Eastern tradition, were the carriers of the knowledge and wisdom that allowed their communities to thrive. Much of this knowledge is incorporated within the sacred texts.

Thus, environmental stewardship is at the heart of all the major religions, as demonstrated by both local communities and powerful religious organizations, ranging from simple recycling projects to the work of, for example, Coalition on the Environment and Jewish Life (COEJL), which focuses on the religious importance of environmental stewardship.

Western Traditions

The Jewish, Christian, and Islamic traditions share the same creation story. In this tradition, the earth was created by God and given to humankind to respect and to care for. The earth remains God's property, but was given to humans to support them in their life and work. Two of the key texts on which this tradition is based are the following:

Be fruitful and multiply, and replenish the earth, and subdue it: and have dominion over ... every living thing (Genesis 1:28).

God ... put him into the garden of Eden to dress it and to keep it (Genesis 2:15).

These texts have been interpreted by religious leaders many times and in many ways, depending on the needs of the people and the stresses they are experiencing. The first verse is usually read as a blessing, rather than an instruction to exploit the earth. This reading is reinforced by the second text and by subsequent texts in Judaism, Christianity, and Islam, all of which offer additional teachings that promote the concept of human's looking after and respecting the earth.

In Jewish belief, religious law forbids the destruction of nature (the Law of Lo Tash'chit), unless the destruction is necessary for the survival of people (the Gemara). People are explicitly placed first in the natural order, and in the past this has created a tension between the ability to exercise control over nature and the duty of mankind to guard the earth's natural resources. It has become increasingly clear, however, that the exploitation of nature endangers the health and welfare of people, and these laws no longer appear to conflict (Berman 2004).

Most Christians accept that without stewardship of the earth's resources there will be nothing to have dominion over. They consider the protection of God-given resources to be a good practice. In spite of this, the connection that is made between lifestyle and the use of natural resources varies greatly among Christians.

In the Islamic tradition, the Qur'an, the book containing the words of God as heard through the prophet Muhammad, is held sacred. The Qur'an teaches that:

The world is beautiful and verdant, and verily God, be He exalted, has made you his stewards in it, and he sees how you acquit yourselves.

Later interpretations of the Qur'an and teachings by Islamic religious leaders have reinforced this message. For example, the fourth Caliph said to a man who had developed abandoned land:

Partake of it gladly, so long as you are benefactor, not a despoiler; a cultivator, not a destroyer.

Further, the giving of charity is considered one of the five pillars of faith, and the Qur'an states that even the fruits of farming can be counted as charity.

If anyone plants a tree, no human being nor any of God's creatures will eat from it without its being reckoned as charity from him.

In summary, the Western traditions of Judaism, Christianity, and Islam all contain teachings that stress the importance of the conservation of the earth's resources as part of their people's religious obligation to God and to each other.

FIVE PILLARS OF ISLAMIC FAITH		
1	Pbut	The belief that there is no God worthy of worship but Allah and that Muhammad is his messenger
2	Salate	Prescribed prayers, which are said five times a day
3	Siyaam	Fasting once a year, during the whole month of Ramadan
4	Zakaat	Charity, which is paid to poor and needy once every year
5	Hajj	The pilgrimage to Mecca once in a lifetime if one can afford it physically and financially

Eastern Traditions

Eastern beliefs are more fluid than Western religions. There are thousands of different religious groups, most of which developed to follow particular teachers. Various branches of Hinduism share sacred texts, including the Bhagavad-Gita, the Vedas, the Brahmanas, the Sutras, and the Aranyakas. For example, the Bochasanwasi Shree Akshar Purushottam Swaminarayan Sanstha (BAPS) is a Hindu organization revealed in the late eighteenth century and one of the mostly widely followed Hindu organizations in the West. BAPS describes its environmental commitment as follows:

We are not the inheritors of this world, but its trustees for our children.

Its members' commitment to environmental stewardship is shown through their dedication to social programs that focus on environmental goals. These programs have included tree planting throughout the world, aluminum recycling in the United Kingdom, water conservation projects in India, and the use of solar energy in many *mandirs,* or temples.

Buddhism grew from within Hinduism, but it does not admit the existence of a specific God or gods. Buddhist philosophy begins with four noble truths, and Buddhists follow an eightfold path to enlightenment.

As Buddhism is a philosophy rather than a religion, the elements of the eightfold path are frequently recast and reinterpreted by different groups of followers. For environmentalists, "right livelihood" is interpreted to mean earning a living without harming living things. Recent followers and interpreters of Buddhism, such as members of the large International Soka Gakkai movement, have recast the precepts and path to specifically include both social and environmental sustainability. The Soka Gakkai International (SGI) charter principles are shown in the table on page 101. These principles clearly reflect concepts of both economic and social sustainability.

FOUR NOBLE TRUTHS OF BUDDHISM

1	Suffering exists.
2	Suffering arises from attachment to desires.
3	Suffering ceases when attachment to desire ceases.
4	Freedom from suffering is possible by practicing the Eightfold Path.

NOBLE EIGHTFOLD PATH	
Three Qualities	**Eightfold Path**
Panna (Wisdom)	Right View
	Right Thought
Sila (Morality)	Right Speech
	Right Action
	Right Livelihood
Samadhi (Meditation)	Right Effort
	Right Mindfulness
	Right Contemplation

SOKA GAKKAI INTERNATIONAL CHARTER PRINCIPLES

1   SGI shall contribute to peace, culture, and education for the happiness and welfare of all humanity, based on Buddhist respect for the sanctity of life.

2   SGI, based on the ideal of world citizenship, shall safeguard fundamental human rights and not discriminate against any individual on any grounds.

3   SGI shall respect and protect the freedom of religion and religious expression.

4   SGI shall promote an understanding of Nichiren Daishonin's Buddhism through grass-roots exchange, thereby contributing to individual happiness.

5   SGI shall, through its constituent organizations, encourage its members to contribute toward the prosperity of their respective societies as good citizens.

6   SGI shall respect the independence and autonomy of its constituent organizations in accordance with the conditions prevailing in each country.

7   SGI shall, based on the Buddhist spirit of tolerance, respect other religions, engage in dialogue and work together with them toward the resolution of fundamental issues concerning humanity.

8   SGI shall respect cultural diversity and promote cultural exchange, thereby creating an international society of mutual understanding and harmony.

9   SGI shall promote, based on the Buddhist ideal of symbiosis, the protection of nature and the environment.

10 SGI shall contribute to the promotion of education, in pursuit of truth as well as the development of scholarship, to enable all people to cultivate their individual character and enjoy fulfilling and happy lives.

SOCIAL SUSTAINABILITY AND RELIGIOUS BELIEF

Because the belief systems for all the major religions were developed at a time when membership in a community was important to personal survival, religious texts all devote attention to the ways in which people should treat other members of their community. Even though personal interactions are generally no longer crucial for survival, research suggests that there are significant social benefits that arise from better social connectivity, including lower crime rates, good health, and happiness.

Even in secular societies, religious organizations form a strong background, motivation, and location for community activity. People who do not usually participate in religious services often use the places set aside for worship for rituals and ceremonies surrounding weddings, memorials, and other rites of passage. The social rituals inherent in each religious tradition will influence the planning and design of its places for worship.

Western Traditions

Within Judaism, there are 613 basic rules, called the *Mitzvot* and detailed in

Leviticus, many of which require that Jews aid other people, both Jewish and nonbelievers. Jewish law includes commandments not to "stand idly by the blood of your neighbor" and to "love your neighbor as yourself." These commandments imply, among other things, a commitment to the good of society and to justice in interactions with others.

Synagogues are the centers of Jewish life. They are used as houses of prayer, places for study, and often as social welfare agencies for the poor within the Jewish community. In the Jewish tradition, it is possible to carry out most daily prayers alone. However, there are some prayers that have to be said with a minimum of 10 Jewish men present, and it is generally considered better to pray as a group than to pray alone. The study of Jewish law is a requirement for the adolescent rite of passage, the Bar Mitzvah, and encouraged throughout a devout life. Synagogues provide some of the best places for such study, frequently housing extensive libraries of sacred texts. As the synagogue is so central to Jewish life, it

sometimes comprises additional facilities—for leisure, for example. Some even include swimming pools (Kaufman 1999).

The Christian tradition originates from Judaism and shares with Judaism the teachings in Leviticus. These teachings were reinforced and emphasized during Christ's ministry. Two of the most well-known and central Christian teachings are the story of the Good Samaritan and the injunction "Love one another as I have loved you," which is an intensification of the instructions in Leviticus. Both teachings emphasize an obligation to one's fellow people, both Christians and non-Christians alike.

In many areas the church is the focal point for community activities. These may include Girl and Boy Scouts, youth groups, Bible study groups, and church parties to celebrate harvest, Shrove Tuesday (Mardi Gras), or Easter. Although praying alone as a Christian is not considered any more or less effective than praying with others, parishioners are expected to attend church services every week. In some denominations Christians also take part in Communion services and other sacraments, administered by ordained priests.

Like Christians and Jews, Muslims are also encouraged to look after their fellows. One of the five pillars of Islam is the requirement to give alms to others. The Qur'an says that all people are equal before God, and alms can be given to both believers and nonbelievers. As the center of prayer, mosques are pivotal to Islamic life. Muslims are encouraged to pray together, although they can pray alone. Because Muslims generally pray five times each day, a mosque will be occupied often.

THE SACRAMENTS	
Sacraments of Invitation	Baptism Confirmation Eucharist (Communion) Rite of Christian Initiation of Adults
Sacraments of Healing	Reconciliation Anointing of the Sick
Sacraments of Vocation	Marriage Holy Orders

Eastern Traditions

"Many ask 'How can you mix spirituality and social service?' We ask 'How can you separate the two?'" (BAPS 2003).

The BAPS Hindu organization, noted earlier, whose members worship at the Neasden Mandir in London, make the link between social service and spirituality explicit. On an individual level they are instructed thus:

The hallmark of the Swaminarayan devotee is that he or she devoutly begins the day with puja and meditation, works or studies honestly and donates regular hours in serving others. No stealing, no adultery, no alcohol, no meat, no impurity of body and mind, these are the five principal vows. Such moral purity and spiritual surety add a deeper brilliance to all the hundreds of social services for better life (BAPS 2003).

At an organizational level, Hindus are encouraged to participate in numerous social programs, most of which have environmental goals. Although their programs cater to many different interests, most have stated social and environmental objectives. This strong element of religious organization will place specific demands on the architectural requirements of the place for worship.

In addition, there are often people living at Hindu temples as part of their religious observance. This provides both a social core and a requirement for specific types of accommodation within the temple.

Places of Buddhist worship are often located at monasteries or retreats. However, there are neither specific requirements for Buddhists to worship together, nor expected times of worship. Buddhists traditionally seek refuge in three things: the Buddha, or teacher; the Dharma, or law; and the *sangha,* or community. The *community* means those who are devoting their lives to the pursuit of the eightfold path, but specifically includes those who are intent on achieving the final step on this path: enlightenment.

As noted, Buddhism is a philosophy rather than a religion, and followers of particular leaders or groups of Buddhists frequently recast the central precepts to emphasize their own concerns. Common to many of these groups and also important in Hindu practice is the idea of karma, or causality. At retreats and worship centers there is often a tradition of karma yoga in which practitioners, to work through their personal karma, will volunteer labor for the good of the community. For a design team, this implies a need to incorporate the ability for practictioners to participate in a building project's construction.

ENVIRONMENTAL CONSIDERATIONS FOR CONSTRUCTION

With so many religions throughout the world and throughout history calling for harmony between the environment, society, and economy, sustainable development is clearly not a new concept. What is considered relatively new is the direct application of these ideas in the context of our corporate, industrial, and information-based society.

The key environmental impacts of building projects are due to energy and resource consumption. As the built environment is a major consumer of energy and resources, both during construction and operation, the adoption of sustainable building practices is essential.

The LEED™ (Leadership in Engineering and Environmental Design) rating system was developed by the United

States Green Building Council (USGBC) to help building design teams reduce their buildings' impact and to set a standard against which buildings can be evaluated. This rating system divides the impacts of buildings into five areas: sustainable sites, water efficiency, energy and atmosphere, materials and resources, and indoor environmental quality.

As the LEED system is becoming widely adopted in the United States, the same general structure is used in the following guidelines. LEED ratings are available for buildings, based on the number of points that they achieve from a checklist of sustainable building design measures. For up-to-date details on the available points, a detailed discussion of each element, and the requirements for achieving a rating, refer to USGBC information.

Site Selection

Sustainable site selection requires consideration of the impact of the development on the local ecology, transportation patterns, and the immediate surroundings. In general, the aim is to reduce the impact of the building in the following ways:

- Minimize disruption to the surrounding watershed; for example, sites should be selected outside of the floodplain.

- Minimize soil erosion, particularly damage caused by rainwater runoff that has been redirected by the building.

- Minimize potential flood damage by using permeable surfaces, collecting rainwater for further use, or holding runoff in detention ponds until it can be released.

- Maximize the open area on-site. The building should be built on as small an area of the site as possible, and any topsoil removed should be recycled rather than sent to a landfill. This is because topsoil holds many nutrients needed for plant growth, which will be lost if the soil is removed. Topsoil takes a long time to generate, and recycling it reduces the amount of matter sent to landfill.

- Minimize transportation energy use. As a worship space often functions as a community hub for the use of people of all ages, the sites must be accessible by public transportation. This is convenient, and it will reduce the energy use associated with bringing people to the building. In many Jewish communities, driving is prohibited on holy days, meaning that synagogues should be located within walking distance of all their attendees.

Water Use

The use of water has an enormous effect on the environment. Much of the water in the United States is provided through large reservoirs and is intensively treated and pumped miles from its source to its points of use. After use, the water is then pumped away and is treated again before it can be released to the environment. Any reduction in use will reduce the impact of these processes and, in rapidly expanding communities such as those in the Southwestern Sunbelt, can eliminate the need for additional expensive infrastructure.

Water demand can be reduced in the following ways:

- By using appliances that consume less water than standard fixtures, includ-

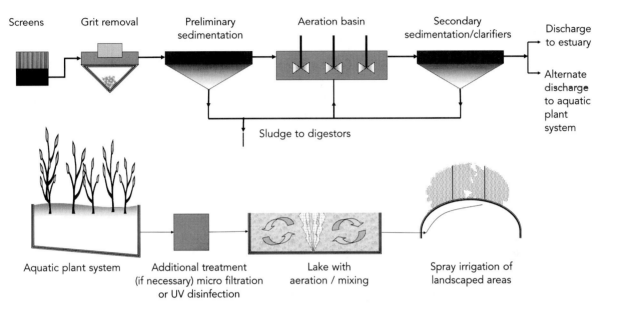

Screens Grit removal Preliminary sedimentation Aeration basin Secondary sedimentation/clarifiers Discharge to estuary

Alternate discharge to aquatic plant system

Sludge to digestors

Aquatic plant system Additional treatment (if necessary) micro filtration or UV disinfection Lake with aeration / mixing Spray irrigation of landscaped areas

ing waterless urinals, low-flow and dual-flush toilets, and aerators on taps, the upstream and downstream processing required can be reduced.

- Rainwater can be collected for non-potable uses in a building to reduce the upstream treatment requirements. The most significant use in a building is likely to be toilet flushing, and in most parts of the United States adequate rainwater can be collected for this need for the whole year.

- Treating sewage locally—for example, using reed beds and leach fields—will also reduce downstream treatment requirements, although it may not be appropriate on urban sites.

Energy Use and Alternative Energy Sources

Forty percent of the energy consumed in the United States is used to heat, ventilate, light, and air-condition buildings. Much environmental damage stems from

the generation of electricity using dirty fuels like coal, which leads to pollution and acid rain and contributes to global warming. Significant energy efficiency measures for new and existing buildings can decrease demand for electricity generation, lessen global environmental damage, and reduce future infrastructure needs.

▲ Conventional and aquatic plant system wastewater treatment strategies. For further information, see US EPA/625/1-55/022.

▼ Building systems that incorporate wind-driven ventilation and solar energy.

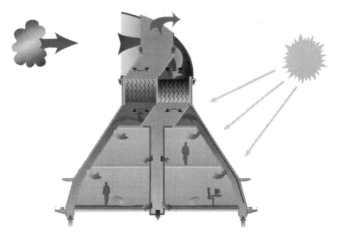

Energy use can be reduced significantly by:

- Envelope design: Energy use for both heating and air-conditioning will be reduced if the building is well insulated and sealed to prevent unwanted air ingress. If the building's windows are sized and designed to admit adequate daylight, while controlling heat from the sun, this can reduce the energy needed to air-condition and light the space.

- Lighting design: Lamps should be as energy efficient as possible to decrease the amount of energy consumed by both the electric lighting system and the heating, ventilating, and air-conditioning system.

- Mechanical systems: High-efficiency components such as pumps, fans, and compressors should be selected. As noted in Chapter 8, the energy-efficient design of the mechanical system will depend on other criteria as well.

The payback period for energy efficiency measures is likely to be longer for spaces for worship that have highly intermittent use than for those in constant use because the equipment will not be run long enough to realize energy savings. However, the costs for running equipment can be a significant portion of a religious organization's expenses, and energy use should be minimized for both environmental and financial reasons.

In addition to reducing energy demand, it is possible to decrease the use

▼ Map showing solar radiation in the United States. In the regions that enjoy high annual solar radiation, there is greater opportunity for photovoltaic power. Renewable Resource Data Center (RreDC). Courtesy of the Department of Energy's Office of Energy Efficiency and Renewable Energy.

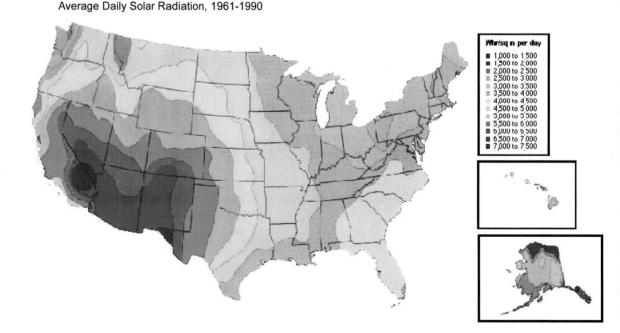

Average Daily Solar Radiation, 1961-1990

| Wh/sq m per day |
| 1,000 to 1,500 |
| 1,500 to 2,000 |
| 2,000 to 2,500 |
| 2,500 to 3,000 |
| 3,000 to 3,500 |
| 3,500 to 4,000 |
| 4,000 to 4,500 |
| 4,500 to 5,000 |
| 5,000 to 5,500 |
| 5,500 to 6,000 |
| 6,000 to 6,500 |
| 6,500 to 7,000 |
| 7,000 to 7,500 |

Energy from the sun on a surface directly facing the sun.

of fossil fuel energy use by generating energy using renewable sources, such as photovoltaic power, wind power, or even waterpower. The equipment can be installed locally or purchased from a power supplier committed to generating electricity from renewable sources. In some areas of the country, high-temperature geothermal sources can also be used to supply power and heat.

One of the major components of most renewable energy systems is the equipment needed for storage of the energy when the power is not being used. The storage system will be larger if energy must be stored for longer periods of time, which is likely in the case of intermittently occupied spaces. If the local utility is required to buy power from owners of photovoltaic systems when the

systems are generating more than the owners can use, then the installation of photovoltaic technology on, say, a church roof may pay for all the power used by the building, especially if midweek power demands are low.

Indoor Environmental Quality

In recent years there has been increasing concern regarding "sick building syndrome." Sick building syndrome usually consists of a collection of minor ailments like headaches, dizziness, sneezing, and chronic tiredness that occur more frequently and with greater intensity after or during occupancy of specific buildings.

Sick building syndrome is unlikely to arise in places of worship, as they are not occupied long enough or consistently enough for symptoms to develop. In any

▼ Map showing availability of wind power in the United States. In the regions where wind forces are strongest, there is greater opportunity for wind power. Courtesy of the Department of Energy's Office of Energy Efficiency and Renewable Energy.

United States Annual Average Wind Power

U.S. Geothermal Provinces

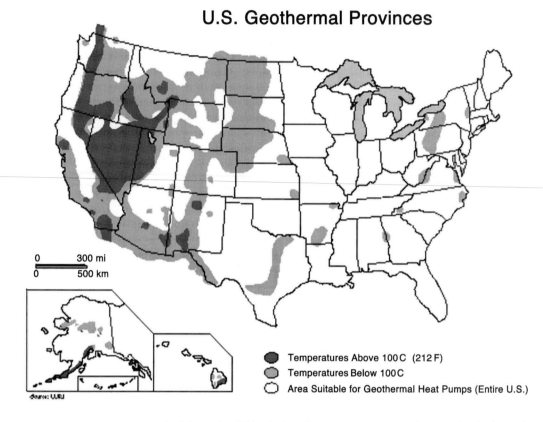

Temperatures Above 100 C (212 F)
Temperatures Below 100 C
Area Suitable for Geothermal Heat Pumps (Entire U.S.)

▲ *Geothermal energy map of the United States, showing regions that could make use of this natural heat source. Courtesy of ASHRAE.*

case, buildings should be designed to use materials that have beneficial effects on the occupants, or at least do no harm. The villains are volatile organic compounds that evaporate from paint, adhesives, foams, sealants, and varnishes as they cure and dry. Variations of all these materials, with equivalent durability, are available and may be specified instead.

In addition, the design of the mechanical system should provide adequate filtration and fresh air, as described in Chapter 8.

Resource and Materials Use

The extraction of materials from the earth's crust and their conversion to building materials requires enormous amounts of energy for both production and transportation. It therefore makes sense to use materials that are naturally renewable or that contain recycled material or have already been extracted and made into industrial products.

Reuse of an available existing building that meets most of the requirements of the proposed place of worship would be the single most effective design decision for the conservation of materials and reduction of resource use. Yet the reuse of existing buildings constructed for other purposes can cause theological or philosophical difficulties for members of some religions, even though there are numerous examples of churches being converted to synagogues or mosques and vice versa.

Another important consideration is the size of the building. Although comfortably accommodating the congregation and providing inspirational space are paramount, the smaller the building, the less its cost and its environmental impact. Similar benefits can be achieved if the space can be designed to be flexible. For example, a church may be designed so that it is usually operated as two spaces, say a church and a meeting hall, but with the ability to open into a single, larger church area for well-attended services.

Once the need for a new building has been established and its size has been carefully considered, then materials should be selected that have a high recycled content, such as structural steel or finishes like recycled carpet or ceiling tile.

A further approach is to reuse elements from existing decommissioned buildings. This may work well for a place of worship replacing a previous one. Components that may be reused include seating, especially for buildings that have fixed seats; doors, notably those that are large or ceremonial; and windows, particularly stained glass.

Additional Concerns

These technical and environmental concerns for the sustainability of a space for worship must be coordinated with the economic and social concerns. There are often links between the social, economic, and environmental impacts of a construction project, and it is important to balance them. For example, low-emitting paints are often more expensive than standard paints, and high-efficiency building systems may be more expensive than standard ones. However, the reuse of building components may save costs.

SOCIAL CONSIDERATIONS IN CONSTRUCTION OF SPACES FOR WORSHIP

To be socially sustainable, worship space design needs to provide for all visitors, from devout worshipers to infrequent attendees. Design that communicates the intended function of particular areas, or helps to direct expected behavior, increases visitors' comfort and improves their experience. The functional design of worship spaces is discussed in Chapter 3, and wayfinding is described in Chapter 15.

ECONOMIC CONSIDERATIONS IN CONSTRUCTION OF SPACES FOR WORSHIP

The ways in which different religious groups use their places of worship influence their economic sustainability. Although all buildings are sized for peak occupancy, many of them are rarely used at that level, particularly by those congregations that gather together only on holy days. This can be an enormous maintenance challenge.

For example, the worship halls in Christian churches and Jewish synagogues tend to be open only for services. Although at odds with the concept of a welcoming, open religious community, there are often serious concerns about security and vandalism, and it can be expensive to keep these spaces staffed and conditioned.

However, even though attendance levels fluctuate, mosques are occupied every day for prayer. Hindu temples are also generally open, with continuous reading of sacred text and people arriving and leaving at will. There are also days set aside for fasting when temples tend to be more heavily used. Yet it is unlikely that a place for worship will be erected in an area lacking sufficient worshipers to support it.

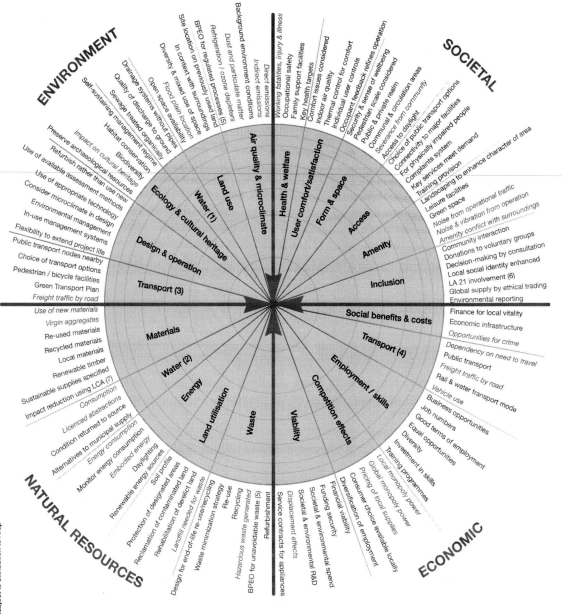

(1) Water within the ENVIRONMENT quadrant is about reducing flood/storm risk and maintaining quality of resource
(2) Water within NATURAL RESOURCES quadrant is about minimizing the use of resources
(3) Transport within the ENVIRONMENT quadrant is about reducing pollution from vehicle use and increasing diversity of transport used
(4) Transport within the ECONOMIC quadrant is about reducing financial implications of travel/transport
(5) BPEO is Best Practicable Environmental Option
(6) LA21 (Local Agenda 21) is local delivery of sustainability strategies involving local authorities and communities
(7) LCA is Life Cycle Assessment

ARUP

THE SUSTAINABLE DESIGN PROCESS

To design a building in a sustainable way, the designer needs to go through a process that includes the following steps.

- Establish the goals of a sustainable plan and the boundaries within which sustainability will be achieved. The criteria for these goals will vary according to the religious group for whom the building is to be built, the primary purpose of the space, and the vision of the client/financier/donor team.

- Establish how most impact can be made on the building sustainability at least cost by using the LEED checklist or another sustainable measurement tool. This will require investigation of the availability and price of local resources, the possibilities for construction to be carried out by volunteers, and the way in which the building will interface with the local community. In working though this stage of the process, it will become clear that there are trade-offs to be made between costs and the social and environmental impacts of choices made during construction. There are also comparisons to be made between very different kinds of costs. For example, is it better to spend money to reduce electricity use or water use? This will obviously depend on the building location, type, and occupancy patterns.

- List as many sustainable measures as possible. These should be as wide-ranging as possible and distributed across design disciplines. For example, energy use can be reduced by changes in equipment, controls, or system design or through building upgrades, including glazing or insulation improvements. Within the building industry there are also a number of broadly recognized incremental modifications that can be made to usual construction methods or materials to minimize adverse environmental impacts.

- Evaluate the sustainable measures against the goals, and balance the financial investment required. Some of the measures will not be economically feasible, others will not cost any more or will repay their costs quickly. Low-cost strategies or strategies with short payback periods should be implemented.

There are a number of ways to ensure that a balance between the different aspects of sustainability is achieved. One of these is the SPeAR™ tool, developed by Arup. SPeAR is a graphical tool that can display both positive and negative results (see the diagram on page 112). The circle is split into four major areas, two dealing with environmental issues and one each for social and economic aspects of sustainability. Within each sector are a number of specific indicators. Good practice in each of these indicators is shown with a light tone, at midpoint between the center and the outside of the circle. Positive sustainability outcomes are shown in a darker tone, closer to the center of the diagram, and negative outcomes are shown in darker tones, closer to the edge of the circle. Data input to the diagram is made through a spreadsheet, and the specific indicators can be altered from project to project, depending on the conditions. This spreadsheet is fully auditable, so that the reasoning behind different decisions can be traced. A completed diagram will highlight specific

◀◀ *Diagram showing the framework of Arup's SPeAR™ sustainability assessment tool. The score in each category is dependent on the indicators listed around the diagram. Indicators shown in italics should be decreased/discouraged and indicators shown in normal text should be increased in order to reach an optimal solution. Courtesy of Arup.*

▶ *Completed SPeAR™ diagram. Courtesy of Arup.*

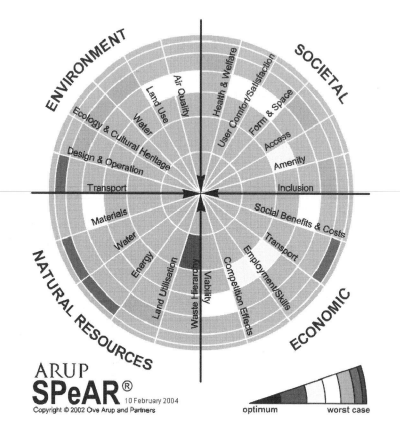

indicators where improvements should be made or where significant advances have already been made.

The most important consideration in selecting a tool for sustainability analysis is that it can show the balance between the social, economic, and environmental impacts of the process, as this is the most complex aspect of the movement toward sustainability.

CHAPTER 7
STRUCTURAL SYSTEMS

Spaces for worship vary as much as religions, presenting the structural engineer with a broad spectrum of possible designs, ranging from the simple to the elaborate.

The illustration and the photograph on pages 114 and 115 show two extremes for such a space: that on the left consisting of a mud floor enclosed by a piled stone wall, and that on the right consisting of a concrete structure employing earthquake-resistant base-isolation techniques.

Both extremes try to achieve similar social needs, namely, to connect with something or someone beyond the bricks and mortar of the building. Consequently, spaces for worship, from the simple to the complex, are perceived as special types of places that transcend and transport. This theme of transcendence beyond the physical realm and the role of the structure itself is of particular interest.

How this theme is realized is a key architectural design issue and shapes the form and detailing of the building. To arrive at a structural solution that both serves the functional requirements and embodies the philosophical intention of the worship space, the structural engineer must understand the design philosophy and collaborate with the architect to identify appropriate structural options and issues. But the revealing question is, where does the architecture stop and the structure start? This is important in understanding the actual role of the structural engineer in this process and how it complements the role of the architect.

Structure should be considered as those building elements necessary for the overall stability of the building, or those building elements for which the risk of structural failure has unacceptable consequences.

STRUCTURAL SYMBOLISM

Elements of the structure that form the spaces for worship may have a symbolic role. For example, the symbolism of towers can represent different aspects in different faiths:

- For Buddhists and Taoists, the multi-level tower temple symbolizes a ladder, linking heaven and earth, as well as the ascent and its associated transformations as a person gets closer to the deity.

- For Christians, steeples denote height or the act of rising above the common level of life and society.

- For Muslims, the minaret represents the call to prayer, and the structure can be as simple as a timber pole with speakers, as shown in the illustration on page 114.

This symbolism is perhaps more apparent in the structure shown in the photograph on page 114, than in the illustration on pages 115. If, however, one were told that the construction on the left is in a new Afghan refugee camp, established in Pakistan after the conflict in Afghanistan following the collapse of the World Trade Center towers on September 11, 2001, then the simple symbolism of this structure becomes clear. This mosque was the first structure the refugees built after erecting their tents.

CHARACTERISTICS OF THE BUILDING STRUCTURE

One cannot draw general conclusions about spaces for worship, given the

▲ Simple mosque in Pakistan.

- The buildings are usually single-story structures, although they often have a mezzanine floor for musical groups, a choir, and extra seating.
- Sometimes extra floors are provided within the main building mass for related worship activities (e.g., religious schools).
- Floors, roofs, and walls used as structural diaphragms are often discontinuous because of the massing of the buildings, thus making lateral load transfer less direct (a fuller description of structural diaphragms is given later).
- The buildings often require a longer design life.
- Heavy, durable materials are often specified.

These issues are more representative of the structure in the photograph on the right, than in the illustration on the left. The assumption throughout this chapter is that spaces for worship require a building of reasonable stature.

DESIGN LOADING

Structural design in its rudimentary form entails the transfer of loads through the structure to the ground. Loads are created by the weight of the building itself (referred to as dead loads), the building occupants (live loads), and the building's environment (such as wind, snow, and seismic loads). The following discussion is based on the 1997 Uniform Building Code (1997 UBC).

Gravity Loads

- The *design dead loads* are permanent and include the weight of all building materials and the weight of fixed equipment.

diversity of building forms, yet the structural issues typically involved in designing spaces for worship can be listed as follows

- The buildings are often dominated by a central space.
- This dominant space is often of high volume, requiring longer-span roof structures.
- The roof over the central space becomes a significant design feature.
- The roof structure is often exposed to view.
- There is often one focal point in the building, and that focal point is reflected by the structure.
- The walls of the space are often high.

- The *design live loads* are produced by the use and occupancy of the building. According to the 1997 UBC, for areas of public assembly the design live load is 50 psf for fixed seating areas and 100 psf for areas without fixed seating. Where schools are incorporated, the live load design requirement is 40 psf for the classroom areas and 100 psf for corridors and general assembly areas (where, in the case of mosques, prayer mats are used rather than fixed seating). Roof live loads depend on the slope of the roof and the area of roof supported by the structural member under design. This load can vary from 12 psf to 20 psf.

Environmental Loads

Environmental loads emanate from the local characteristics of the site. Building codes express these loads as having a small probability of being exceeded in a given return period, usually 50 years.

- *Design wind loads* are a function of the building's location, its exposure, and its height. Such wind loads are based on wind measurements taken at 33 ft (10 m) above ground level and have an annual probability of 0.02. This means that this wind load can be expected to be exceeded once every 50 years. A higher design life than this may be achieved by using statistically higher estimates of wind speeds for the determination of wind loads. Wind loads are taken as being perpendicular to the surface of the material and can act inward or outward on the building.

- *Seismic loads* are caused by tectonic movements of the ground creating horizontal and vertical accelerations and, consequently, forces on the

building structure. The horizontal forces are the most significant in seismic design. The design seismic load depends on the location of the building, the soil profile of the site, the

▲ *Cathedral of Our Lady of the Angels, Los Angeles.*

building's assigned importance factor, and the type of seismic resisting system selected. The aim of the code provisions is primarily to "safeguard against major structural failure and loss of life, not to limit damage or maintain building function." In addition, the design forces derived from the code have a 10 percent chance of being exceeded in 50 years, as determined by a site-specific hazard analysis. As for wind loads, higher seismic loads, based on a statistical analysis of the expected ground accelerations, can be calculated and applied for a longer building design life. Current building code seismic design procedures are based on simplified empirical methods. Future codes will adopt performance methods where the structure is designed to perform to a specified performance level when subjected to various loading scenarios, with the intent to provide owners and designers with the capability to select alternative performance goals for the design of their buildings.

- *Snow loads* depend on the location of the building, its exposure, the shape of the roof, and the building's assigned importance factor. Such loads are based on statistical data and have a 10 percent probability of being exceeded once in every 50 years.

- Importance factors are based on the use of the building and the need for the structure to perform well under earthquake and other loads. For example, hospitals and other emergency facilities have high importance factors.

Loading relates to the particular characteristics of spaces of worship thus:

- The requirement for a longer design life will increase the snow, wind, and seismic design loads above those stipulated in the code.

- The use of high unbraced walls around spaces for worship will mean that lateral loads, such as the wind and seismic loads, will have a greater impact in the design of these elements.

- Long-span roofs are more sensitive to high dead and live loads and snow loads, and attempts should be made to minimize these where possible. For example, heavily articulated roof forms can attract drifting snow in certain regions.

- Discontinuities in the wall, roof, and floor diaphragms will either result in larger diaphragm stresses or require more bracing elements to withstand the wind and seismic loads.

- The use of heavier, more durable materials will impact the dead loads and the seismic loads.

STRUCTURAL SYSTEMS
Gravity Systems

The gravity system includes the parts of a structure that carry forces due to gravity, such as floor beams and slabs and columns. The choice of system will depend on a number of factors, including required span, loading, stiffness requirements (e.g., perception of vibration of suspended slabs by the congregation), availability of materials, and whether the system fits the architecture, both conceptually and dimensionally. The table on page 117 compares various roof systems and lists examples of their use in spaces of worship. Similarly, the table on page

118 compares various floor framing options. Although these are presented as individual systems, combinations of systems and materials are possible. Notice that some of these systems are inherently stable and can also carry lateral forces, as noted below.

- *Roof structures:* The architecture of spaces for worship can yield complex roof forms. Buddhist buildings, for

GRAVITY SYSTEMS FOR SPACES FOR WORSHIP			
Gravity System	**Advantages**	**Disadvantages**	**Span Range**
Simple beams (timber and steel)	Simple construction, easy connection details	Relatively small spans. Size is larger than if beams are continuous. Lateral bracing system still to be resolved.	Timber (5–22 ft) Steel (10–80 ft)
Trusses (timber and steel)	Larger spans, although relatively light weight.	Building height is increased. Roof space is created. Lateral bracing system still to be resolved.	Timber (25–150 ft) Steel (25–300 ft)
Portal (moment) frames (timber, steel, and concrete)	Economical structure. Inherent bracing. Often exposed.	Tend to be long, linear buildings. Future development difficult.	Timber (25–125 ft) Steel (25–325 ft) Concrete (25–125 ft)
Trussed portal	Incorporates a lateral bracing system.	Tend to be long, linear buildings. Future development difficult.	Same as for portals.
Arches (timber, steel, and concrete)	Minimizes weight of structure. Inherent bracing. Often exposed.	Diagonal braces or shear walls required along the sidewalls of the space for worship.	Timber (50–300 ft) Steel (50–550 ft) Concrete (50–350 ft)
Shells (steel and concrete)	Minimizes weight of structure. Large-span structures possible.	Acoustics. Specialist contractor required.	Steel (50–300 ft) Concrete (50–300 ft)
Domes (timber, steel, and concrete)	Minimizes weight of structure. Large-span structures possible.	Acoustics. Specialist contractor required.	Timber (50–550 ft) Steel (50–600 ft) Concrete (50–300 ft)
Lightweight structures	Usual roof shapes.	Relatively short life span.	Plastic (25–400 ft)

FLOOR SYSTEMS FOR SPACES FOR WORSHIP			
Floor System	**Advantages**	**Disadvantages**	**Span Range**
Timber deck	Exposed underside can be finished ceiling.	Short spans.	2–11 ft
Timber joists	Larger spans than timber deck. Easy construction.	Short spans.	5–22 ft
Timber box beams	Easy to construct.	Connections can be problematic.	20–60 ft
Timber laminated beams	Good appearance.	Connections can be problematic.	15–100 ft
Steel composite beams	Reduces space required for floor.	Needs to be covered over.	20–90 ft
Steel beams	Availability.	Connections can be problematic.	10–80 ft
Concrete beams	Can be exposed.	Connections can be problematic.	10–60 ft
Concrete slab and beam	Underside can be finished surface. High load capacity.	Heavier construction.	10–60 ft
Concrete flat slab	Flush ceiling useful for straight service runs.	Heavier construction.	5–20 ft

example, traditionally have an odd number of roofs. Christian churches often reflect the progression from the outside world to the inner space for worship in the different roof structures above the various spaces. Mosques frequently use a dome-shaped roof over the prayer areas. Thus, the roof often becomes the signature of the space for worship and can require careful design and detailing.

- *Lightweight roof structures:* Structural fabrics (tents) and cable nets carry in-plane membrane forces and adjust their geometry to maintain equilibrium with the applied forces. They are characterized as thin membranes, with a thickness that is very small as compared with their dimensions, and a three-dimensional load-carrying behavior determined by geometric shape and level of prestress. These usually have interesting doubly curved surfaces to resist positive and negative loads and have potential for large-volume, light structures.

Lateral Systems

For the majority of spaces for worship, the best system is the simplest. Where lateral load-bracing elements are clearly identified, the load paths and the connections to those elements become well defined. The advantages of different lateral resisting systems are outlined in the table below.

A commonly used form of lateral system is the portal frame and three-pin arch. Portals are often used in industrial buildings where a clear space is required. These portals are effective in only one direction (normally across the building), and often use diagonal bracing along the building. Such a system may intrude into the building, and this condition is often treated by exposing and expressing the structure, as with glue-laminated portals.

Diaphragms

Diaphragms are an essential part of the lateral system, used with framing elements called drag-struts to tie the vertical elements of the structure together and to deliver horizontal forces to the vertical elements of the lateral system. They are, in effect, horizontal beams that transfer lateral loads within a building. Roofs and floor slabs are typically used as diaphragms and are sometimes supplemented by cross bracing if they are not adequately configured. In spaces for worship, diaphragms are important to transfer roof loads out to lateral resisting

LATERAL RESISTING OPTIONS FOR SPACES FOR WORSHIP		
Lateral System	**Advantages**	**Disadvantages**
Cantilevered columns or buttresses	Simple connections to roof. Open movement below.	Heavy foundations and heavy columns required. Columns are closely spaced.
Portal frames	Economical structure.	Large member sizes intruding into worship space.
Diagonally braced frames	Economical.	Require wall spaces. Restricted movement through braced area.
Shear walls	Walls often detailed, hence double use.	Transfer members to get loads to the walls.
Arches	Easier construction.	Roof shape set.
Domes	Light and special aesthetics.	Complex structure.
Special Seismic Designs		
Base isolation	Highest level of seismic protection.	Expensive.
Energy dissipaters	Higher level of seismic protection	Structure more complex.

▲ Wood trusses.
Thorncrown Chapel,
Eureka Springs, Arkansas.
Architect: E. Fay Jones.
Photo: Timothy Hursley.

elements, to transfer loads from mezzanine floors or upper levels, and to reduce the loading on high unbraced walls.

Diaphragms can be constructed from timber, steel, or concrete and typically take the following forms:

- Timber or plywood floors and roofs
- Concrete floor slabs or roofs
- Metal decking
- Diagonal steel rods or straps

Metal cladding, other than aluminum, may also be used as a diaphragm, provided it carries a Underwriters Laboratories (UL) load rating for shear.

Diaphragms are often penetrated, making them discontinuous in localized areas. For example, there may be a need for clerestory lighting in the roof. In such instances, the opening can often be reinforced and the diaphragm split into a series of subdiaphragms. Alternatively, diagonal steel members can replace the dia-phragm action yet still allow light through, or drag members such as beams and struts can be used to transfer loads away from the clerestory location.

MATERIALS

One of the first decisions that the architect and engineer have to make is the selection of materials. The process of selecting materials to satisfy structural as well as architectural requirements is complex. One must gauge the suitability of the material for the proposed structural form, its cost in the local marketplace, and the available local construction expertise. Issues of costing usually require feedback from local contractors and prospective bidders for the project.

Structures for spaces for worship often employ a mix of materials. The design team tries to exploit the distinct advantages and avoid the disadvantages of the material combinations used. The 1997 UBC allows, for instance, the use of plywood diaphragms to prop masonry walls, but only for single-story construction. A mix of materials should be avoided where it will increase the complexity of construction or where there would be a mismatch of material stiffness.

Timber

Timber is used principally for its visual and tactile qualities. Because of its good strength-to-weight properties, it is often used for roof structures, where modern connectors and gluing techniques can allow long spans. Timber can also be used for a wide range of structural applications:

- Roof or floor beams

- Plywood bracing walls

- Timber trusses

- Long span glue-laminated timber beams

- Glue laminated portal frames and arches

The advantages of timber are as follows:

- Inexpensive for simple framing

- Easy to construct

- Allows off-site fabrication

- Warm appearance

See the photographs on pages 71 and 72.

A potential disadvantage is its susceptibility to insect and fungal attack, which can be overcome by:

- Using appropriately durable species

- Using it within the weather envelope

Timber pole structures, typical of Eastern faiths, have been used where smaller timber sections were inadequate. Poles are used in the gateways and roof structures but, other than in these specific structures and this geography, are not widely employed. (See the illustration on page 3.)

An impressive use of timber is for long spans, using glue-laminated timber sections. These sections are formed by pressing and gluing together smaller timber to form one composite timber section. Large curved, intricate sections can be achieved with this material in spans of up to 525 ft (160 m). Economies are realized by using lower-strength graded timber in the center of the glue-laminated sections (where stresses are lower) and reserving the better-strength material for the outer layers.

Glue-laminated arches are almost universally of the three-pin variety. This is because of the practical transport restrictions on size. Moreover, the two-pin option would present difficulties in on-site

▼ *Wood clerestory detail. St. Matthew's Church, Pacific Palisades, California. Architect: MRY. Courtesy of Assassi Productions.*

connection. Sketches of the two types of arch systems are shown below.

The durability of timber relies on its protection from water, pest treatment, well-engineered connections, and protection from the weather. The moisture content of timber changes depending on the ambient environment and the season. Moreover, glue-laminated timber is usually oversized to provide a level of fire resistance. Thus, in a fire the outer layers char, protecting the structural core of the section.

Steel

Like timber, steel has a wide range of structural applications, including:

- Simple post-and-beam framing
- Trusses
- Fabricated plate girders
- Portal frames and arches

Steel has several advantages over other materials:

- Steel has better strength-to-weight and stiffness-to-weight characteristics than most timber species and hence will yield lighter section sizes.

- It can be fabricated off-site and easily erected on-site.
- It is a known material to contractors, though not as common as timber.
- It can be shaped to fit complex and unusual shapes.

The main disadvantage of steel is that it is perceived as an industrial material and is not often exposed in spaces for worship; when used it is usually covered over. When carefully finished, steel can be exposed to great effect, as in the Herz Jesu Kirche in Munich, Germany. (See color plate 6.)

Masonry

Masonry has been used throughout the ages for spaces for worship. Masonry construction today includes reinforced load-bearing block and brick masonry and reinforced non-load-bearing stone masonry. Brick and block masonry can be found in building exteriors in both load-bearing and veneer applications. Masonry is also used inside where structural support and internal partitioning are required.

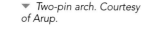
▼ *Two-pin arch. Courtesy of Arup.*

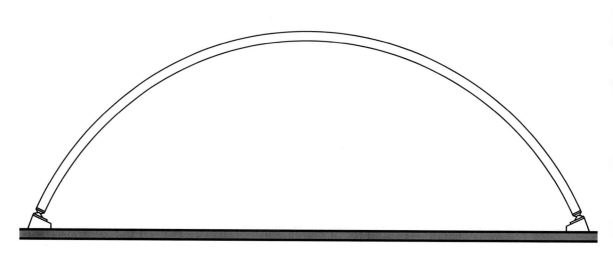

The advantages of this material are as follows:

- Economical building form where building modules fit the block size
- Excellent fire resistance
- Good sound attenuation
- Very good durabability

Masonry is also useful in providing lateral resisting elements such as reinforced shear walls. The main disadvantages are that it has a low tensile strength, which can be overcome by the introduction of reinforcing steel or, less commonly, by prestressing, and that its heavy weight generates large seismic forces. (See color plate 18.)

Concrete

Reinforced concrete gains tensile capacity from reinforcing steel, allowing it to be used in many applications:

- Foundations, retaining walls, and grade slabs
- Conventional beam and column frames and suspended slabs
- Long-span beam sections, which can be achieved by prestressing or post-tensioning
- Arches
- Shells

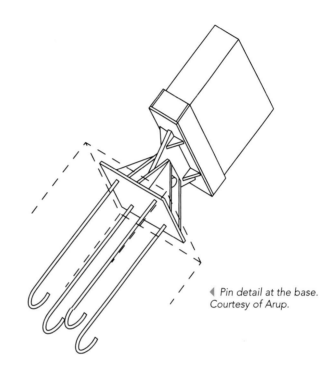

◀ Pin detail at the base. Courtesy of Arup.

▼ Three-pin arch. Courtesy of Arup.

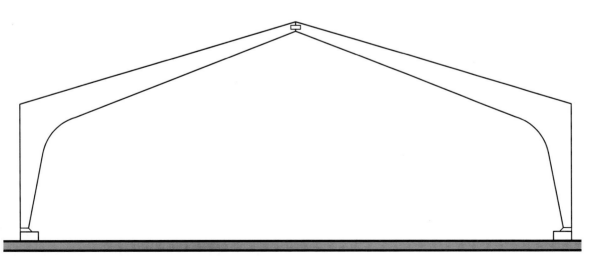

▲ *Padre Pio Church, San Giovanni Rotondo, Italy. Granite blocks threaded through with steel wires form the arches supporting the roof. Architect: Renzo Piano Building Workshop. Photo: M. Denance, courtesy Renzo Piano Building Workshop.*

Concrete has many of the same qualities as masonry. Its advantages are as follows:

- It is pourable and thus can take the shape of the forms into which it is cast.
- It is very durable.
- It may be precast, permitting off-site fabrication.
- It can be detailed to provide good ductility, which is useful for seismic applications.
- Its high thermal mass can be useful for passive heating/cooling schemes.
- It offers excellent fire resistance.
- It has good sound attenuation.

(See the color plates 1-3.)

The main disadvantage of concrete is that its weight can generate large seismic forces. For cast-in-place concrete the speed of construction is generally slower than that of other materials fabricated off-site.

DURABILITY AND DESIGN LIFE
Durability

Durability can be defined as the ability of a material, element, or structure to perform its intended function for its required life without the need for replacement or significant repair, but subject to normal maintenance (*Encyclopedia of Architectural Technology* 2002). In the case of spaces for worship it is likely that this intended function would include provision of, at least:

- An enclosed area that is safe for the occupants
- Some degree of protection from the weather
- A pleasing, or at least acceptable, visual appearance

The required life could conceivably lie between two extremes, ranging from a few days or weeks, a temporary structure for a particular festival or rally, to many centuries, for major cathedrals or temples.

The need for durability will thus have a large influence on the design philosophy—that is, whether elements should be replaceable, maintainable, or lifelong—and on the selected materials. Obviously, the structural frame and the foundations will have to be designed to last the whole life of the structure, but other elements may be designed to be replaced. Indeed, it may be uneconomic, inappropriate, or even impossible for all parts of the structure to be designed to last for its entire intended life. Such replaceable elements may include window frames, cladding, or roof coverings, for example. For structures with long design lives it is very likely that fixtures and fittings such as lighting and heating systems will need to be replaced in time because of obsolescence, and the design should take this into account.

Some religious buildings achieve their longevity by continual rebuilding. For example, the Shinto shrines of Ise, Japan, although built as relatively short-lived wood structures, have survived for 15 centuries by being rebuilt every 20 years.

Most materials deteriorate with time, albeit at a greater or lesser rate, depending largely on their physical characteristics and environment. The anticipated rate and form of deterioration should therefore be major considerations, taking into account the required performance and life of the structure. The architect/designer needs to have at least a basic understanding of the durability of materials and, where a very long life is required or where the exposure environment is particularly severe, this should be supplemented by more extensive specialist materials knowledge.

The durability of a material is not an inherent property as such, unless considered within the context of time and exposure. For example, most building stones will be durable for lifetimes measured in decades, but when building life is expressed in centuries or when stone is used under severe conditions such as flooring, their performance can vary widely. Factors such as acid rain or general weathering may lead to progressive loss of surface, which, although not necessarily threatening to structural integrity, may result in an unacceptable change in appearance.

With many materials it is possible to control the rate of deterioration by taking special measures or even by controlling the environment itself. Consider the case of reinforced concrete, for example. The exposure of concrete to air, as will almost inevitably occur where it is used in a building superstructure, will result in the reaction of the concrete with carbon dioxide in the atmosphere. This will lead to the gradual but progressive neutralization of the naturally high alkalinity of the concrete, working from the outer surface inward. If this neutralization reaches the reinforcement, and if there is sufficient moisture present in the concrete, the reinforcement will corrode, eventually leading to cracking and spalling of the surface. A concrete of sufficiently high quality and a sufficient depth of concrete cover to the reinforcement, as provided by most design codes for normal building structures, should mean this process is sufficiently slow to ensure durability for a life of at least between 50 and 100 years.

If a significantly longer life is required extra precautions will probably be needed, which may include:

- Higher-quality concrete and/or increased depth of cover to reinforcement

- Replacement of normal carbon steel reinforcement by corrosion-resistant stainless steel

- Redesign of the structure so that the concrete elements are within the building envelope, where the level of moisture in the concrete will generally be insufficient to support sufficient corrosion of the reinforcement to cause damage

- Regular sealing of the exterior with a penetrating sealer that prevents moisture penetration

- Cathodic protection, whereby a small electric charge, continuously applied to the reinforcement, repels water molecules and minimizes corrosion

Other materials will require different measures, such as the painting or other protective coating of timber or steel, but the general philosophy remains the same—that it may be possible to tailor the performance of the materials to meet specific requirements, based on knowledge of the appropriate deterioration mechanisms. Certain measures may require periodic maintenance to ensure their continued efficacy, and if so this maintenance needs to be programmed. Durability performance, however, is not always easy to predict, such as for natural stone because of its inherent variability, or for new materials such as fiber-reinforced polymer composites because of their relatively brief experience record.

The structural form and design of details, in particular for the runoff of water and the interfaces between elements or materials, can also have a large influence on durability. Often it is the failure of such details, rather than the choice of materials themselves, that leads to premature deterioration or durability failure.

Thus, in summary, one must identify the required life of the structure, the exposure conditions to which it will be subjected, and the level of performance (including appearance) required over that lifetime. It must then be determined which parts of the structure are required to last for its whole life and which need to be designed to be replaceable. The materials, necessary maintenance and other protective measures, details, and structural form can then be selected and designed to meet these requirements and provide a durable structure.

Design Life

1. The Building Code implies a design life of 50 years with proper maintenance. The client should be consulted early in the design to enable him or her to make an informed decision as to whether a longer design life is required.

2. In some countries, places of worship are seen as secondary civil defense centers and therefore need to be more robust than other community buildings.

3. In some faiths, such as the Islamic faith, once a building has been designated as a particular place of worship (e.g., a mosque), the land cannot be changed nor the building used for anything other than a place of worship (a mosque). Hence, mosques automatically have a long life expectancy.

OTHER CONSIDERATIONS
Constructability: Simplicity of Fabrication and Speed of Erection

The cost of on-site construction is a significant component of the overall building cost. Designers typically try to organize as much off-site fabrication in controlled factories both for quality and for speed of erection. Connections made on-site must be quick, practical, and straightforward.

Steel construction probably has the highest degree of off-site fabrication and is usually erected very quickly in the field with the use of cranes. Timber fabrication off-site is also common, and elements such as glue-laminated beams, box beams, trussed beams, and larger timber roof trusses are all fabricated off-site. Protection from UV rays and rainwater is required until the building is closed in.

Concrete can be precast off-site. The high cost of forms, however, means that they should be reused as much as possible to realize economies, which is difficult unless the project is large. An alternative to precasting off-site is casting tilt-up panels on the slab floor of the building, then lifting them in place and tying them back to their foundations. (See the photograph on page 183.)

Dimensions of off-site-fabricated sections vary but are usually specified so that they can conveniently fit on a truck. Hence, a width of 12 ft and a length of 60 ft are typically used. In addition, cranes must be able to easily access the site, avoid overhead power lines, and get as close as possible to the final location of the fabricated section. This is not always achievable, particularly on urban sites. In these situations larger cranes, with the required lifting capacity, may be employed.

Therefore, to create an economical building, the designer must strive to simplify on-site detailing and construction, simplify the configuration, and provide practical detailing that considers the specific material advantages and disadvantages.

Building Flexibility

Future adaptations of any new building affect live load requirements, length of span, and mechanical systems. For instance, it may be prudent to increase the live load to 100 psf or more over all suspended floors to allow for changes in occupancy from, say, a classroom to an assembly hall. A design that employs fewer columns allows greater flexibility if the building interiors are to be changed.

Building Obsolescence

Mechanical, electrical, and, more recently, audiovisual requirements for spaces for worship have a shorter design life than the structure. Thus, the structure needs to incorporate allowances and access for these changes over its lifetime. These may, for example, involve floor knock-out panels and under-floor trenches sized for cabling and ductwork.

STRUCTURAL UPGRADE AND REPAIR OF EXISTING BUILDINGS

In one sense, the work of appraisal and repair is the reverse of the design sequence. The building as it exists is the starting point, and the design team works back from there to define the necessary remedial work.

A general methodology of repair is as follows:

Carry out a survey to:

- Understand the structural form
- Determine the condition

Appraise the adequacy of the structure according to the following performance criteria:

- Safety
- Serviceability
- Durability

Determine the remedial work necessary to achieve the required service life.

Existing Information

For "younger" buildings, say, from the 1950s onward, the original construction drawings are often available from the designers and are an invaluable aid to the understanding of such buildings. For older buildings there is less chance of obtaining the originals, but record drawings may have been made at some time and held by the owner or the local authority.

The Survey

The aim of the survey is to obtain the information relevant to the repair of the structure, which, in general, falls under two headings:

- The construction
- The condition

It is important to distinguish between these two aspects of the structure and to recognize their independence. It is possible that a sound structure is in poor condition, and vice versa. The amount of information gathered under each heading must be sufficient to allow a conclusion to be reached when the structure is appraised. A visual inspection may suffice, but in many cases some investigative work, requiring local opening-up, will be necessary.

The Appraisal

The appraisal is the most important stage of the process, when an assessment is made of the potential for the various parts of the structure to perform satisfactorily for their desired service life. An appraisal may have to be made under the following headings:

- Safety
- Serviceability
- Durability

Consider a timber structure as an example. It may be found that some beam ends have rotted, leaving the floor unsafe. Long, shallow floor beams may have suffered creep deflection over time, and although still adequately strong, the alignment of the floor as a serviceability criterion may not be acceptable in a pub-

lic building. And as an element becomes intermittently wet, the durability of the timber species may not allow sufficient design life to be realized.

The appraisal concludes with a decision on the form of remedial work that is appropriate. It is essential to see the complete picture before making a decision. If, for instance, some rafters require remedial work below a tiled roof that is sound, then the most appropriate repair may be splice plates fitted from below. If the tiles are to be renewed, then the rafter may more simply be replaced when the old tiles have been stripped.

Historic Buildings

The sequence described in the preceding discussion applies to all existing buildings. For historic buildings, however, the original fabric is of great importance, and design teams are not free to remove it as they wish. It is generally required that a "cultural audit" be carried out to determine the significance of the various parts. This should be taken into account in the choice of remedial work to maximize the retention of significance. This will often mean retaining the maximum amount of original material—repairing the end of a beam, for example, rather than simply replacing it—which will not always be the cheapest option.

Remedial Work

When the appraisal has shown that some parts of the structure will not perform adequately for the required service life, remedial work may be necessary. Remedial work can be classified under the following headings—the "five Rs":

- *Retain.* In effect, concluding that, for parts of the structure in sound condition, no remedial work will be needed generally.

- *Repair.* If a large part of a structure, or an element, is sound, only local repairs may be needed in the affected areas.

- *Reinforce.* Adding structure to a defective element to increase its strength. This is a particularly useful technique for historic structures, because it allows the retention of the original fabric.

- *Replicate.* If a structure is found to be generally defective, then it may be appropriate to replace it with a facsimile, such as, for example, an exposed roof truss of a historic church

- *Replace.* Again, for a defective structure, replacing it with a new structure of different form, as may be done for a concealed roof truss. (See the photograph on page 254.)

For any particular building, however, the final decision will involve aesthetics as well as structural logic, particularly for historic buildings where the structure is expressed. Generally, the form and condition of the adjacent fabric will also have to be taken into account.

CONCLUSION

It would be easy to assume that the structural design of a space for worship is the solution of a series of problems and that when each individual issue is resolved, the building emerges (Artemis 1994). That is not the case, however, as many issues are interlinked, not isolated concerns. This is common to all structural design projects. What makes spaces for worship different is the number of related design issues and the extent of their potential influence on the overall design solution.

CHAPTER 8
MECHANICAL SYSTEMS

GOALS OF MECHANICAL SYSTEM DESIGN

The main purpose of the mechanical systems for places for worship is to provide comfortable and hygienic conditions for the occupants. The secondary purpose is to protect the building and its contents from frost, heat, or moisture damage during unoccupied periods. The selected systems have to achieve these goals within acceptable capital and operating budgets.

Most religious spaces have high occupancies and are used intermittently, but although these design constraints are common to most religions, there are significant differences in the details of how the spaces are used. To select the most appropriate system, it is important to consider and balance the following factors:

- Form of the space
- Local climate
- Noise criteria
- Occupancy patterns
- Artworks and artifacts
- Existing conditions, if any
- Capital cost
- Operating cost
- Maintenance capability and building life
- Additional program elements such as meeting space or residential acommodation at the same location as the worship space

Comfort

The actual conditions that provide comfort will depend on the activities that take place within the building and the clothing of the building occupants. These need to be evaluated carefully, based on the religious practices associated with the building. The following are the most important variables that influence thermal comfort:

- Air temperature (dry-bulb)
- Humidity
- Mean radiant temperature
- Relative air velocity
- Activity level (heat production in the body)
- Thermal resistance of the clothing (clo-value)

Thermal comfort can be achieved with many different combinations of these variables. The dry-bulb temperature, humidity, and relative air velocity are controlled by the mechanical system. The mean radiant temperature is dependent on the system, its operation, and the architectural finishes, while the activity level and thermal resistance of the clothing are determined by the occupants and the activity within the space.

Indoor comfort criteria are most usually defined using the American Society of Heating, Refrigerating, and Air-Conditioning Engineers (ASHRAE) guidelines (ASHRAE Standard 55-1992), which are based on research into human comfort. To determine the correct design conditions for the spaces, the designer must understand the likely clothing levels within the building and the likely activities. These can be surprisingly variable and are related to the form of worship, the seasons, the role of the worshiper in the service, and his or her location in the worship space.

The activity level of the people will depend on the form of worship. For example, in a Christian gospel service people may move around a lot, dancing and singing, for which a cooler design temperature is preferred, whereas in most other forms of worship people are relatively static and warmer temperatures are preferred. For a full-immersion baptism service, a specific area of the building must be kept warm enough for people in wet clothing.

Clothing level will depend on the time of year and any specific clothing required for the form of worship. In most building types, seasonal clothing variations are usually allowed for by designing the cooling system to achieve a temperature of approximately 78°F (25°C) on the "warmest" design day and designing the heating system to achieve a temperature of approximately 72°F (22°C) on the "coldest" design day.

This approach assumes that people dress in lighter clothes in summer than in winter, but depending on the type of religious building, this assumption may not be valid. For example, an Orthodox synagogue should be cool enough for people dressed in full suits at all times of year. Similarly, priests and choristers in most

Psychrometric chart showing the range of thermal comfort conditions accepted by most people. Courtesy of Arup.

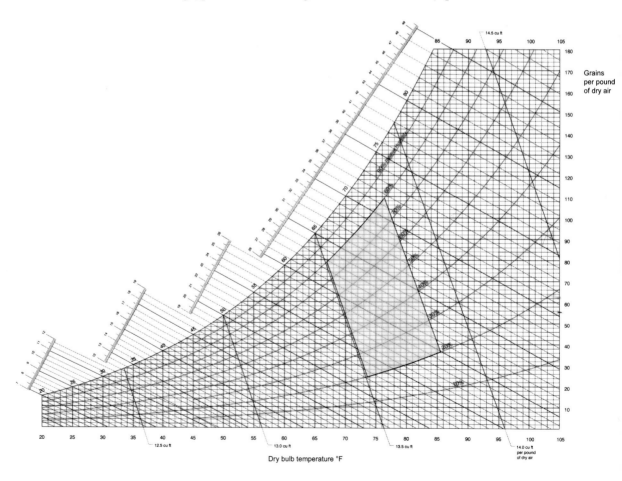

Dry bulb temperature °F

Grains per pound of dry air

Christian denominations wear ceremonial robes that will increase the warmth of their clothing and reduce their preferred temperature. The type of footwear also significantly affects the temperature at which people are comfortable.

In most buildings a combination of heating and cooling will be required to ensure comfort. The amount of heating and cooling and the design of the system will depend on the climate and the building use. The advantages and disadvantages of different systems are discussed later in this chapter.

Ventilation

Outside air is required to prevent the buildup of odors and chemicals in the air. Outside air is also required for healthy breathing.

The minimum outside air ventilation rates are given in ASHRAE Standard 62-2001. These values are sometimes amended by local codes. Typically, a minimum outside air supply rate of 15 cu ft per minute (cfm), or 8 l per second, is required for each occupant. If the building is occupied intermittently, defined as being for periods of less than three hours, and if contaminants are able to disperse between periods of peak occupancy, then the codes usually allow the ventilation rates to be reduced.

Spaces for worship for most religions share two characteristics that affect the design of the ventilation system. Worship halls generally have very high occupancy densities during major religious services, and these services are generally shorter than three hours. A high occupancy density means that the outside air supply rate has to be high. The outside air supply rate has a large effect on the energy use of the building, and in most areas of the United States, at most times of year, the lower the outside air supply rate, the lower the energy use will be.

The ventilation system also has to reflect the type of worship occurring in the space. Some religious celebrations, notably "high church" Christian services, use incense. Other services may use candles. In both cases, the ventilation rate must be high enough to remove the smoke from the air.

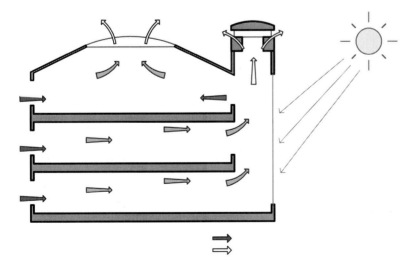

◀ The principle of buoyancy-driven natural ventilation. As air is heated, it rises, drawing in cool air at low level. Natural ventilation may also be wind-driven.

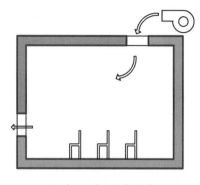

The principle of mechanical ventilation, in which fans are used to circulate air.

Mechanical supply with natural exhaust

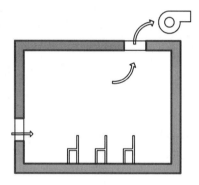

Mechanical exhaust with natural air make-up

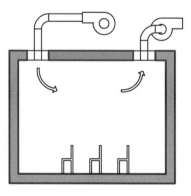

Mechanical exhaust and supply

Ventilation air is also used as a heat transfer medium in air-based mechanical systems. Ventilation can be in the form of either natural ventilation or mechanical ventilation.

Low Energy Use

Most places of worship have limited budgets for the management and operation of their mechanical systems. Religious organizations also frequently have objectives that are broader than the operation of their worship halls, and funding for these competes with building operations budgets. Any system should be efficient and affordable to operate.

SUMMARY

To achieve comfortable conditions throughout the year, a combination of heating, cooling, and outside air ventilation is usually required. The selection of the most appropriate mechanical system will depend on the size and type of space, the occupancy pattern, and the local climate. System selection will also depend on whether the project is a renovation or to be newly built, the available capital and operating budgets, and the types of spaces included in the building, other than the worship space.

MECHANICAL SYSTEM CONSTRAINTS FOR PLACES OF WORSHIP

Some characteristics of places for worship are common to many religions and present particular challenges for the correct design of the mechanical systems. Primary among these is the fact that places for worship are essentially large meeting rooms. Services are usually led by a small number of people located in a particular place, and it is important that all the attendees can see them. The rooms are typically large and without columns, with a high ceiling, often a balcony, and usually a raised dais or stage area.

The arrangement creates three challenges for the mechanical design:

- The size and openness of the room limits the locations for air distribution equipment. The ventilation demand for the space, however, is high because of the occupancy density. Congregations also need draft-free comfort, particularly when seated for long periods of time.

- The volume of the space is large, but since much of it is unoccupied, it is both unnecessary and expensive to heat and cool the entire space.

- The space for worship is a large room that requires very low noise levels. Acoustic performance depends on the size of the space, the construction materials, and the building's mechanical systems. The mechanical systems must be designed to be appropriate for the required acoustic performance. Further details on acoustic design considerations for worship spaces are found in Chapter 12.

Facility management practices dictate several other concerns that should be addressed through the programming stage of the project to avoid the specification of special systems and future expense. These include building life span, appearance, special contents, and the availability of maintenance staff.

- Religious buildings are often built from high-quality materials for a long life. This means that it is likely that mechanical systems will have to be replaced within the lifetime of the

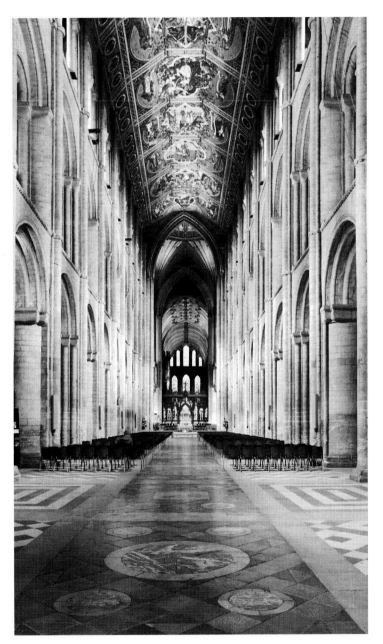

building and they should therefore be designed to be fully removable, or accessible for cleaning and maintenance, with as little disruption to the original finishes as possible.

▲ Ely Cathedral, Cambridgeshire, England, showing the tall ceilings and limited surfaces for mechanical distribution. Courtesy of Arup.

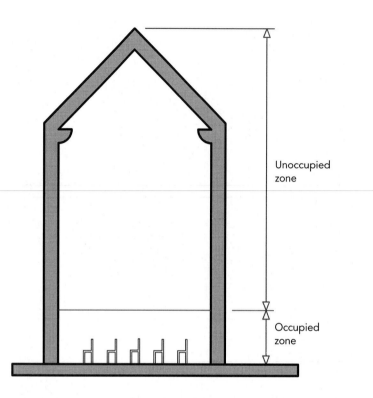

Unoccupied zone

Occupied zone

▲ A large portion of a worship space may be unoccupied.

- The mechanical systems should be simple to operate and not require sophisticated controls, because they will frequently be operated by unskilled volunteers and maintenance budgets are usually small.

- Finally, artwork or other precious materials in spaces for worship may have requirements for temperature or humidity control that are more stringent than those for human comfort. (See color plate 4a.) In this case, removing these items at times when the building is unoccupied and storing them in a thermally controlled location can significantly reduce energy use. For similar reasons, finishes for buildings that are likely to be unoccupied for long periods of time should be chosen to be robust enough to accommodate large swings in temperature and humidity so that the building does not have to be heated and cooled at all times to preserve the finishes.

- The appearance of worship spaces frequently owes much to tradition, so that mechanical systems often need to be disguised or concealed. This can be particularly difficult in renovation projects, where the designer of the mechanical system must work within the architectural concept of the building while aiming to provide a modern standard of comfort for the building's occupants.

- The systems should be as long-lasting as possible. The budgets available for building operation and the intermittent use of many kinds of places for worship means that systems should be designed to require little maintenance and to be reliable.

Churches

The predominant religion throughout the history of the United States has been Christianity. In many areas, churches have existed for years, but church attendance has declined, leaving many congregations reduced in size. Thus much mechanical design for churches is likely to be renovation, and is often designed to focus the worship for a smaller congregation. This will impose a number of constraints on the design of the mechanical systems.

Primary Christian worship takes place on Sundays. Most churches have three services: early morning, late morning, and evening. The most heavily attended is the late morning service. In most rural and suburban areas, churches are barely used during the week, although there may be prayer meetings and Bible study groups within the church. In between these events, church buildings are generally locked. In urban areas, church use can be more intensive and buildings tend to be open for private devotion throughout the week. Churches may also be rented out for other uses, such as classical music concerts. Attendance varies widely. Christmas and Easter services can fill churches with several hundred people, whereas other services may have only a few worshipers.

Most Christian worship requires sitting, kneeling, and standing only. Many people dress up for church and are well covered by clothing. In some denominations people may leave their seats to receive communion. Comfort conditions should therefore be appropriate for seated people with moderate levels of clothing. Seating is usually fixed, and this can provide opportunities for concealing mechanical systems.

The mechanical systems for churches, therefore, need to be designed for infrequent but high levels of occupancy and should also be able to provide comfort for much smaller groups. There should be some mechanism for freeze protection or severe overheating prevention during long unoccupied periods. The systems should react quickly so that comfort conditions can be achieved with the least energy use.

Urban churches are also likely to have outreach and community support programs in auxiliary spaces around the worship space. These spaces are likely to be occupied during normal business hours and early evenings. The design of these spaces depends on their use, but in

general their mechanical systems should be kept separate from the main worship hall system, as the occupancy profiles and required conditions are likely to be different.

▲ Coventry Cathedral, Coventry, England. Modern spaces of worship often maintain some characteristics of historic structures. Courtesy of Arup.

Synagogues

There have been Jewish worship spaces in urban areas of the United States since it was first settled by Europeans. There are many existing synagogues, and therefore some of the mechanical design for these spaces is likely to be renovation. With the migration of Jewish people from urban centers into suburban developments, a number of underused churches have been converted to synagogues. As with churches, the fact that many of the projects are renovations of existing spaces will impose a number of constraints on the design of the mechanical systems. New synagogues are also being built, and some unused synagogues are being converted to churches as well.

Primary Jewish worship takes place between sunset on Friday and sunset on Saturday. The most heavily attended services occur on Saturday morning. Attendance at synagogue is variable, depending on the time of year, with peak attendance at Yom Kippur, the day of atonement, the most solemn day of the Jewish year, and Rosh Hashanah, the Jewish New Year. The High Holy Days have very long services, up to five hours. In between these events, synagogues are generally locked, as the worship halls in synagogues are used exclusively for services.

Jewish worship requires sitting and standing. People generally remain in their seats throughout the service. Many people dress up for services and are well covered by clothing. Comfort conditions should therefore be appropriate for seated people with moderate to heavy levels of clothing. The seating is usually fixed, and this can provide opportunities for concealing mechanical systems.

The mechanical systems for synagogues should be designed for infrequent but high levels of occupancy and should also be able to provide comfort for much smaller groups. There should be some mechanism for freeze prevention or overheating protection during long unoccupied periods. The systems should react quickly so that comfort conditions can be achieved with minimum energy use.

Synagogues may have Hebrew schools and community programs associated with them, and these activities are usually housed in auxiliary spaces in the same building as the worship space. The occupancy schedules and conditions required in these spaces differ from those of the main worship hall, and the systems should be separated.

Mosques

Islam is the most rapidly growing religion in the United States, but there are few Islamic communities outside the major urban centers. As communities have

▼ UNESCO Mission to India Temple, Konarak, Prissa, India. Courtesy of Arup.

been small, many existing Islamic places of worship are accommodated in existing buildings that were not specifically designed for the purpose and that may be unsuitable. Mechanical design for these spaces is driven by the available space and the high occupancies.

Devout Muslims pray five times a day; they are encouraged to worship together as often as possible. Attendance at a mosque is highest on Friday, but Muslims will go there at other times as well. Buildings are generally locked other than during worship periods. Attendance during Ramadan, the ninth month of the Muslim year, when Muslims fast and follow strict restraints in order to focus on their faith, is higher than at other times of year. The pattern of frequent worship means that mosques should be kept comfortable for most of the time.

Moslem prayer involves prostration. There is usually no seating, and shoes are removed on entering the space. Traditional Islamic dress is layered and modest, but appropriate for hot climates. Comfort conditions should be appropriate at floor level and for people standing, and special attention should be paid to the temperature of the floor surface.

The mechanical systems for mosques should be designed for frequent, high levels of occupancy and should be able to provide comfort for much smaller groups.

Hindu Temples

There are only about one million Hindus in the United States. They are concentrated within urban areas. Hinduism is flexible; there is no one single founder or single system of morality. Hinduism is an aggregation of different religious groups

◀ *Hindu temple, sculptural detail. Courtesy of Arup.*

that share a number of sacred texts, including the Bhagavad-Gita. Because of the variations among different kinds of religious groups, the type of worship that occurs in the space should be carefully described during the programming stage of design.

Within the United States and Europe there are very few buildings that have been built specifically for Hindu worship; many temples are in old churches. There is no specific Hindu day of worship, but temple attendance is higher on traditional fast days. The most popular fast days are Tuesday and Thursday evenings and all day Sunday. A full meal is usually served in the ancillary, a hall located next to the worship space. Because of the meals being served, the ancillary can have increased heat gain and odors in the air. Within the temple, incense is burned all year, the sacred texts are read continuously, and worshipers arrive and leave according to their own schedules. Weddings take place within the temple on Saturdays, with services lasting up to four hours. Weddings typically have a large number of attendants and a meal is served. Other rites include blessings, also with a large number of attendants and a meal.

Hindu worshipers are generally seated on the floor. Shoes are removed before entering the space, which is usually carpeted over the sitting area. Special attention should be paid to the temperature of the floor surface. Priests and meditation staff are usually located on an elevated platform. From the platform they read from the holy books. A group of musicians who participate in the service also sit on the platform. Worshipers cover their heads. Traditional Hindu dress is layered and extensive, but appropriate for hot climates.

The most popular times of attendance are in the cooler months. Diwali (Divali, Dewali), a five-day festival, is usually in November. *Diwali* means "rows of lighted lamps," and this special time, often referred to as the Festival of Lights, is celebrated with many lit candles, evening dancing, services, and festive meals. The actual Diwali date varies according to the lunar cycle, but even on a weekday attendance is very large and the following Sunday is also well attended. Smaller peaks in attendance occur in January during the Indian new year, the Festival of Color, and when the Sikh community celebrates its founder, Guru Ravi Dass. These are one-day events.

Buddhist Temples

Buddhism places more emphasis on meditation than worship. Meditation can be done anywhere, and Buddhist shrines and meditation spaces are often personal rather than public. The most public places of worship are monasteries. Buddhists are encouraged to spend time in monasteries to deepen and improve their meditation.

Within the United States there are both monasteries and retreat centers. These are often built outside major urban centers. People may attend for short breaks or

▼ *Amaravati Buddhist Center, Great Gaddesden, Hertfordshire, England. Interior. Courtesy of Arup.*

long retreats, but they may stay at a center 24 hours a day. Peak times are likely to be on weekends.

Buddhist meditation is usually done sitting on the floor, and people may meditate for a few minutes or several hours. Some people will reach advanced meditative states, in which case environmental temperature control becomes less important, but this should *not* be used as the design criterion! Comfort conditions should be appropriate for very low activity levels. Special care should be taken with the temperature and treatment of the floor surfaces. Mechanical systems should be extremely quiet so as not to interfere with meditation.

Buddhist centers may also include education and training spaces. These will have different design conditions and occupancy schedules. As noted, people are usually at the centers continuously, so the design of Buddhist spaces must include major support areas.

MECHANICAL SYSTEM DESIGN AND SELECTION

The purpose of a mechanical system is to provide heating, cooling, and ventilation. There are two main types of mechanical systems that may be used: air-based systems and mixed systems.

- Air-based systems use air as the medium for all the heating, cooling, and ventilation necessary.

- Mixed systems use chilled or heated water for cooling and heating the space and provide only the necessary amount of ventilation. In mixed systems the ventilation can be provided through natural ventilation or forced ventilation.

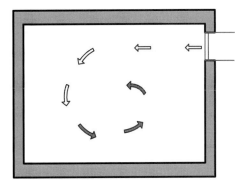

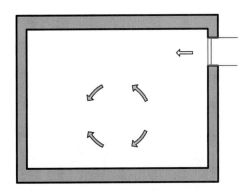

◀ *Air-based cooling system.*

⬅ Warm air
⬅ Mixed air
⬅ Cool air

Air-Based Systems

Air-based systems are rapid reacting; they generally have ventilation rates that exchange all the air in the space several times an hour and can therefore achieve comfortable air temperatures in very short periods of time. Comfort depends approximately equally on the air temperature and the temperature of the room surfaces. In designing for spaces with intermittent use located in cool climates, surface materials that warm up quickly, such as wood benches or seating with fabric, should be chosen. In warm climates, materials selection is less important because the temperature difference between the surfaces and the air is likely to be smaller. In high-volume spaces with slow-reacting surfaces, air-based systems will have to be turned on several hours in advance of occupancy.

The rapid reaction times of air-based systems can be problematic in intermittently used spaces that contain artwork or other artifacts, as these are often sensitive to variations in temperature and humidity.

Air-based systems rely on heat transport using air, meaning that heating and cooling are transported solely by air. As air has a low specific heat capacity, large quantities of air need to be moved in order to provide the required amount of heating or cooling for each space. As a result, air-based systems can require a significant amount of space.

In an air-based system only air is provided to the space. The air is heated by gas or oil boilers, heat pumps, or electric coils. It is cooled by gas or electric

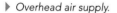
▶ Overhead air supply.

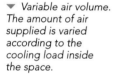
▼ Variable air volume. The amount of air supplied is varied according to the cooling load inside the space.

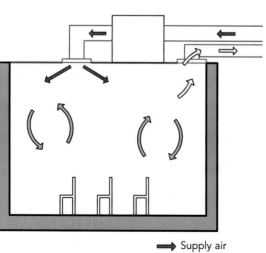

➡ Supply air
⇨ Return air

▼ Sidewall supply.

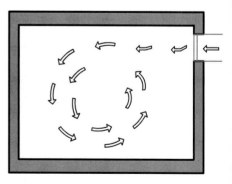

chillers, direct expansion (DX) coils, or an absorption cycle chiller. The selection of heating and cooling sources will depend on cost, availability, energy use, and whether there are other spaces within the worship building. All the equipment associated with the system should be located outside the worship space to minimize any disruption due to noise.

There are two main types of centralized air-based systems, which have different advantages and disadvantages: overhead and low-level supply systems.

Overhead supply systems

In an overhead supply system the air is provided at high level in the space. Air is provided through ceiling or high-level wall grilles at approximately 55°F or 12°C. The momentum of the air is used to mix the air throughout the space and achieve uniform conditions throughout.

The space is heated and cooled by varying the temperature of the supply air. If different areas of the building have different loads, these are met by using multizone units that allow different supply temperatures in different zones or by varying the air quantity using variable air volume (VAV) boxes.

▲ All Souls Langham Place, London, England. Interior, showing a situation where air distribution could be provided from the balcony levels. Courtesy of Arup.

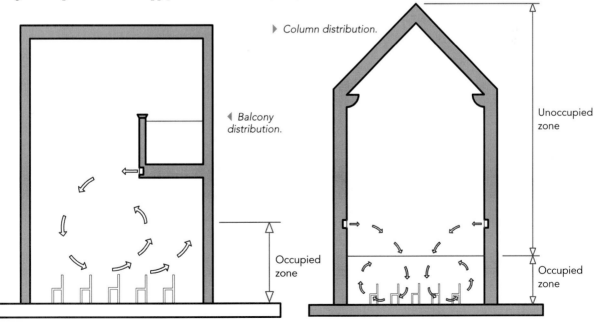

▶ Column distribution.

◀ Balcony distribution.

Unoccupied zone

Occupied zone

Occupied zone

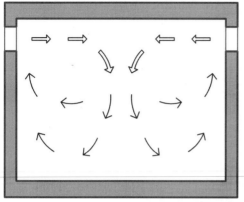

⇒ Higher velocity air
→ Lower velocity air

▲ *Air pattern developed by displacement ventilation.*

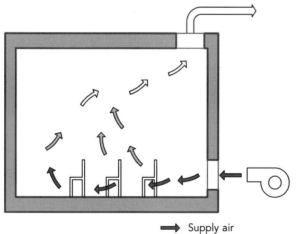

⇒ Supply air
⇒ Return air

▲ *Air pattern developed by "throwing" air into the center of the space.*

can cause discomfort and can also blow out candles. If the ceiling height is greater than 10–12 ft (3–3.6 m) this type of system will also use a significant amount of energy to condition air that is not in the occupied zone.

A variant of the system is sidewall distribution, which can be used economically in spaces taller than 12 ft (3.6 m). In this case, air is blown from sidewalls, columns, or balcony edges at about 10 ft (3 m) above the floor.

Air is removed from the top of the space, creating a condition in which the bottom layer is mixed and cool and the upper layer of air is warmer. If the space contains many columns and balcony edges for air distribution, or if the space is narrow, then a sidewall distribution system may be appropriate. Again, the system's main disadvantages are noise and drafts, particularly if the air distribution points are too far apart. When the air distribution points are located farther apart, the air has to travel at a higher velocity to ensure adequate mixing and reach the central portion of the space.

The main advantage of both overhead and sidewall supply systems is that they can be built successfully using commercially available, mass-produced equipment. Packaged air-handling units can be used to provide heating, cooling, and ventilation with one purchased item so that chillers, boilers, and other components are not required. As commercial packaged air-handling units are generally designed for situations with lower occupancy loads, and therefore lower outside air requirements, than are found in most spaces for worship, additional heating or cooling may be required in some circumstances. If a packaged unit is used, both maintenance and warranty issues will be simplified.

An overhead system is appropriate in spaces where the ceiling heights are 10–12 ft (3–3.6 m) or less. If the ceiling height is greater than this, it becomes difficult to mix the air within the space without providing air at very high velocities, which can cause noise and drafts. Mechanical system noise can interfere with religious services, especially if there is no sound reinforcement system. Drafts

If the space used for worship is poorly insulated, however, or requires multiple zones, or is located in an extreme climate, simple overhead supply systems will not be effective. If additional zones are required, the system will require VAV boxes and variable-speed drives, and, possibly, perimeter heating, which will complicate the system design. Although the system will remain within the range of commercially available prepackaged units, a greater level of skill will be required to operate it. If sidewall supply systems are used for heating in a tall space that is poorly insulated, warm air will tend to rise, forming a warm layer above the occupied zone, and fail to heat people at floor level.

Low-level supply systems

In a low-level supply system the air is provided at a low level and removed at a high level. The air can be provided either through diffusers placed in a pressurized floor plenum (a raised-floor system) or through large displacement diffusers located at the side of the space (a sidewall displacement system). Very low velocity air is supplied to the space at temperatures of about 65°F (18°C), close to the temperature required in the occupied zone. As the air enters the space, it moves across the floor, forming a pool of conditioned air.

As the air picks up heat from people and other heat sources (such as produced by the effect of the sun or lights on the temperature of the floor), it rises and is removed at a height above the occupied zone. Low-level supply systems are very good at providing cooling and can provide adequate heating in well-insulated buildings and those in mild climates.

In buildings where people are barefoot or sitting on the floor, a raised floor system is inappropriate because it will make the floor too cold. A sidewall displacement system may be appropriate, provided that the space is uninterrupted by partitions and is less than approximately 80 ft (25 m) wide. In spaces wider than this it would be difficult for a sidewall system to provide adequate ventilation to the center of the space.

In buildings with fixed seating, where people sit or kneel, a raised floor system can be used. Sidewall displacement systems will not work well because the seats will act as a barrier to air movement. A raised floor system can be configured to supply cool air below the seats, and this will provide good levels of comfort. This type of displacement system has been widely used in cathedrals and concert halls.

The main disadvantage of low-level supply systems is that they are still

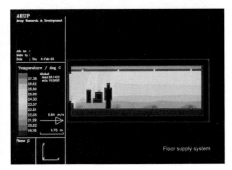

Floor supply system

Cathedral of Our Lady of the Angels

◀ Computer-generated models showing air temperature profiles for spaces in which air is supplied at low level by either natural or mechanical means.

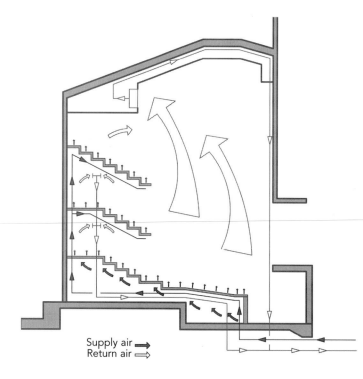

Supply air ⟹
Return air ⟹

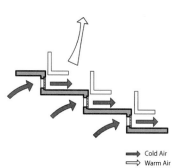

⟹ Cold Air
⟹ Warm Air

▲ Detail of underfloor air supply typical for auditorium ventilation.

◀ Overall air pattern developed using underfloor air supply and high level return in an auditorium with balconies.

▶ Computer-generated model showing air temperature profiles, Jubilee Church, Rome, Italy. Naturally cooled air is supplied from the crypt below the church using buoyancy and natural ventilation. Courtesy of Arup.

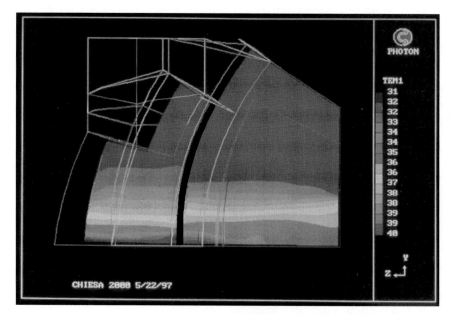

unusual in the United States. It is possible, with significant care in design, to achieve good results using modified versions of commercially available packaged air-handling units. Although these modifications slightly complicate system operation, the quiet, unobtrusive air supply and lower energy use achieved with low-level supply systems may outweigh the disadvantages.

Mixed Systems

As stated earlier, air-based systems can require a lot of space and sometimes do not provide adequate comfort for a building's occupants. These problems are especially likely in renovation projects, particularly for historic structures. In these circumstances it may be better to use a mixed system. Mixed systems contain two elements, the heating/cooling element and the ventilation element. Mixed systems generally use water as an alternative heat transport medium. Unlike air, water has a high specific heat capacity, and only a small amount of water needs to be moved around the building to provide the heating or cooling required. In a mixed system the minimum amount of ventilation is supplied to the space, generally requiring smaller ducts. These two factors generally result in a lower space requirement and lower energy use, although the need for two systems can increase the initial cost.

Mixed systems can be used to provide either supplementary heating or supplementary cooling, or both, as required. There are two types of mixed systems: static and active.

In "static" systems (such as radiant flooring or ceilings) the air system and the water system are separate. These systems are generally quiet and use little energy, but they react slowly. This can be both an advantage and a disadvantage. The main advantage is that the water-based system can be operated continuously to provide protection against freezing and overheating in intermittently occupied buildings, at low energy cost. The main disadvantage is that the systems have to be turned on hours before the building is occupied to provide comfortable conditions during occupied periods.

In "active" systems the air interacts with the heating or cooling elements. In such systems, which include fan convectors and active chilled beams, the air is forced to pass through the element. "Active" systems will react rapidly to changes in the occupied space. The main drawbacks of "active" systems are noise and drafts.

Mixed systems can be used with either natural or mechanical ventilation systems. However, in all cases, ventilation air has to be provided. Natural ventilation is often appropriate in high-volume spaces with intermittent occupancy, in moderate

▼ *Displacement diffusers located under seats.*

climates, and where outside noise levels are low so that large ventilation openings can be provided. Otherwise, a forced ventilation system using an air-handling unit that also conditions the air will be required.

Static heating systems

As noted earlier, it is difficult to provide adequate heating to the occupants of poorly insulated spaces with high ceilings using overhead air supply systems. In these conditions, a supplementary system using perimeter heating, under-seat radiators, or heated radiant floors can provide heating in the occupied zone. In intermittently occupied buildings, static heating systems are appropriate for providing low-energy-use freeze protection. Static heating systems are often suitable for renovation projects or naturally ventilated buildings, because such systems are easy to conceal. They may also be used in conjunction with minimum ventilation systems. In all cases heating should be achieved with hot water, rather than

steam, to reduce the risk of system noise and improve comfort in the occupied space. Further restrictions are noted in the following paragraphs.

Perimeter heating

In a perimeter heating system, heating is provided at the outside walls and windows of the building to offset heat loss through the windows and walls.

Perimeter heating, which can be achieved using hot water or steam, reduces the risk of cold downdrafts at the outside walls. It is particularly appropriate in buildings that are infrequently occupied and require freeze protection because of the climate. The system works mainly through convective heat transfer, heating the air and allowing it to travel through the building using natural convective currents, and is therefore very slow reacting. As a result, the system must be turned on several hours before the space is occupied. (See the figure at right.)

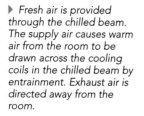

▶ Fresh air is provided through the chilled beam. The supply air causes warm air from the room to be drawn across the cooling coils in the chilled beam by entrainment. Exhaust air is directed away from the room.

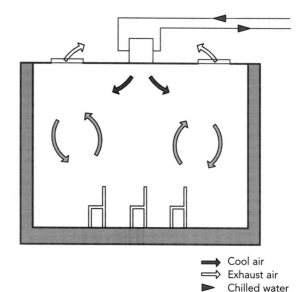

⟹ Cool air
⟹ Exhaust air
▶ Chilled water

Additional equipment may be needed for the production of hot water or steam. Water systems are preferable because steam systems can be noisy and because the surface temperature of steam heaters can be dangerously high.

Under-seat heating

An alternative location for heating elements is below the fixed seating common in synagogues and churches. An under-seat system will not provide as good freeze protection as a perimeter system, because the heating elements are not located at the perimeter, which is where most of the heat is lost.

However, this arrangement will provide heat directly to the people through both radiation and convection and will provide comfortable conditions more quickly than a perimeter system. Steam should not be used in this type of system, as the heat emitters will become dangerously hot.

Radiant floor heating

The third main type of static heating system is a radiant floor system. Heat is provided by circulating warm water through plastic pipes embedded in the concrete of the floor or concealed below a wooden board system. A radiant floor system raises the floor temperature to approximately 80°F (29°C). Because the heat transfer surface is the floor surface, and because this may be thermally massive (in the case of concrete) or insulating (in the case of wood), these systems need to operate for most of the time. They work better with mechanical air supply systems than either of the other two types of active system because the heat is distributed more evenly. The use of radiant floors is particularly appropriate in colder regions for spaces like mosques, Hindu temples, and Bud-

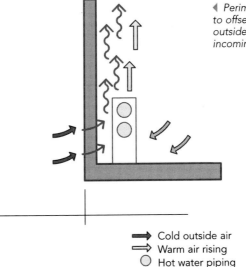

◀ *Perimeter heating used to offset heat transfer at outside wall and to heat incoming fresh air.*

➡ Cold outside air
⇨ Warm air rising
○ Hot water piping

dhist monasteries or retreats, where people will typically be barefoot.

Overhead radiant heating

Overhead radiant heating systems may also be used. These systems may be electric, gas-fired, or water or steam based. Overhead radiant systems should be used only in spaces where other alternatives will not work, as they can be noisy and obstruct the view across the space. The layered air temperatures that result can provide an uncomfortable feeling of "hot head and cold feet."

Active heating systems

The type of active heating system most likely to be used in a place of worship is a fan convection system. A fan convection unit has a heating element and a fan. The fan blows the air across the heating element to speed up the response time, increase the rate of heat output, and improve the air mixing, as shown in the figure at right, but with the addition of a fan.

Fan convection units are typically located at the building perimeter to offset the heat loss through the windows and walls. They reduce the risk of cold downdrafts both through heating and by blowing air upward. Hot water is the usual means of heat transfer, but steam may be used in this type of system. These units are appropriate for use in intermittently occupied buildings in cold climates. Fan convection units may be more suitable than static systems in existing buildings made from stone or other materials with high thermal mass, because they will heat the buildings more quickly. The main disadvantage of fan convection units is that they are very noisy; therefore they are often switched off before worship services. Fan convection units are recommended only as a retrofit for an existing building.

An alternative to a perimeter system is a direct-fired gas unit heater. This system is not recommended except as a retrofit or in case of severe budget restrictions. Direct-fired unit heaters are noisy, drafty, and inefficient and do not provide good comfort for the occupants in the space.

Static cooling systems

Static cooling systems, such as chilled ceilings, chilled floors, and chilled beams, include an element containing chilled water that is a few degrees above the dew point temperature of the air. This cooling element provides a heat transfer surface area that cools air by convection. The element is usually located overhead, as the air will pass over the surface, cool, and then drop to a lower level.

People are also kept cool through the radiant effect of chilled ceiling panels. These systems are not yet common in the United States and are therefore expensive. The presence of cool surfaces within the space means that the dew point temperature of the air in the space, and the temperature of the chilled water, have to be carefully controlled to avoid condensation. Static cooling systems must be used in conjunction with a mechanical cooling system that cools air to a known dew point temperature. The main advantage of these systems is that they are quiet. As with overhead radiant heating panels, the cooling panels may block the view across the space. These systems are most appropriate for low-ceiling spaces with moderate occupancy. Static cooling systems do provide comfortable conditions and are likely to be suitable for retrofit and conversion projects with constrained space. This is a common retrofit in urban areas for mosques, Buddhist centers, and Christian Science meeting spaces.

Active cooling systems

Active cooling systems include split systems, chilled beams, and fan coil units. In an active cooling system a fan moves air across the cooling element. Split systems provide cooling using a refrigerant-cooled element that rejects heat to an outdoor condenser.

▼ *Static cooling using chilled ceiling.*

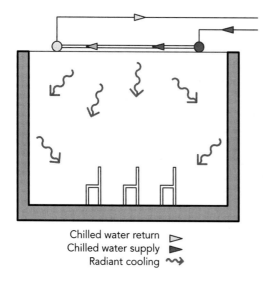

Chilled water return ▷
Chilled water supply ▶
Radiant cooling ⌇➤

Chilled beams and fan coil units provide cooling using chilled water generated at a central plant. Active cooling systems are most appropriate for cooling specific areas of a place for worship where the occupancy is low and the cooling load or the need for temperature control is high. Fan coil units and split systems that incorporate reversible heat pumps can be used for heating as well as cooling.

Systems for Preservation of Artwork/Artifacts

In most buildings, and particularly those that are occupied for short periods of time, the range of temperatures and humidity can be wide. However, many religious buildings contain precious artwork or artifacts that need to be kept in an environment in which both temperature and humidity are controlled throughout the year.

Most artwork and artifacts will be damaged most by rapid changes in temperature and humidity. The presence of such items in the main space of a place for worship demands systems that provide humidity control and are operated continuously. The combination of a humidity control system and continuous operation may be expensive. In new buildings these art objects are best confined to a small area, such as the sanctuary of a church or synagogue. The area can then be conditioned separately, provided that it can be physically separated from the rest of the building. The physical barriers should be kept closed when the conditions in the rest of the building differ from the conservation conditions required for the artifacts.

For moderate conservation goals a split system air conditioner, similar to those used in computer and server rooms, capable of providing heating and humidity

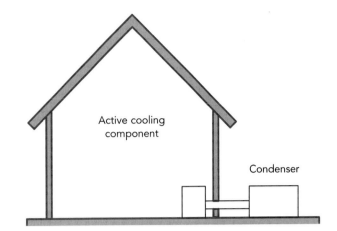

Major system components for a system in which heat is rejected to an outdoor condenser.

control, is most appropriate. If a worship space contains artwork and artifacts, the design team should work closely with a conservationist.

CONTROLS

The controls system, also called the energy management system or the building automation system, must provide the necessary tools and features to achieve the energy-saving goals included in the mechanical systems design and ensure the occupants' comfort at all times and under various conditions.

Energy Management System Requirements

Adaptability

An energy management system must be able to adapt to occupancy levels and to indoor and outdoor conditions.

The system should be able to analyze the indoor and outdoor conditions and determine the most economical way to condition the space. The percentage of outside air and the amount of mechanical cooling or heating may all be varied to achieve this goal.

The quality, calibration, and proper location of temperature sensors are very

▲ *Fresco Chapel, Houston, Texas. Architect: François de Menil; engineers: Arup. Courtesy of Arup.*

short period of time. It is necessary for the system to start before the scheduled time, and it may have to slightly overcool the space prior to the scheduled event,

- *Weddings.* The requirements will depend on the number of guests.
- *Baptisms.* Occupancy is usually less than at regular masses or weddings. Baptisms may be performed in a special area, where a separate system may be provided. In winter or summer, a warmer temperature mode should be available in order to keep a baby warm.
- *Major events.* Similar to weekly services.
- *Prayer groups.* Usually smaller groups; no preheating or precooling of the larger space is usually necessary, but small areas will need to be heated or cooled.
- *Unoccupied time,* during periods when the church may be accessible to the public or during the night when the church is closed.

For high-occupancy densities, large amounts of outside air must usually be provided to satisfy the local codes and standards, and mechanical systems are designed accordingly. However, outside air levels can be reduced during low-occupancy events by providing CO_2 sensors and monitoring CO_2 levels within the space. This measure will allow for energy savings (since most of the energy is usually used to condition the outside air being introduced in the space), while not compromising occupants' comfort.

For each of these conditions, the control system must be able to provide an appropriate system control strategy. Each strategy should be identified with a name or number and associated by the operator with a specific day and time.

important. The sensors should not be located in areas where they will be subject to drafts or stagnant conditions.

It is necessary to program the system to recognize the requirements for different types of events or for when the space is unoccupied. For example, for the Christian traditions:

- *Weekly services.* Usually the space will be full, and the cooling loads will rise fairly quickly to the design values in a

Ease of Use

Controls systems may be operated by untrained staff and must therefore be easy to use. They may also need to be operated by trained maintenance personnel who do not work at the worship space site. During design it is important to understand how the system will be operated and to specify an appropriate interface with the controls system.

SUMMARY

The factors in this chapter will determine the selection of the most appropriate mechanical system. For most new buildings the choice is likely to be a type of air-based system. For most retrofit projects and for special spaces within a building, it is most likely to be a mixed system that will provide supplementary heating, cooling, or both.

CHAPTER 9
ELECTRICAL AND COMMUNICATION SYSTEMS

GOALS OF ELECTRICAL SYSTEMS DESIGN

The electrical system of a worship space provides a source of energy to allow the space to function. Electrical system design for places of worship must consider the following:

- Occupant safety is of critical importance, as with any premises occupied by large numbers of people. Planning for safety should include consideration of the security of the electrical supply and the provision of electrical energy for ordinary lighting and emergency lighting.

- Reduction of electrical energy consumption and maintenance cost is important, as many such premises operate on small budgets and running costs can be a significant part of their expenditure.

- The functionality of the electrical system must be considered in relation to the type of operation being carried out. For example, there must be consideration of a sensible switching system and the locations for receptacles to enable close control for different tasks.

- There must be an appropriate design for security, fire detection, and evacuation systems, taking into consideration the type of worship, the potential levels of occupancy, and building-specific requirements.

- Audiovisual (AV) and communications systems for places of worship are increasing in significance as presentation and interactive systems develop. The electrical design should not only incorporate the specific requirements for modern AV and communications systems but also consider planning for adaptation or extension of the designed systems.

Prior to considering electrical design for spaces for worship in detail, it is worth noting the role such a building performs for its community: the symbolism of the venue as a sanctuary, a safe haven at times of hardship, a refuge when disaster strikes. People gather at a space for worship after earthquakes and floods, for example, for news, for food, and for shelter, and to ease the experience simply by being together. To provide for the community at such a time, the worship space must be designed with the ability to maintain power. Effective electrical engineering design is critical in ensuring the building's ability to function for the community in this way.

ELECTRICAL SYSTEM CONSTRAINTS FOR PLACES OF WORSHIP

The National Electrical Code (NEC), along with any applicable local amendments, governs the design and installation of electrical systems within any building type; however, there are no specific requirements in this document for places of worship. Although the general design of electrical systems for buildings of this type will not vary from that of any other building type, certain areas should be given special consideration.

Maintenance

As with any large place of public assembly, generally involving a large open area with high ceilings, places of worship can present particular problems in providing access to overhead electrical equipment—for example, light fittings, speakers, fire detectors, or alarm devices. Careful consideration of the methods available for access to replace or maintain equipment is required to avoid future disruption and further costs to the facility.

Temporary Equipment

Power supplies for temporary equipment, such as musical instruments or local sound equipment, should be considered at strategic points within the general public spaces. The design of such supplies should always consider the various types of equipment that may require connection, as well as the relatively nontechnical users. Particular attention should be given to provision of ground fault interrupting protective devices to minimize risks to the public or the presider.

Hours of Use

The nature of places of worship is that they will usually be heavily occupied at certain times and will have limited or no occupancy for other periods. Such usage means that special consideration and discussion should focus on security issues related to the building and any requirements for remote monitoring or control.

ELECTRICAL SYSTEMS

Electrical design for places of worship should consider the following systems:

- An incoming power supply to the buildings

- An emergency power supply for the buildings
- Lighting and emergency lighting
- Receptacle services for general power
- Power connections to main equipment
- Fire safety system
- General voice and data communications systems
- Audiovisual systems
- Energy conservation systems and controls

All of these systems will require close coordination with the other engineering disciplines and the architect.

Lighting

Lighting is required within a space to allow occupants to move around safely, and perform tasks such as reading texts and to help define a desired atmosphere for the space, appropriate to the service or activity. The design of lighting is discussed in detail in Chapter 13. This section considers the provision of energy to a lighting system.

Switching

Careful planning of the switching of the light fixtures throughout the premises is important, not only to ensure that the user has maximum flexibility for the tasks to be done, but also to enable light fixtures to be turned off when not required. These two considerations are particularly critical in considering places of worship.

First, the planning of light switching for functionality must consider levels of occupancy at various times, from potentially full occupancy during a service to almost no occupancy at other times. The switching plan should also enable the user

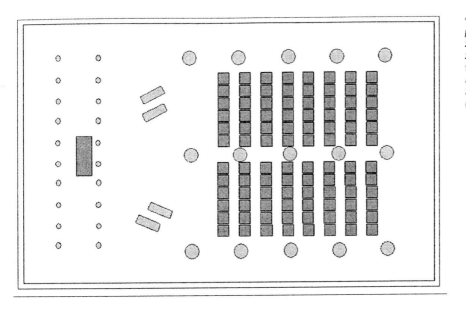

◀ *Worship space lighting plan showing control zones. Separate control zones will be required for the sanctuary (at left), the altar spotlights (at center), and the nave chandeliers (at right).*

to manage the switching to best enhance the service and provide simple close control in locations best suited to the task.

Second, the switching of fixtures for the purpose of minimizing energy consumption is an important consideration for any public premises, but in particular for places of worship because of the times of very low occupancy. In addition to the NEC requirements, a switching plan must consider the use of natural light and simple, obvious ways for occupants to turn off, or not turn on, light fixtures to save energy.

In summary, careful planning for light switching is essential, not only for enhancing the functionality of the building but also for minimizing energy and frequency of lamp changing. For practical purposes, control of the lighting systems and dimming capability should be given to the presider or the person who is managing the service—that is, either at the lectern position or within a stage-type control room for larger operations.

General ambient lighting should remain "on" in the main hall during times of occupancy, but all other lighting for the purpose of specific tasks or stage effects should be independently operated by the ceremonial manager. This may include stage spot lights, dimming of general lighting, enhanced or reduced stage lighting, and even control of daylighting during a sermon.

In individual rooms or small offices, local switching allows occupants to control their own lights. Adopting automatic devices such as motion sensors conserves energy and increases lamp life. Such sensors should be used only to switch lights off, within a predetermined time, ranging from a few to 10 minutes, after the room empties. It should always be a conscious decision of the occupant to use lighting if required. Other devices such as photocells can be used to monitor internal lighting levels. When lighting levels reach a certain value, the photocells switch off the artificial lighting. This is particularly useful for rooms with many windows and usable daylight.

Consideration of the quantities and locations of light fixtures for use as nightlights or security lighting should balance the need for building protection and user safety with energy consumption and light pollution control.

When large public spaces that have relatively defined periods of occupancy need to be lit, centralized switching is a sensible approach to lighting controls. This allows preprogrammed lighting control for large open spaces, which triggers lighting fixtures off and on using criteria such as occupancy, type of event, time, duration, and available daylight. Controls should be extended to encompass external lighting for architectural accenting, feature lighting such as displays, or parking lots, where times of need or use are well defined. Such systems enhance ease of use and energy savings.

Basic lighting control systems comprise lighting control panels, incorporating relays that turn lights on and off, and a microprocessor unit that provides the intelligence. The lighting control panels can be linked by computer to program or reprogram the system. This system is often integrated with the mechanical controls system and forms a component of the overall building management systems.

Other special lighting control systems, such as dimmer systems, are often required in this type of building. Dimmer systems can range from a simple wall-mounted dimmer, which allows the occupant to dim the lights in an individual office, to a large centralized dimmer system consisting of racks of dimmers con-

trolling the lighting in large public areas. Dimming systems allow for the manual or automatic control of the light intensity from the fixtures, increasing or decreasing light levels to create various moods within the space.

Centralized dimmers are typically located in dedicated dimmer rooms, which will require both good ventilation and acoustic treatment. Dimmers often generate substantial heat, as well as low-level acoustic noise or vibration.

Power

The local utility company normally provides an external source of power. Depending on the complexity and size of the building, it will normally be rated at 480/277/120 V or 208/120 V. Typically, the local power utility company is obliged to provide the building with a single dedicated supply.

Power supply to the building

Depending on the size of the building and the restrictions of the local utility, power may be provided in the form of a high-voltage supply via a step-down transformer. Consideration must be given to the space required for a step-down transformer and access for transformer replacement. Typically, transformers are placed on a concrete pad in a service yard, in a nearby parking lot, or, when space is limited, in an underground vault or within an electrical vault outside the building. The building takes the power from this transformer into a main electrical switch and the utility meter, which becomes the point of connection.

The construction of a concrete pad or vault is typically provided by the building development project. The utility company then installs the cables from the street and provides the transformer as part of its service.

Main distribution

The main distribution system for places of worship must consider many factors that are common to all buildings, but must also consider the type of occupancy of such buildings. For instance, places of worship must be designed for maximum peak occupancy and therefore maximum peak load at, perhaps, intervals of one or two hours per week. During these times the stability of the electrical supply is important, not only for functional reasons but also for reasons of safety, as complete or partial power failure may cause panic and/or injury.

As for any building, the main switchboard should be located in a secure room accessed only by the building's trained personnel. It is important that adequate ventilation and maintenance access are provided for this main electrical room to prevent the equipment from overheating and to provide the electrician with easy access.

Typically, the main electrical room is located on the ground floor or in the first basement below grade. Generally, this location is close to the incoming service from the utility company. It is a good practice to avoid locating the main electrical room at the lowest level in the basement to forestall any risk of flooding the equipment.

Several supply voltages can be used within the building. The following voltages are usually considered to be the most cost-efficient:

- 480 V three-phase for heavy motors such as air-handling units, elevators, pumps, etc.

- 277 V single-phase for fluorescent lighting
- 208 V single-phase for smaller motors
- 120 V single-phase for receptacle outlets and smaller equipment

Transformers are required to step down voltages from 480/277 V to 208/120 V, and these transformers will need to be in secure, ventilated locations.

Panel boards should generally be located in a closet or electrical room where maintenance access is permitted to trained personnel only and access does not affect the general operation of the premises.

Cables and equipment must be sized on the basis of future maximum occupancy of the building to ensure that circuits do not become overloaded over time. For places of worship it is important that the designer of the electrical systems understand the anticipated use of the building, both immediately after completion and in the future if growth or expansion is likely. If potential growth is not considered, overloading of cables and equipment can occur, generating significant heat and posing a risk to the building and its occupants.

Receptacle outlets

Much equipment inside the building will require power—for example, desktop computers, fax machines, coffeemakers, and desk lamps, as well as building maintenance equipment such as scrubbers and polishers.

Planning of receptacles requires an understanding of the operation and function of the building, so the electrical systems designer must work closely with the users to understand their specific needs. Otherwise, there may be a tendency to either over- or undersupply outlets in locations required for normal day-to-day functioning.

As for any building, there will be code requirements to consider, such as provision of ground fault interrupters near sinks or outdoor areas. There will also be specific requirements for isolated ground receptacles for sensitive equipment such as computers and audiovisual and communication equipment.

The design should also consider the visual impact of receptacles, and the faceplate finish should be designed with the architect to integrate with the interior design.

Power connections to equipment

Besides receptacle outlets, there are many items of equipment requiring power connections. These can include air-handling units, trash compactors, elevator motors, exhaust fans, supply fans, and pumps for various uses. Typically, this equipment requires different types of connection, often provided through a fused or nonfused disconnect switch. This is similar to a light switch, but a rather more heavy-duty type for the application and load.

Kitchens have unique servicing requirements that need detailed coordination with all members of the design team. Generally, a full working kitchen will require many varied power connections, ranging from simple wall receptacle outlets, through direct connections from a junction box, to disconnect switches. In addition, many differing voltage configurations maybe present, depending on particular equipment suppliers. All of these connections often occur in restricted areas, and the connections have to be well coordinated to remain accessible. Emergency shutoff buttons may also be

required, depending on the design and the equipment.

Audiovisual and communications systems

It is likely that audiovisual systems for sound reinforcement and projection, communications systems such as the telephone, data network, public address, broadcast, cable TV network, intercom, or two-way multichannel communication systems will be required in renovated or newly designed places of worship. Selection and integration of such systems requires close liaison with the user to ensure that specific needs are planned for and incorporated into the systems' design. Multiple system requirements can produce problems of compatibility, and close attention to the separation and segregation of systems design within the overall network is critical to avoid such issues and minimize interference.

Special signal systems

Security systems are generally provided for places of worship. Artwork and valuables, such as sacred vessels and money from the collection, may require special protection. Security systems can range from simple door and window alarm units to sophisticated closed-circuit television (CCTV) monitoring systems.

The components of a basic alarm system may consist of local alarms, placed at all external doors, that detect doors being opened at unauthorized times or by unauthorized personnel. Alarms can be triggered to sound locally at the doors as well as at a central station.

More sophisticated systems may use card access controls and electronic door locks to manage access to building areas.

CCTV allows remote monitoring of activity occurring in and around a building. It permits the viewer to determine the need to send manpower to investigate and can provide the ability to play back any events that have caused concern.

CCTV systems consist of strategically positioned single or multiple cameras. Cameras can be located outdoors in parking lots, around the building, and in interior lobbies, corridors, and sensitive areas. The input can be monitored using single or multi-screens depending on the number of cameras in the system. Signals can be recorded in electronic digital storage or with conventional tape.

The presence of CCTV cameras can be a significant deterrent to minor crime. To achieve a solution that gives the client complete peace of mind, it may be necessary for the security system to include elements of all of the aforementioned equipment. In areas that are designated as posing a high security or safety risk, it is important to consult local police for advice to ensure that adequate protection is provided for the occupants and the building. Good lighting is also an essential component of effective security design.

Broadcasting

During the programming phase, the client will have to decide how the facility is to act as an origination point of programming for broadcasting purposes. This decision will determine, to a large extent, the architecture of spaces and, to some extent, the shape and form of the buildings.

Understanding client needs

It is important to identify who, within the client organization, has the vision for the project's broadcasting role, so that the design team can complete its work effectively.

If it is desired that the facility will, at some point, be a venue for broadcasting, the next critical step is to determine specific broadcasting requirements. A master plan should be developed in conjunction with the client and the design team to address the specific needs. This will allow the architectural team to move forward with the design of the facility with clear and precise direction from an informed client. Not only will the master plan act as an invaluable resource to the design team, but it will also serve as a living document for the client, a road map that can be reviewed and revised throughout the life of the organization to reflect its evolving mission.

Once the initial programming has been completed by the design team, the architectural, engineering, and cost implications of the broadcast program requirements will become clearer. At this point, the client's vision for the venue's broadcasting potential in relation to budget realities may be clarified.

Technical considerations for a broadcast facility

With clearly identified broadcasting needs established, specific technical modes of broadcasting should be considered. Some methods of signal transmission are not compatible with specific broadcast programming desires or financial resources, which will influence the design. For example, 20 or 30 years ago obtaining television stations for religious broadcasting purposes (via either UHF or broadband cable networks) was relatively inexpensive and a viable option for many religious organizations. Today the cost associated with obtaining a TV station is prohibitive.

Although the development of a religious cable network is still a viable option financially, there is the current hurdle of procuring space on local cable systems—a result of the vast amount of programming as compared with the number of channels or the physical amount of bandwidth available. A cost-effective option may be to consider streaming programs on the Internet via a client-operated website.

In all decision making, it will be important to consider the implications of the broadcast method(s) in support of the client's stated outreach mission. The client's mission must be considered in relation to its financial capacity to procure and operate an external television transmission, as the first cost in making such provisions is high and should be spent only if absolutely necessary.

There are a number of further technical considerations in designing a house of worship with broadcasting requirements:

- Physical space requirements to support programmed broadcasting activities

- Types of production and postproduction activities both within the venue and off-site

- Desired programming (e.g., live musical groups, religious education) determines stage and studio sizes, including voice-over booth, dressing room space requirements, and green room considerations

Determining the client's needs at the outset of a project can add immeasurable value to the end product and help to ensure a successful deployment of broadcast capabilities within the facility.

Safety

There are particular requirements for the safety of occupants in places for worship that govern certain features of the electrical system. It is important, however, to first consult local codes and addenda, as requirements can vary. In general, such requirements include the following:

- Safe evacuation of occupants in the event of an emergency, which affects the emergency lighting and fire alarm/voice alarm design and must be coordinated with the architectural design of the means of escape

- Security systems such as CCTV, which increase the safety of the occupants, especially those using the car park

- Security and reliability of the electrical supply, taking into account peak occupancy when electrical failures can have the greatest impact

Emergency power

Even though power supplies from utility sources within the United States are relatively reliable, there are times when the power for a building may be interrupted. Alternative sources of power for the building allow people to evacuate it safely or to continue essential tasks. Emergency power may be provided via an electrical generator.

A generator may be sized to consider only the essential loads or, possibly, the continued operation of the premises in the event of a power failure. This decision will have to be made in conjunction with the client, as it must be made with both initial cost and anticipated use of the premises in mind.

If a generator is needed the design should consider the potential noise from the generator, as well as accommodations for fuel storage and fuel deliveries.

Typically, the generator is diesel fueled and is normally standing idle for the most of its lifetime, coming on only when the utility supply fails or for regular testing. Testing is essential and is typically conducted for $\frac{1}{2}$ to 1 hour per month, depending on the generator manufacturer's recommendations.

Electrical generators are inherently noisy and require substantial quantities of air for both cooling and combustion. Generators are usually located outdoors in a weatherproof acoustic enclosure or indoors adjacent to exterior walls where ventilation and acoustic noise reduction can be adequately provided.

An emergency generator generally requires a diesel fuel storage tank. This tank can be located in a separate fuel storage vault or in a tank mounted below the generator in the frame. A nearby low-capacity fuel tank may be required if the main storage tank is remotely located. Wherever the storage is located, it is important to consider sensible access for fueling from a truck.

In some instances it may be possible to obtain a backup power supply from the utility company so that in the event of a momentary power failure, the building can be automatically switched over to the secondary power supply. This can be very costly.

Fire safety system
Places of worship are places of public gathering and will be occupied by people not familiar with the premises and not necessarily familiar with escape procedures. Thus, the electrical systems designer should consider how the building will operate in an emergency, in addition to applying the code requirements for fire detection and evacuation.

A fire detection system is, in effect, an advance warning system to detect a fire as quickly as possible, to evacuate the occupants, and to enable the fire to be dealt with by trained personnel before too much damage is done. Moderns systems are "intelligent" and operate on a microprocessor design to pinpoint the fire location and enable fast response.

The system normally includes manual break-glass units, links to other systems such as sprinklers, and the use of automatic heat and/or smoke detectors. In places of worship there will likely be large assembly rooms, which may utilize beam detectors mounted at either end of the main space to avoid ceiling-mounted smoke detectors.

Alarm or evacuation systems for places of worship are usually linked to an announcement system, utilizing the audiovisual equipment already in place. However, this is a design decision that must also take local code requirements into consideration.

Audiovisual alarm units should be placed in corridors and egress paths, as well as large open spaces, offices, and conference rooms. In addition, visual alarm units are required to be posted in all bathrooms, whatever their size. The final locations of audiovisual alarms often require fire marshal approval, and it is advisable to obtain the fire marshal's input as soon as possible to avoid late changes or additions during the final building commissioning stage.

Emergency lighting
Emergency lighting is required in a building to allow occupants to leave it safely in the event of a power failure.

Emergency lights are the lighting fixtures that will be designated to turn on when the emergency generator is turned on. These emergency lights can be separate lighting fixtures but are often normal light fixtures that have also been connected to the emergency power source. Exit signs must be provided to indicate to the occupants the egress path determined by the architect and code official.

Energy Efficiency

Electricity consumption is typically measured in kilowatts per hour (kWh). This is the amount of power consumed in one hour, measured by the utility company via the utility meter that records the prime consumption, as a result of which a bill will be sent to the occupant.

As energy consumption has a direct relationship to the cost of operating the building, careful consideration should be given to factors influencing this consumption, such as the following:

- Sizing and selection of mechanical systems

- Energy sources used for heating

- Use of daylight to minimize the need for electric light

- Selection of electric light sources for maximum energy efficiency

- Selection of energy-efficient motors and starters

Within the majority of buildings the two most direct contributors to energy consumption are the mechanical systems for heating and cooling and the electric lighting.

Although tungsten lighting is generally preferred for use in areas requiring mood control or scene selection, it is important to consider that fluorescent or discharge-based sources use a fraction of the energy of tungsten. Careful targeting of low-efficiency light sources in areas that count, along with the use of high-efficiency sources in back-of-house or support areas, can dramatically reduce energy consumption.

Alternative energy sources may be appropriate or available, such as wind power or photovoltaic energy, and many utility companies and cities offer incentive programs for their incorporation. Sustainable design is discussed in detail in Chapter 6.

1. *Cathedral of Our Lady of the Angels, Los Angeles, Design Architect: Rafael Moneo; Executive Architect: Leo A Daly.* This cathedral, completed in 2002 to replace the earthquake-damaged St. Vibiana's Cathedral, shows the use of procession, light, and materiality to create a sacred space within the language of modern architecture. A crescendo of light from the subdued entry to the brightly lit sanctuary accompanies a procession from the profane world of the street to the sacred space of the Eucharist. Massive poured-in-place concrete walls dignify the interior; alabaster windows filter the natural light and turn the building into a glowing lamp by night.

The sanctuary, showing the organ, choir seating, great cross window, tapestries, and acoustic baffles. (Photo: Grant Mudford.)

▲ *2. Entry plaza showing the pool and fountain by artist Lita Albuquerque, the grand stairs, and the procession to the great doors. The Guadelupe Shrine can be seen in the distance on the right. (Photo: Julius Shulman and David Glomb.)*

◀ *3. South ambulatory showing the use of light to lead the congregation. (Photo: Julius Shulman and David Glomb.)*

▲ **4a.** Tapestries of the Communion of the Saints by artist John Nava, and the great altar with frieze by M. L. Snowden. (Photo: Tom Bonner.)

The artwork for the Cathedral of Our Lady of the Angels in Los Angeles, which also includes the crucifix by Simon Toparovsky, bronzes by Max de Maas, ambo and cathedra by Jeff Tortorelli, and Guadelupe Shrine by Lalo Garcia, was commissioned from local artists under the guidance of Rev. Richard S. Vosko.

▼ **4b.** Great bronze doors. Artist: Robert Graham. (Photo: Tom Bonner.)

▲ **5.** St. Ignatius Church, Seattle University, Washington. Architect: Steven Holl. View of altar showing the light from the lenses of color. The metaphor of a "gathering of different lights" that the architect used for this small, 6,100 sq ft chapel describes the mission of Seattle University and its multiracial community. It also refers to St. Ignatius's vision of the spiritual life as comprising many interior lights and darknesses.

The chapel was conceived as seven bottles of light in a stone box, each one corresponding to a different liturgical space. Light bounces off color fields painted on the backs of baffles suspended in front of the windows, and shines through colored lenses in the windows and in openings in the baffles. As the sun moves around the building, it illuminates the different liturgical spaces and projects shafts of colored light onto the walls and floor. At night the chapel radiates colored light out to the campus. (Photo: Paul Warchol.)

Herz Jesu Kirche (Church of the Sacred Heart), Munich, Germany. Architect: Allmann Sattler Wappner. An immaculately detailed cube of maple slats enclosed by a silk-screen-printed glass cube, one side of which opens completely, with a pair of 46 ft high glass doors designed by glass artist Alexander Beleschenko. The ethereal cross over the altar is woven into the metal mesh tapestry, designed by Susanne and Bernard Lutzenberger, which covers the back wall of the sanctuary.

◀ **6.** View from outside with doors open. (Photo: Harf Zimmermann.)

▼ **7.** View of sanctuary. (Photo: Harf Zimmermann.)

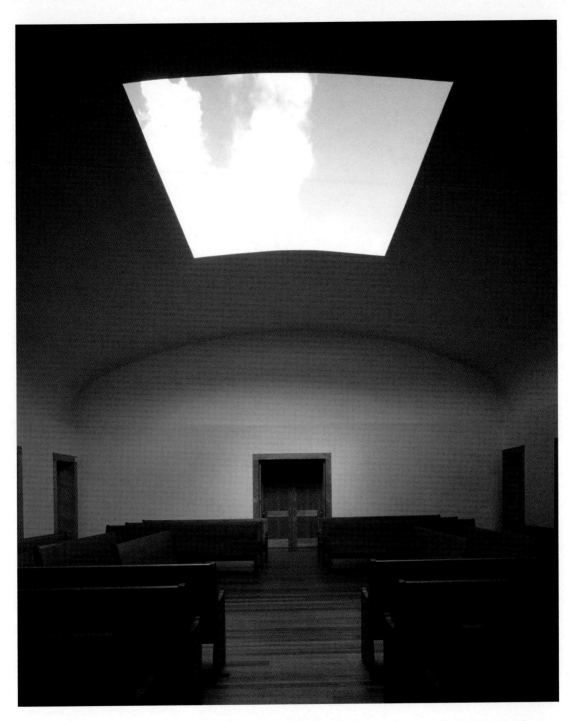

▲ *8. Live Oak Friends Meeting House, Houston, Texas. Architect: Leslie Elkins Architecture. Daytime interior view showing Skyspace by artist James Turrell. The meditative space of this 75-seat meetinghouse is crowned with a 12 ft square opening to the sky. Artist James Turrell designed the opening so that the edge between ceiling and sky is imperceptible, extending the space of the room into the void of the sky. At night, when a retractable roof covers the opening, the opening is lit by seamless blue light that creates the appearance of another infinite space. (Photo: Paul Hester, Hester & Hardaway.)*

▲ **9.** Church of Jesus Christ of Latter-day Saints, Salt Lake City, Utah. Architect: Zimmer Gunsul Frasca. Interior view with congregation. This multiuse assembly space seating 21,000 is one of the largest spaces used for worship in the United States. Two balconies reduce the distance from the worshipers to the podium, and sophisticated lighting and audiovisual systems engage the congregation. (Photo: Timothy Hursley, courtesy ZGF.)

◀ **10.** York Minster Restoration, York, United Kingdom. Architect: B. M. Feilden; Structural Engineer: Ove Arup & Partners. Foundations during restoration.

Surveys of York Minster, a cathedral dating from the thirteenth century, revealed serious cracking, endangering the central tower, east wall, and western towers. An extensive restoration was completed in 1975 that included underpinning the structure with new foundations to spread the loads on the overburdened ground, strengthening the superstructure with stainless steel reinforcement, and elimination of deathwatch beetle from the roof structure. (Photo: Ove Arup & Partners.)

▲ *11. Font. (Photo: James F. Housel.)*

St. James Cathedral renovation, Seattle, Washington. Bumgardner Architects; Liturgical Advisor: Rev. Richard S. Vosko. Bumgardner Architects, with Rev. Richard S. Vosko as liturgical consultant, renovated the cathedral, moving the altar to the center of the crossing, replacing the lighting and adding an oculus over the altar, and creating a new Blessed Sacrament Chapel for private prayer. A new baptismal pool for full immersion includes the old font in its design.

▲ *13. Nave. (Photo: James F. Housel.)*

▲ *12. Blessed Sacrament Chapel. (Photo: Stephen Lee.)*

▲ **14.** *View of ark with doors open.*

▲ **15.** *View of interior.*

Synagogue, North Shore Hebrew Academy, Kings Point, New York. Architect: Alexander Gorlin. This multiuse synagogue and auditorium, with classroom wings flanking the sanctuary, is an addition to the North Shore Hebrew Academy. A large door covered with brass panels rotates to protect the ark and acts as a backdrop for films and dramatic productions when the room is used as an auditorium.

The fractured cube of light over the ark evokes the Kabalistic creation myth, in which the original order of the universe is shattered, and also serves as an acoustic device to reflect the voices of the congregation. The Eternal Light is suspended and floats within the cube of the ark as a microcosm of the same geometry. The pattern of the stained glass, which takes its cues from the ark and the circular pattern of the seating, represents the seven days of creation and rest. (Photos: Peter Aaron, ESTO.)

▲ **16.** *Detail of stained glass.*

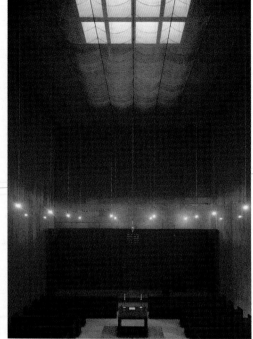

▲ **17.** Interior showing ark.

Dresden Synagogue, Dresden, Germany. Architect: Wandel Hoefer Lorch + Hirsch. Although the construction of this new synagogue marks the rebirth of Dresden's Jewish community from a tragic history, its defensive design illustrates the continuing concern for security. The 15-degree rotation of the synagogue plan allows the space to be oriented correctly for worship, and the concrete block construction refers to the surviving western wall of the Temple in Jerusalem. Inside, a tentlike structure of metal fabric encloses the worship space and refers to the historical dichotomy of Jewish places of worship, from the temporary structure of Moses' tabernacle in the desert to the massive stonework of Solomon's Temple in Jerusalem. (Photos: Roland Halbe-Artur.)

◀ **18.** Exterior view.

Central Synagogue Restoration, New York City. Architect: Hardy Holzman Pfeiffer Associates. Central Synagogue, originally built in 1872, is the oldest building in New York City continuously used as a synagogue. Severely damaged by fire in 1998, this National Historic Landmark was carefully restored, recreating historic details lost for many decades. Alterations such as a section of movable pews, enhanced acoustics, and modifications to the lobby allow the space to better serve contemporary needs. The women's gallery can be clearly seen on either side of the worship space. (Photos: Peter Aaron, ESTO.)

▲ **19.** *Interior view after restoration.*

▲ **20.** *Interior detail.*

▲ 21. Exterior with dome and minaret.   ▶ 22. Interior of prayer hall.

Islamic Center of New York City. Architect: SOM. The first religious center for the Islamic community of New York includes a mosque, an assembly room, and a minaret. Rotated on the site to face Mecca, it includes traditional elements such as the copper-clad dome, the nine-square decorative window geometry, and Kufic inscriptions over the doors. Inside the prayer hall, the mihrab denoting the qibla wall is embellished with cut-glass panels and a frieze of verses from the Qur'an. Men's and women's ablution spaces are located on a level below, and a women's gallery is above the main prayer hall. (Photos: Wolfgang Hoyt, ESTO.)

International Buddhist Progress Society, Hsi Lai Temple, Hacienda
Heights, California, a large rural Buddhist temple with courtyards,
gardens, and extensive community facilities. (Photos: Ellen Kuch.)

▲ **23.** Entry pavilion.

▼ **24.** Central courtyard.

Hindu Temple Society of Southern California, Sri Venkateswara Temple, Calabasas, California. (Photos: Ellen Kuch.)

▶ **25.** *The garbagriha with its characteristic pyramidal form.*

▼ **26.** *Sculpted images adorn the garbagriha.*

27–30. Storefront churches of Los Angeles. On Sunday mornings in Huntingdon Park and South Central Los Angeles, the converted storefront churches ring out with sermons and songs of praise. These churches attract worshipers from the African-American community and, increasingly, recent Hispanic immigrants, for whom they provide social services such as job networking, youth outreach, and immigration counseling. (Photos: Monica Nouwens.)

CHAPTER 10

SPECIAL EQUIPMENT

In addition to the furnishings described in Chapter 14, most worship spaces have special equipment, which may incorporate pumps, motors, plumbing, blowers, and controls. The equipment is usually furnished by specialist vendors and requires careful coordination with the building design and engineering.

The building architect generally provides a schematic design for the equipment and reviews the specialist contractors' shop drawings. Mechanical and electrical engineers design and specify the required electrical, mechanical, and plumbing connections, and the structural engineer must make sure that sufficient structural support is provided.

BAPTISMAL FONT

For Baptist churches, Churches of Christ, and many Evangelical churches, the baptismal font is designed as a pool, with steps leading down into the water on one side, and up on the other side. Bathrooms and changing rooms for men and women are located nearby. A screen conceals the candidates until the ritual; after immersion they step behind a screen, or a screen is slid to conceal the font and the candidates from the congregation.

In Episcopalian, Presbyterian, and other Protestant churches, where infant baptism by sprinkling is the norm, the font provides an elevated bowl for the water.

In Catholic churches built or renovated since the Second Vatican Council, the font assumes a renewed importance in the church ritual. The font should be deep enough for the pouring of water over an adult; it should be intimidating, not pret-

ty. It signifies death and resurrection: "Baptism into Christ demands enough water to die in" (Kavanagh 1978, pp. 109, 126).

It is important that the water that greets the congregation be moving, refreshing, living water (Giles 2000, p. 168; Mauck 1990, p. 49), which calls to mind its value as a precious commodity and the source of life in an arid climate such as the Holy Land. In some font designs, the water issues from an upper basin and flows down, splashing and gurgling, into the main pool. For baptism, there should be a sufficient amount of water to allow the congregation to see and hear the splashing water.

◀ Font for infant baptism carved from Alaskan cedar. The ambry holding the holy oils and the paschal candle are seen beyond. Chapel of St. Ignatius, Seattle University, Washington. Architect: Steven Holl.

SPECIAL EQUIPMENT

▶ *Section of baptismal font, Holy Trinity Church.*

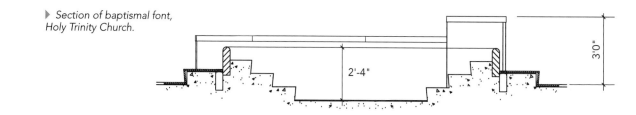

2'-4"

3'0"

▶ *Plan of baptismal font, Holy Trinity Church.*

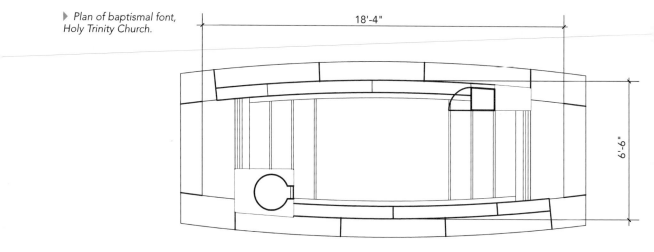

18'-4"

6'-6"

▶ *Font for Roman Catholic full immersion, showing shafts of sunlight from the overhead skylight illuminating the glass ambry and the water in the font. Holy Trinity Church, San Pedro, California. Architect: Leo A Daly. Photo: Erhard Pfeiffer.*

A font for a contemporary Catholic church should have a basin at waist height for infant baptism, and for members of the congregation to purify themselves, in addition to a main pool. The pool for immersion should be approximately 5' × 5' at the bottom, with steps leading down into the water and up on the other side. Ideally, the path through the water should lead toward the altar. The equipment needed to circulate, warm, and filter the water will require space approximately 5' × 5' in a separate enclosed room equipped with water, gas, power connections, a flue, and vents.

In the Catholic Church, the font water that has been blessed should be returned to the earth by means of a dry well, not connected to the sanitary sewer system. Such a well generally requires a building code modification provided by the local authority.

If a baptismal pool is provided, it must be designed to prevent children from falling into the font when the font is not in use. This prevention may take the form of enclosing walls with gates or a stainless steel or plexiglass screen just below the surface of the water.

A small table is required close to the font for placing the oil for baptism, dry towels and pitchers for pouring water.

The holy oil used for anointing the candidates for baptism and the oils used in other rituals are generally kept adjacent to the font in a lighted vessel called an *ambry*, where they are clearly visible.

THE ORGAN
Introduction
The pipe organ is quite likely the largest and most expensive furnishing in a church. Its musical success or failure depends on its placement and the acoustics

▲ *Ambry, St. Ignatius Church, Seattle, Washington.*

of the room in which it speaks. It is also a very complex piece of machinery whose mechanical stability and reliability are affected by the building environment.

Types of Organs
Pipe organs can be divided into two classes, those with electric key action and those with mechanical key action. Electric action organs have their consoles remote from the pipes and have electrical cables that carry signal information from the console to the organ. Mechanical action organs have their consoles built right into the organ case, or in a very close proximity to it, and have mechanical connections from the keyboard to the valves that play the pipes.

Many organists like the direct and intimate artistic quality of the mechanical action organ. Electric action organs are often less sensitive to the player, somewhat akin to driving a car with an automatic transmission and power steering as opposed to the manual controls of a fine sports car.

Electric action organs have an advantage in allowing greater flexibility in the placement of the console or even providing a movable console. Mechanical action organs have nonmovable consoles.

▲ Mechanical-key-action organ, University of South Carolina, Columbia, South Carolina (2 manuals, 29 stops, 36 ranks). Organ builder: Dobson Pipe Organ Builders, Lake City, Iowa. Photo: Dobson Pipe Organ Builders.

have an advantage in being inexpensive and not requiring the space of a pipe organ. Their sound lacks the richness of a genuine pipe organ, however, and the electronic components have a limited life.

Organ Location

Experts believe that an organ should be freestanding within a room, not housed in a separate room or "organ chamber," as it sometimes was during the early twentieth century. This freestanding location allows the sound of the organ to project into the room and develop freely in an unforced way.

It is best to locate an organ where its sound can have a direct line of projection to the majority of people in the room. Because the organ alternates with the presenter's spoken word, accompanies the choir in service music and solo anthems, and leads the entire congregation in song, it must be carefully related to all parts of the church to successfully perform its duties. The choir and organ must be together and not separated by great distance if they are to work musically together. Likewise, they must be positioned where they can best fulfill their alternating roles as solo performers or leaders of the congregation. This often means that the choir and organ are behind or to the side of the liturgical center of the church and facing the congregation. Besides speaking directly to the majority of the people in the church, the organ should be placed high in the room so that its sound is not obstructed by people or furnishings. Heavy solid walls behind the organ, open floor space in front of it, and a heavy, hard ceiling over the organ to reflect sound into the room enhance the sound projection. (See the diagram at right.)

However, electric action organs have bulkier valves under each pipe in their wind chests, causing the organs to be less compact than mechanical action organs. The electrical and electronic components in electric action organs are less durable over the long term than the parts of a well-built mechanical action organ.

Electronic organs, in which the sound is digitally synthesized and played through the building's sound system, are occasionally used for worship spaces, usually as a temporary measure until the congregation can afford a pipe organ. Electronic organs

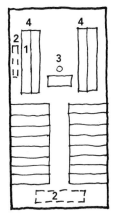

Electric-action organ, Cathedral of Our Lady of the Angels, Los Angeles (4 manuals, 104 stops, 105 ranks). Organ builder: Dobson Pipe Organ Builders; organ consultant: Manuel Rosales; design architect: Rafael Moneo; executive architect: Leo A Daly. Photo: Dobson Pipe Organ Builders.

Floor plan showing desirable organ locations.
1 *Organ console*
2 *Organ pipes*
3 *Altar and celebrant*
4 *Choir*

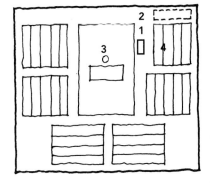

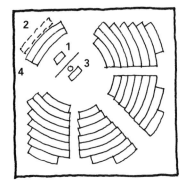

Construction of the Organ

An organ consists of the following components:

- The organ case, which encloses the *wind chests* and the *pipes*
- Pipes, including facade pipes, exposed on the front of the case, and others, the vast majority, inside the case
- The wind chests, on which most of the pipes are mounted, and which provide air to each pipe through the valve at its base

- The *console,* which contains several keyboards or *manuals,* a set of pedals, and the *stops,* which control which *rank,* or set of pipes, is being played
- The *blower,* which provides compressed air to the pipes through the wind chests

The desired musical characteristics establish the size and number of pipes in an organ, which in turn determine its layout and space requirements. The musical resources are measured by the number of ranks. A rank of pipes is made up of one pipe for each key on the keyboard. Pipes of each rank are graduated in both length and diameter. A 10-rank organ would be a very small organ, perhaps suitable for a chapel, and a 100-rank organ would be considered large and suitable for a church seating more than 1500 people. Each rank is designated by the length (pitch) of its longest pipe. Most organs have pipes of either 16 ft or 8 ft pitch as the longest pipes in each division. Very large organs may contain pipes of 32 ft pitch.

Space Requirements

Each organ is custom designed, but the following are general guidelines to help in providing adequate space. A pipe organ is usually thought of as a vertical structure. Typically, a two-manual and pedal organ needs a case no less than 25 ft high. Three-manual organs require at least 34 ft for the case. These figures are based on having the manual divisions stacked one over the other, with the lowest division no less than 7 ft off the floor (higher than a person's head) and allowing about 9–10 ft of height for the mechanisms and pipes of each division.

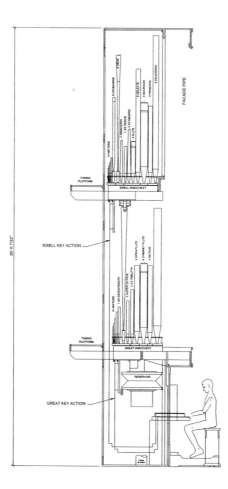

▶ Cross section of an organ showing components.

With sufficient height allowed, the width and depth of the organ case are considered next. In normal-sized organs manual divisions commonly take up 8–10 ft of width and are stacked one over the other with the pedal division at one or both sides. This arrangement would make the organ 18–20 ft wide. Larger organs may have more than one manual division at a level, making the organ even wider. It is always best, from an acoustical standpoint, to have the organ case at least twice as wide as it is deep.

In average-sized organs, if the manual divisions are 8–10 ft wide, the case would have to be 3–5 ft deep. This means that a two-manual organ of say, 35 ranks, would require a case about 18–20 ft wide, 3–5 ft deep, and 25–30 ft high. Some types of organs with electric action require more space than mechanical action organs. In special circumstances the organ may be arranged differently, but if given a clean slate most organ builders would prefer this simple vertical arrangement.

Larger organs require more space. For instance, the 105-rank organ in the Cathedral of Our Lady of the Angels, Los Angeles, is in a case 11 ft deep, 36 ft wide, and more than 55 ft high. Because organs require periodic service, the organ case must have access space behind it. Usually an organ case has at least 24 in. between it and the wall behind it.

Another factor of importance to architects and engineers is the weight of the organ. Although exact weights depend on the number and size of the pipes, it can be estimated that each rank of pipes and the associated mechanism weighs about 500 lb. That means that an organ of 35 ranks may weigh 16,500 lb. An organ of 75 ranks would weigh more than

19 tons. This could easily equate to 400–500 lb per sq ft of floor loading or point loads of several tons.

Blower Location

A blower generates compressed air for the pipes. Many smaller organs have modern, quiet high-speed blowers that fit into a space of 9 cu ft and can be

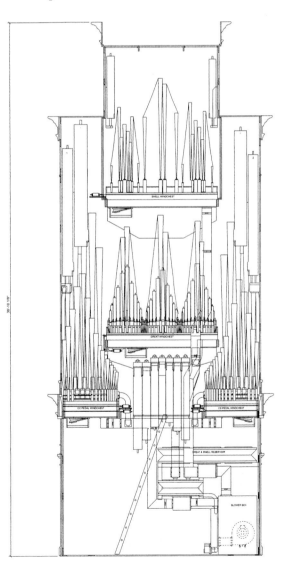

▼ Elevation of an organ showing divisions.

placed inside the organ case. In larger organs, blowers are larger and noisier and must be in a remote location. If a remote location is provided, the blower room will need a return air duct extending to it from the room the organ is in, so that the organ will draw air of the same temperature and humidity as the air it stands in. In addition, a duct for compressed air extending from the blower to the organ case must be provided.

Environmental Conditions

Providing steady temperature and humidity without sudden swings is important in planning an organ installation. This will ensure the stability of the tuning during the use of the organ. It is important that there be no air registers for the heating, ventilating, and air-conditioning (HVAC) system positioned

so that they blow air directly on the pipes or create air currents through them. Air currents create uneven temperatures that make the pipes go out of tune. It is also desirable not to have direct sunlight from windows or skylights fall on the organ case or the front pipes, because this will heat the pipes unevenly at different times of day, causing the organ to be perpetually out of tune.

Finally, in this era where lighting is often provided for television broadcasts or theatrical lighting is used in the context of a worship setting, it is important not to have lights hanging near the organ. These lights produce considerable heat and will change the tuning of the organ when they are turned on and off during a service.

The Role of the Organ Builder

Because pipe organs are always custom designed to meet the musical needs of a client and the architectural conditions of the buildings they will occupy, it is important to involve an organ builder early in the design process. Coordinating the organ design with the building design can ensure success for both the architect and the organ builder. Today many organ builders will work in a consulting capacity during the design process, helping the client to plan for an organ in the church long before the client is ready to sign a contract for the purchase of a fine pipe organ. The Associated Pipe Organ Builders of America (APOBA), a national trade organization, has a booklet entitled *Planning Space for Pipe Organs*. It is available to help architects and church building committees with their planning. This booklet can be obtained through APOBA's Website (http://www.apoba.com).

▼ The world's largest swinging bell, the World Peace Bell, cast by the Verdin Company in Nantes, France, in 1998 and installed at the Millenium Monument, Newport, Kentucky. The bell weighs 66,000 lb and can be rung by either swinging or striking with an electric striker. The clapper itself weighs 6,878 lb. Photo courtesy of the Verdin Company.

BELLS

In Western religions, church bells are either hung in freestanding towers or mounted on the church building and may be swung or struck. Historically, the mechanism was activated by pulling on ropes; bells are now operated electrically, and preset controls provide several different ring patterns.

The following factors should be taken into account in planning a bell installation:

- The bells must be located so that their sound is free to propagate and not constrained by buildings. An acoustician experienced in bell design should be consulted early in the design.

- The bells should be located so that they are readily visible. The excitement of seeing them in motion is an important benefit of investing in church bells.

- The bells should be selected with a view to both pitch and tone. The notes the bells ring when struck must harmonize, and their sound quality, a function of the bells' geometry and tuning, must be compatible. An acoustician specializing in bell design should be consulted when specifying the bells.

- The structure supporting the bells must be engineered to support not only their weight, but also the dynamic load of swinging bells and, in earthquake areas, the lateral forces they create under seismic movement. Church bells can weight up to 6–8 tons. The heaviest in the United States is 20 tons, in the Cathedral of St. John the Divine in New York City.

- The motors for swinging the bells should be protected from the weather;

▲ Carillon, Cathedral of Our Lady of the Angels, Los Angeles.

appropriate electrical power should be provided and space allocated for the control equipment. Access stairs and ladders, protected by safety rails, should be provided to the bells and all the equipment.

- Carefully consider the impact of bell ringing on the surrounding environment, particularly in residential areas. In today's diverse communities, the traditional Sunday morning peal of Christian church bells may now be experienced as an unwelcome intrusion. When environmental impact studies are performed for a new church building (see Chapter 5), the anticipated intensity of bell sound as a function of distance should be included in the report. A large bell can generate 100 dB of sound 100 ft away, and although sound intensity diminishes with the square of the distance, the peal can be audible over background noise for more than 3 miles.

Although foundries in Europe are casting new bells, churches may also choose from a range of pre-owned bells. Before purchasing a bell, however, churches should bear in mind the musical considerations discussed here.

Carillons are sets of bells tuned in chromatic order and designed for playing music. They are played from a keyboard, and the clappers that ring the bells may be mechanically connected to the keyboard or, as is more common now, electrically operated. Electrical operation permits the keyboard to be located remotely or even incorporated into an organ console, but lacks the musical expression conveyed by the player's touch.

▶ Bell motor and frame shop drawing, plan. Courtesy of the Verdin Company.

▶ Bell motor and frame shop drawing, elevation. Courtesy of the Verdin Company.

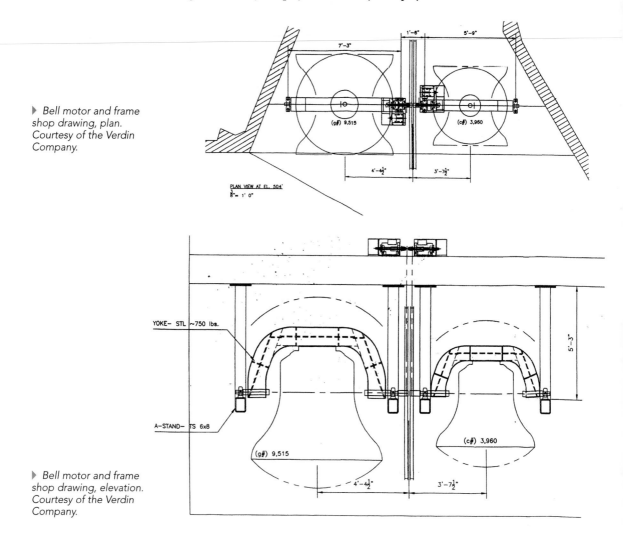

174

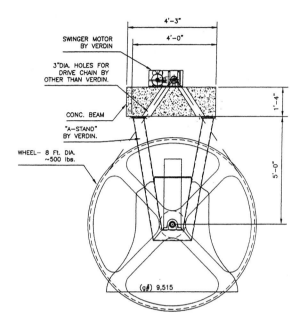

SWINGER MOTOR
BY VERDIN

3"DIA. HOLES FOR
DRIVE CHAIN BY
OTHER THAN VERDIN.

CONC. BEAM

"A—STAND"
BY VERDIN.

WHEEL— 8 Ft. DIA.
~500 lbs.

4'—3"

4'—0"

1'—4"

5'—0"

(g♯) 9,515

◀ *Bell motor and frame
shop drawing, section.
Courtesy of the Verdin
Company.*

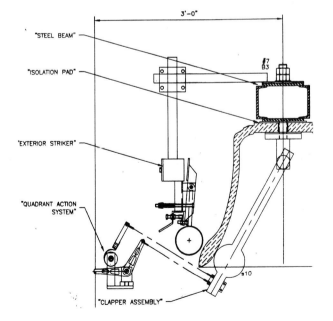

3'—0"

"STEEL BEAM"

"ISOLATION PAD"

"EXTERIOR STRIKER"

"QUADRANT ACTION
SYSTEM"

"CLAPPER ASSEMBLY"

#7
B3

#10

◀ *Striker detail. Courtesy of
the Verdin Company.*

SPECIAL EQUIPMENT

▶ Wuzu, *plan with dimensions.*

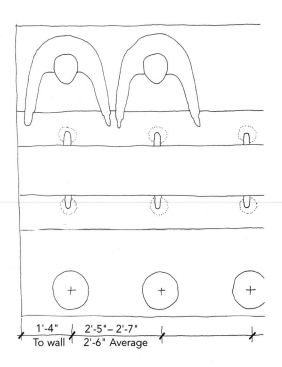

1'-4"
To wall

2'-5"– 2'-7"
2'-6" Average

▶ Wuzu, *section with dimensions.*

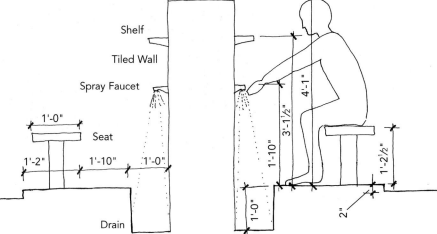

Shelf

Tiled Wall

Spray Faucet

1'-0"

Seat

1'-2"   1'-10"   1'-0"

Drain

4'-1"

3'-1½"

1'-10"

1'-0"

1'-2½"

2"

JUDAISM

Because the Orthodox Jewish faith forbids the use of mechanical devices on the Sabbath, synagogues do not generally have equipment for use by the congregation.

The Mikvah

Some congregations have a *mikvah,* or pool for ritual purification, in a separate building. Adults converting to Judaism use the *mikvah;* it is also used by women, and occasionally by men, for ritual cleansing. The design considerations are similar to those for a full-immersion baptismal pool.

ISLAM
The Ablution

Muslims must wash their hands, elbows, faces, behind the ears, and their feet before praying. Traditionally, a pool in the outer courtyard of the mosque fulfilled this purpose; the contemporary mosque has a *wudu* or *wuzu,* an ablution facility. Separate spaces are provided for men, women, and children.

Detailed dimensions required for the *wuzu* are shown in the illustrations at left.

Toilets are also included in the *wuzu,* and they must be designed carefully:

- Toilets should be in compartments with solid walls.

- Compartments should not open or back toward Mecca.

- Toilets should be the squat type.

- Toilets and their associated piping must not be located under or over the prayer hall.

▲ *Wuzu, King Fahad Mosque, Culver City, California. Photo: Ellen Kuch.*

CHAPTER 11
MATERIALS

Finish materials clothe and give form to a worship space; they define the surfaces that members of the congregation touch, and they give character to the interior. They convey a sense of the sacred by their difference from everyday domestic or commercial materials. As mentioned in Chapter 1, it is material qualities like the weight of the door, the resistance of the handle, and the sound of footsteps on the floor that signal that the visitor has entered a special place. Materials create a carefully calibrated reflection of light and sound, and they have a symbolic role in the literature of the faith and the history of the community. Above all, the materials used in spaces for worship must be durable; they must withstand heavy use over a long period of time. They should be easy to maintain and convey an appearance of elegance and dignity.

Materials for worship spaces should display the passage of time as they wear and weather gracefully, just as a worn stone step shows centuries of foot traffic or a bronze handle is polished bright by the touch of thousands of visitors.

Authentic materials reaffirm the honesty and integrity the congregation demands of its members. Modern synthetic materials such as plastic laminate and vinyl tile have a place in their own right, but not as imitations of other materials such as wood or stone.

Despite the importance of quality and durability, cost is also a significant factor in material selection. Life-cycle costing, as discussed in Chapter 19, should be used to evaluate the true cost of a material, including maintenance and replacement over the life of the building.

Materials frequently have a symbolic role in religious iconography—for example, the acacia wood for the tabernacle listed in Exodus 25 and the stone required for an altar in a Catholic church. Historically, materials reflected the locale where they were found. Now, despite the globalization of building materials, congregations can still support sustainable design by using indigenous materials. Materials can also make connections to the craft traditions of the community, whether they are brick masonry, carpentry, or metalwork. For example, at Holy Trinity Church in San Pedro, California, the curved nave ceiling finished in cherry wood refers to the boat building and fishing tradition of this maritime community.

Finish materials also serve important technical functions:

- They reflect or absorb sound to control echoes and provide the correct reverberation time, as discussed in Chapter 12. Hard materials such as stone, concrete, and brick create strong reflections that fortify choral and congregational singing and provide the appropriate reverberation time for organ music. However, some absorbent surfaces are usually needed to control echoes and keep reverberation time within limits for speech intelligibility.

- They reflect light. As discussed in Chapter 13, the surface reflectance contributes significantly to the overall brightness of a space.

FLOORING MATERIALS
The most popular worship space flooring materials are shown in the table below,

ranked by cost, durability, ease of maintenance, slip resistance, acoustic reflection, and light reflection. The sixth column shows the perceived warmth of the floor, an important factor in Hindu and Islamic worship, in which the participants sit and kneel on the floor, and for all forms of worship in cold climates.

Hard Flooring Materials

Despite their cost, stone finishes are desirable as they last a long time, are easy to maintain, and create an acoustically live environment. Granite, limestone, sandstone, and marble can be laid in slabs or smaller tiles in a weak cement-sand mix over a concrete subfloor.

CRITERIA FOR MATERIALS SELECTION: FLOORING

Material	Cost	Durability	Ease of Maintenance	Moisture Resistance	Slip Resistance	Warmth to the Touch	Acoustic Reflection	Light Reflection
Granite	4	4	4	4	3*	1	4	2
Marble	4	4	4	4	1	1	4	3
Limestone	3	4	4	4	3*	1	4	3
Sandstone	3	3	4	4	3	1	4	2
Slate	3	3	4	4	3*	1	4	2
Terrazzo	3	3	4	4	3*	1	4	2
Ceramic tile	2	3	4	4	3*	1	4	3
Wood parquet	3	2	3	1	3*	3	3	2
Wood strip	3	2	3	1	3*	3	3	2
Cork tile	3	2	3	1	3	4	2	2
Linoleum	2	2	2	3	3*	2	3	3
Vinyl sheet	2	3	2	3	3*	2	3	3
Rubber sheet	2	3	2	3	3*	2	3	3
Vinyl composition tile	1	3	2	3	3*	2	3	3
Carpet	1	1	1	1	4	4	1	2
Colored concrete	1	4	3	4	2	1	4	3

High: 4
Moderately high: 3
Moderately low: 2
Low: 1

*Note: Assumes the use of honed finish or slip-resistant sealer as appropriate

Floor materials must have the appropriate slip resistance to carry heavy foot traffic safely, to avoid accidents, and to allow worshipers in wheelchairs to maneuver comfortably. Building codes typically require a coefficient of friction of 0.6 for public areas, which can be achieved by using a honed finish on limestone, marble, or granite. Around the font, slip resistance should be increased by using a flame finish on granite, or walk-off mats on marble and limestone, to avoid accidents when the floor is wet.

Modern terrazzo provides the durability of a stone finish at a lesser cost and may be used for steps and vertical surfaces in addition to flooring. It is laid as a ⅜ in. thick epoxy resin matrix over a concrete subfloor. Terrazzo should be laid in panels of less than 100 sq ft, separated by zinc or plastic divider strips, and the wide variety of terrazzo colors and divider strip designs make inlaid patterns popular. Slip-resistant traffic wax provides the required coefficient of friction for dry conditions. Terrazzo is also used for font interiors, provided that an aggregate such as granite or crushed glass that resists corrosion by pool chemicals is used.

Ceramic, stone, and slate tiles, which are often used as 12" × 12" pavers laid in a mortar bed over concrete, are a durable and less expensive alternative to stone. Ceramic pavers are naturally slip resistant and may be provided with a surface texture to increase their coefficient of friction. Slate is generally used with a natural cleft finish.

Colored concrete is a low-cost floor material that may be upgraded later by applying other finishes. The concrete is finished with a steel trowel and lightly sandblasted for slip resistance, and a clear sealer is applied. Saw-cutting the

◀ Limestone floor, Cathedral of Our Lady of the Angels, Los Angeles.

▼ Terrazzo font; marble floor adjacent to the font and cork floor in front. Holy Trinity Church, San Pedro, California. Architect: Leo A Daly. Photo: Erhard Pfeiffer.

IN THE NAME OF THE FATHER AND OF THE SON AND OF THE HOLY SPIRIT

floor into 4 ft squares while the concrete is still "green" can regularize the cracking, which frequently develops in concrete floors as the material cures and the building settles.

When hard flooring materials are used, it may be advisable to introduce acoustic absorption under the seats to control noise from shuffling feet and dropped objects. Some congregations use a carpet runner in the aisles to control the noise of foot traffic.

Wood Flooring

Wood materials are popular floor finishes. They add warmth to the space in cold climates and are quieter underfoot than stone. Hardwood strips or parquet shapes ⅜ in. thick are usually fixed by concealed nailing onto a plywood subfloor. They are sometimes laid in mastic on a cement-sand leveling subfloor. Cork tiles, laid in mastic over a wood or concrete subfloor, provide a warm, quiet, and hard-wearing floor finish. (See the bottom photograph on page 181.)

With all wood flooring materials, the subfloor must be absolutely level and dry. Concrete subfloors are usually sealed to prevent moisture penetration. Wood and cork floors are sanded smooth before being sealed with a urethane sealer and finished with a traffic wax.

Synthetic Materials

Synthetic floor materials such as vinyl sheet or tile, linoleum, and rubber are comfortable, quiet, and durable. They are not generally used in worship spaces, but are popular for service spaces such as kitchens, storage, and preparation rooms.

Carpet is not usually suitable as a floor finish for Christian worship spaces that include unamplified music, because its high acoustic absorption deadens the space. It is, however, used extensively in large worship spaces, such as Evangelical Christian churches, that rely completely on sound reinforcement, and for Muslim, Hindu, and Buddhist worship spaces where members of the congregation sit on the floor. Carpet is also appropriate for meeting rooms, classrooms, and small rooms for private prayer.

▼ Concrete floor, Chapel of St. Ignatius, Seattle, Washington. The colored concrete is polished with wax to reflect the light from the colored "bottles of light." (See also color plate 5.) Architect: Steven Holl.

WALL AND CEILING MATERIALS

The finish materials used for walls and ceilings are dictated to some extent by the type of construction, which, as discussed in Chapter 5, is controlled by the building code and depends on the size of the building and its siting. Appropriate materials and their characteristics are shown in the tables on page 184.

For moderate-sized buildings, wood frame construction is appropriate. The exterior walls may be wood siding, metal panels, or plaster, and the interior walls and ceiling finished in wood or acoustic paneling or painted gypsum board. Wood paneling, which may be perforated and backed with acoustic insulation, usually consists of wood veneer over plywood or particleboard. Acoustic panels may be wrapped in fabric. Gypsum board should be installed with control joints at corners and at a maximum of 30 ft on center in straight runs.

More substantial buildings may be built of concrete masonry, poured-in-place concrete, or brickwork. Masonry may be left exposed on the interior or the exterior, provided that it is sealed with a penetrating sealer. In cold climates, one side of the wall must be furred out to allow space for thermal insulation.

Concrete may be exposed on the exterior. The experience of the last 50 years, however, has shown that concrete does not weather well, particularly in cold, polluted, or coastal environments, unless it is carefully designed for durability. Appropriate measures include:

- Maintaining adequate (3 in.) coverage over reinforcement
- Using a mix design that controls cracking by minimizing water content
- Designing formwork and placing concrete carefully to minimize flaws
- Covering exposed parapet walls with flashing
- Sealing the exterior with penetrating sealer

A range of concrete colors and finishes, which include sandblasting, washing, and bush-hammering, are available.

▲ Exterior precast tilt-up concrete walls and curved metal roof, Chapel of St. Ignatius, Seattle, Washington. Architect: Steven Holl. The "pick-pockets" used to lift the wall panels are covered with bronze caps.

CRITERIA FOR MATERIALS SELECTION: EXTERIOR WALLS

Material	Cost	Durability	Ease of Maintenance
Granite	4	4	4
Marble	4	4	4
Limestone	3	3	4
Sandstone	3	3	4
Slate	3	4	4
Brick	3	4	4
Ceramic tile	2	4	4
Exposed concrete	2	4	3
Precast concrete	3	4	3
Concrete masonry	2	4	2
Wood siding	2	1	1
Metal panels	2	2	1
Cement plaster	1	2	1

High: 4
Moderately high: 3
Moderately low: 2
Low: 1

CRITERIA FOR MATERIALS SELECTION: CEILINGS

Material	Cost	Durability	Ease of Maintenance	Moisture Resistance	Slip Resistance	Warmth to the Touch	Acoustic Reflection	Light Reflection
Wood paneling	4	3	2	1	n/a	n/a	2	2
Exposed concrete	3	4	4	4	n/a	n/a	4	3
Plaster	2	4	4	1	n/a	n/a	4	4
Gypsum board	1	3	3	1	n/a	n/a	3	4
Acoustic tile	1	2	2	1	n/a	n/a	1	3

High: 4
Moderately high: 3
Moderately low: 2
Low: 1

CRITERIA FOR MATERIALS SELECTION: INTERIOR WALLS							
Material	Cost	Durability	Ease of Maintenance	Moisture Resistance	Warmth to the Touch	Acoustic Reflection	Light Reflection
Granite	4	4	4	4	1	4	2
Marble	4	4	4	4	1	4	3
Wood paneling	3	3	3	2	4	2	2
Ceramic tile	2	4	4	4	1	4	4
Brick	3	4	2	4	1	3	1
Exposed concrete	3	4	2	4	1	4	2
Concrete masonry	2	4	2	4	1	3	1
Plaster	1	3	2	1	1	4	4
Gypsum board	1	1	1	1	3	3	4

High: 4
Moderately high: 3
Moderately low: 2
Low: 1

Alternatively, masonry and concrete may be covered with finish materials both inside and out, including stone slabs, precast concrete panels, ceramic tile, or plaster.

Very large worship spaces are generally built with a concrete or steel frame. The frames can be infilled with the following materials:

- Poured-in-place concrete
- Precast concrete panels
- Masonry
- Lightweight steel frame with stone, brick, tile, metal panel, or plaster facing

ROOFING MATERIALS
Roofing material selection generally means balancing first cost against the projected life of the material. The appearance of sloping roofs, and the weight of the material and its effect on the structure, should also be taken into account. A list of suitable materials and their characteristics is shown in the table on page 186.

The most durable materials, such as copper and slate for pitched roofs and lead for flat roofs, are also the most expensive. If they are carefully installed in accordance with the trade association recommendations, allowing for ventilation, thermal movement, and separation of dissimilar materials, they will last more than 100 years.

Good-quality clay tiles, if properly installed, will last for at least 50 years.

Galvanized, factory-painted metal standing seam roofing, as well as compo-

CRITERIA FOR MATERIALS SELECTION: ROOFING

Material	Cost	Durability
Lead	4	4
Slate	4	4
Copper	4	4
Clay tile	4	3
Concrete tile	3	3
Coated metal	3	3
Wood shingles	2	2
Composition shingles	2	2
Painted metal	2	1
Single ply	1	2
Built-up	1	1

High: 4
Moderately high: 3
Moderately low: 2
Low: 1

▼ Concrete pressed pavers
and precast concrete bench.

sition shingles, are available in a wide range of patterns and colors and can provide a 20-year bonded roof covering. (See the photograph on page 183.)

Current technologies provide single-ply and built-up finishes for flat roofs that come with a 20-year warranty. Although flat roofs are designed to keep water out when completely flat, they should always be designed to slope at least ¼ in. per foot (2 percent). In wood-framed buildings, where long-term structural deflection could cause ponding, this slope should be increased to ½ in. per foot (4 percent).

EXTERIOR PAVING MATERIALS

The exterior paving materials frame the worship space. Together with trees and planting, they define the character of the journey from the public space of the street or the parking lot to the doors of the worship space. The table at right lists suitable exterior paving materials and their characteristics.

Stone slabs, set on a sand bed, provide the most durable and dignified paving material for the approach to a worship space.

Concrete pavers are available in a wide range of colors and shapes. Finished in sandblasted, stamped, or exposed aggregate, they are also set in a sand bed.

Poured-in-place concrete finishes range from a simple broom finish, through sand blasting, stamping, and washing, to seeding with a decorative aggregate. The keys to the success of a poured-in-place concrete installation are as follows:

- Reviewing mock-ups to check on workmanship, color, and finish
- Saw-cutting to control cracking, preferably every 4 ft
- Sealing the concrete, and applying graffiti coating if necessary, to make it easy to keep clean

CRITERIA FOR MATERIALS SELECTION: EXTERIOR PAVING				
Material	Cost	Durability	Ease of Maintenance	Slip Resistance
Granite	4	4	4	3
Marble	4	4	4	2
Limestone	3	3	4	3
Sandstone	3	3	4	3
Slate	3	3	4	3
Brick	3	3	4	4
Terrazzo	3	3	4	3
Ceramic tile	2	3	4	3
Concrete pavers	2	3	3	4
Colored concrete	1	3	3	3
Stamped concrete	1	3	3	3
Seeded concrete	1	3	3	3
Asphalt paving	1	3	3	4
Decomposed granite	1	2	2	2

High: 4
Moderately high: 3
Moderately low: 2
Low: 1

Because a large area of concrete paving can be monotonous and show every stain and blemish in workmanship, this material works best if the finishes are varied. For example, broom-finished bands may be used to frame panels of seeded or sandblasted concrete.

Decomposed granite (DG) paving is an inexpensive material made from finely ground stone that is used for walks and plazas. When stabilized with polymers and properly drained, it provides a hard-wearing and nonslip surface. Care should be taken to provide an area of hard sur-

◀ Stone pebble and wood decking, Center of Gravity Meditation Center, Jemez Springs, New Mexico. Predock Frane Architects.

▶ *Seeded concrete with broom-finished bands, Holy Trinity Church, San Pedro, California. Architect: Leo A Daly.*

face such as concrete or stone between the DG and the building interior to remove the grit particles carried on the congregation's shoes.

Wood decking is frequently used in Buddhist worship spaces to denote paths of travel, and stone pebbles are used to separate paths from landscape areas.

CONCLUSION

Materials selected for a worship space should reflect a careful balance of durability, appearance, and cost, and a concern for their effect on acoustics, lighting, and thermal comfort. Although finish materials are frequently targets of last-minute cost cutting, congregations should always bear in mind that materials selection has a crucial effect on the appearance, ease of maintenance, and acoustic performance of a worship space.

CHAPTER 12

ACOUSTIC AND AUDIOVISUAL CONSIDERATIONS

"In the beginning was the Word," says the book of John—then came music. The sensitive balance between speech and music for worship facilities subsequently became a concern for clergy, worship leaders, architects, and acoustical consultants.

THE UNIQUENESS OF WORSHIP SPACE DESIGN

The acoustical and audiovisual aspects of worship spaces differ from those of most other building types in a number of ways:

Projects are unique in that their "spiritual" nature often results in architectural forms and volumes that are individually distinctive and acoustically challenging. There are often conflicting and extreme acoustical requirements for the same major worship space—for example, a "live," reverberant space (long reverberation time) to enhance and support music and singing and, at the same time, a "dead" space (short reverberation time) to allow for clarity of speech.

Whenever acoustics and audiovisual systems are a high priority, it is important to involve the acoustical and audiovisual consultant early in the architectural design process. This will forestall incorporating insurmountable problems into the project later. Once the client, sponsors, and/or the public see any initial conceptual image(s) of the building, they are often unwilling to change the basic design concept.

Acoustics, audio, and video system designs are based on well-founded laws of physics. The success of the ultimate solution will depend on how well these prin-

ciples are understood and implemented by the design team. The degree to which the consultant can communicate creative recommendations, both aesthetically and technically, will undoubtedly influence the final solutions. A successful design is a collaboration between acoustical consultant, architect, and engineering design team. Effective communication and close collaboration are essential for reaching a good acoustic design. (See the diagram on page 48.)

▼ Temple Emmanuel, San Francisco, California. Architect: RMW; acoustical consultant: Shen Milsom Wilke + Paoletti. Photo: Robert Swanson.

▲ Soaring interior volumes create acoustical challenges. Jubilee Church, Rome, Italy. Architect: Richard Meier and Partners. Photo courtesy Richard Meier and Partners.

▼ Cathedral of Christ the Light, Oakland, California. Design architect: Skidmore Owings + Merill; executive architect: Kendall-Heaton Architects. Image courtesy Skidmore Owings + Merill.

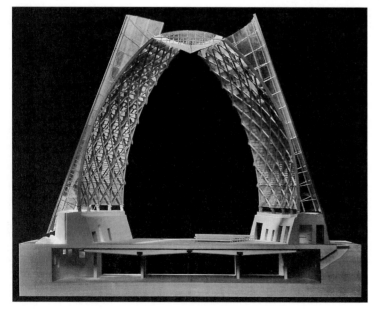

THE ULTIMATE ACOUSTICAL CHALLENGE

From a purely technical viewpoint, the religious denomination is not the issue in the acoustical design of a worship space. Because speech and music are present in most worship environments, the decision that must be made at the beginning of a project is the balance between how acoustically "live" or "dead" the space should be. Will the space be more reverberant for music, singing/chanting, instruments, and/or organ, or less reverberant for the spoken voice and only limited music? Once this criterion is established, the task is to apply the appropriate acoustical principles to the physical design created by the architect.

Mosques, cathedrals, and worship facilities for Greek Orthodox denominations are typically more reverberant than facilities for the Church of Jesus Christ of Latter-day Saints, which emphasize the spoken word, or Evangelical worship spaces where the emphasis is on sound amplification and the room acoustics are geared to those of a broadcast studio.

THE ROLE OF THE ACOUSTICAL CONSULTANT IN THE DESIGN OF A WORSHIP SPACE

The design team for a new worship space, or the renovation of an existing one, typically includes an architect, an acoustical consultant, a music minister or choir director, a liturgical specialist, representatives from the pastoral staff, an organ builder, and interested laypersons of the congregation, most often known as a building committee. During the programming phase of the project, the building committee and the rest of the design team are questioned by the acoustical consultant to determine what

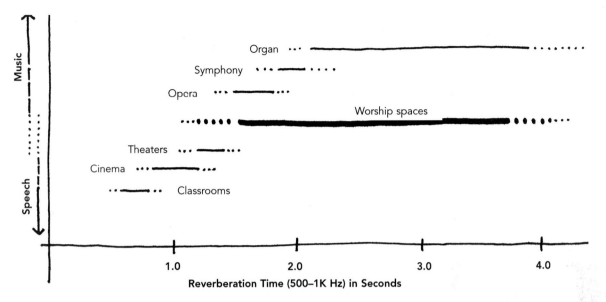

Reverberation Time (500–1K Hz) in Seconds

constitutes good acoustics for their congregation.

Questions for the music minister include:

- What is the relative importance of music versus speech?

- Is electronic reinforcement for the choir, soloists, or instrumentalists desired?

- What style and liturgical function of music is preferred during worship?

- What are the size and configuration of choirs, hand bell ensembles, organ, pianos, other instrumental groups, etc.?

A calendar of past years' activities can be examined for the number and types of special musical programs, including Christmas pageants, Easter cantatas, concerts, recitals, as well as purely speech-oriented programming such as drama or lectures. The music minister is a good source of information as to the direction of the musical program, and the pastoral staff and congregation are key references concerning speech reinforcement within the worship space.

The acoustical consultant questions the building committee regarding the acceptability of visible sound reinforcement elements in the worship space. The consultant provides an explanation of good sound system design based on speech intelligibility, sufficient loudness of speech and music, and the desirability of "directional realism," which is the perception that the amplified sound is coming from the person speaking. Topics of additional concern include the visibility and reinforcement of the choir and the importance of congregational singing.

The acoustical impact of carpet and pew cushions on reverberation, and the control of reflected energy in the case of partial audience seating capacity, are important issues. The requirements for flexible seating within the sanctuary and the use of fixed pews, seats, or movable chairs should be determined.

The consultant does the following:

- Questions members of the pastoral staff as to their public speaking styles in relation to the congregation.

▲ *Reverberation time criteria varies for different use functions.*

- Confirms their requirements for speech reinforcement.

- Discerns whether a wireless microphone system is desirable or necessary.

- Determines requirements for recording, for example, for archival purposes; duplication for availability immediately after a service; distribution to shut-ins; lectures or guest sermons for distribution and sale; weddings or other important events in the worship space.

- Attends a worship service to observe the style and content of the liturgy and to note conditions or practices that differ from the information supplied during interviews with the music minister, the building committee, the preaching staff, and the organ builder. Much can be learned from direct observation and partici-pation.

- Helps to shape the sidewalls and ceiling of a space to promote natural reinforcement of sound, when appropriate, and begins to identify potential locations for the sound reinforcement loudspeakers.

THE ORGAN AND THE CHOIR

When an organ is included in the project, the organ builder should participate in the design process. The goal is to accommodate the acoustical elements that will optimize organ playing and listening conditions. The organ builder has preferences for room finishes and ideas about reverberation and diffusion and the historical nature, content, and tonal design of the organ. Typically, the acoustical requirements for an organ include a very long reverberation time. This is the antithesis of the requirement for speech clarity and intelligibility. See the illustration on page 191. Detailed requirements for the organ are discussed in Chapter 10.

The choir should be located close to the organ and choirmaster or music director and to any other musical instruments used during the worship service. Preferably, the organ and choir are located on the centerline of the worship space, facing the congregation. Many older worship spaces have the organ and choir at the rear, often in the balcony. Many close-in sound-reflecting ceiling and wall surfaces make this location desirable acoustically; however, recent liturgical decisions prefer to have the choir in the vicinity of the altar but not directly behind the altar, except when the choir is singing. Often the decision is made to locate the choir to the side of the altar, in the transept, where the choir does not have to change its location during the worship service. This calls for the design of appropriate sound-reflecting surfaces to help project the sound of the choir toward the congregation, especially if the organ is also located in the transept. (See diagrams on page 169.)

THE DESIGN PROCESS

The importance of a thorough programming phase to set a project on solid footing cannot be overemphasized. After programming, the acoustical consultant develops a master plan to identify areas of concern with respect to room acoustics, reinforcement of speech and music, and control of noise and vibration. A review of the site often includes acoustical measurements of potential environmental noise impacts (e.g., aircraft fly-overs, vehicular traffic, neighboring mechanical equipment, etc.). The acoustical consultant next works with the architect to produce a matrix of room names and acoustical design criteria with narrative descriptions of the functioning of the audio, videos, and broadcast systems.

This is the time to plan for critical adjacencies (i.e., choir rooms, fellowship halls, mechanical rooms, organ blowers, etc.) and to provide appropriate volume in spaces where room acoustics are important. Choir rooms and fellowship halls, for instance, require adequate ceiling heights to allow the appropriate acoustical quality.

It is important to prevent the encroachment of unwanted noise into the worship space from the exterior environment, the building mechanical systems, adjacent toilets and lavatories, organ blowers, and adjacent spaces such as choir rooms, classrooms, other rehearsal rooms, fellowship halls, kitchens, playgrounds, and so forth.

Likewise, adequate space for technical equipment should be integrated with the floor plan, such as equipment racks and control positions for the sound reinforcement and audio and video recording equipment.

Infrastructure

The infrastructure for these systems entails a number of considerations:

- Coordinate the acoustical relationship between the organ console, organ pipes (or loudspeakers), choir, vocal soloists, and other instrumentalists with important visual elements, including altars, crosses, baptisteries, lecterns, open Bibles, statues, etc.

- Integrate the loudspeakers of the sound reinforcement system into the architecture of the space, taking into account the individual requirements of central loudspeaker clusters, distributed loudspeaker systems, line arrays, pew-back loudspeaker systems, column loudspeakers, etc.

- Distribute microphone receptacles throughout the worship space according to the requirements of music reinforcement, the number and flexibility of speaking and singing positions, and the seating configurations within the worship space for various modes of worship.

- Design, orient, and distribute sound reflecting, diffusing and absorbing surfaces/elements to maximize the natural reinforcement of speech and music, including congregational singing, instrumental performance, organ accompaniment, and recital. When natural reinforcement of music and speech is not a primary concern, sound-absorbent materials are located so as to avoid unwanted reflections, echoes, and the buildup of excessive reverberant sound within the worship space.

The follow-up final design process involves working out the details and specifications and reviewing progress sets of architectural and engineering drawings. During construction administration, the acoustical consultant will respond to questions from the field, keep current with construction progress, review sketch details, and make occasional visits to the site, prior to conducting a final commissioning exercise.

The Ultimate Goal

Establishing the appropriate acoustical and audiovisual criteria and basic design concepts are paramount to the success of a project. The follow-up design phases of a project consist of working out the detailed solutions for all the project conditions, and include the acoustical consultant, architectural designers, engineers, and other specialty consultants.

What Makes Good Acoustics?

"Good" is a subjective term that needs to be defined for each project by the client and the design team. Acoustically, some of the basic characteristics known to contribute to the generally accepted quality of "good sound" are as follows:

- Quiet
- Live
- Diffuse
- Loud
- Spacious
- Uniform
- Clear

A synopsis of each of these acoustical characteristics follows.

A quiet environment

Definition
Freedom from high background sound levels and annoying intrusive sound (e.g., traffic noise or hums, buzzing, rattles, and so forth, from HVAC equipment or sound or lighting systems).

Acoustical criteria
Noise criteria NC 20-35.
Noise criteria are a set of contours that describe maximum decibel levels at frequencies ranging from 31 to 4000 Hz.

Architectural consideration
Control of noise and vibration from heating, ventilating, and air-conditioning (HVAC) systems and sound-isolating building constructions.

How to get a "quiet" environment

From exterior sources
- Observe local site conditions at numerous times of the day and night.
- Ask local residents about potential offending noise sources and inquire at the local planning office about future plans that might impact the site (e.g., transportation systems, land use compatibility, etc.).
- Obtain maps of the local site and look for major roadways, airports, etc.

▼ *Noise criteria curves.*

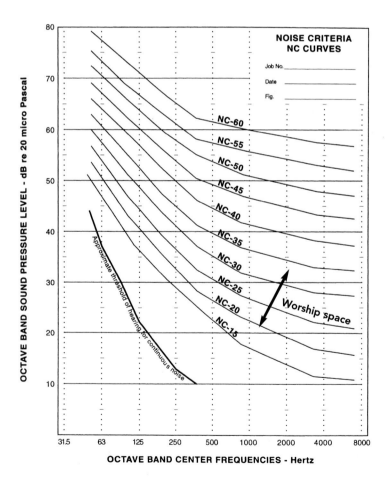

- Make environmental noise measurements. Based on the expected time of use of the facility, determine whether long-term measurement data are required or short-term representative samples are sufficient.

- The space plan should buffer critical spaces from exterior noise exposure whenever possible.

- Windows, although highly desirable for natural light and views, are typically the weakest acoustical components in the exterior building shell. If used, expect double glazing with 4 in. ± airspace.

- Avoid single doors at exits directly to the exterior; use vestibules with two sets of fully gasketed doors. *Note:* Special high-performance sound-isolating doors are available, but they often do not perform up to expectation because of limitations of door gasketing, poor installation, and long-term wear and tear.

- Exterior wall constructions require mass (brick, concrete, plaster, stucco).

- Additional airspace and separate interior walls are often necessary.

- The roof requires a similar degree of sound isolation as the walls.

- Special double-panel acoustical smoke vents (automatically operable during a fire via fusible links) are frequently required.

From interior sources

- Provide vestibules with two sets of gasketed doors at all points of ingress/egress to major assembly (and other acoustically critical) spaces, as noted earlier for doors.

- The space plan is critical. Locate mechanical equipment rooms away from acoustically sensitive spaces. Use corridors as sound isolation buffers. Avoid noncompatible adjacencies.

- Use floor slab joints, on grade, to minimize structure-borne transfer of sound and vibration.

- Vertical stacking of noncompatible spaces, such as parking and worship spaces, will require complex building construction solutions such as floated floor slabs.

- Windows at acoustically critical spaces (e.g., at worship rehearsal rooms, recording rooms, control rooms) will typically require double glazing. (See the preceding comments on glazing.)

- Double wall constructions, using 8–16 in. of depth, are commonly used to isolate noncompatible space adjacencies.

A live environment

Definition

Provides sound that lingers in a space while our ears enjoy the decay of acoustic energy.

Acoustical criteria

Reverberation time = 1.5 – 2.0 – 3.0+ seconds.

Reverberation is the characteristic that defines the degree of liveness of a particular environment. Note that for non-music, speech events, an acoustically "dead" environment (RT = 1.0 second) is desirable, where sound does not linger but is absorbed via the use of soft, fibrous, sound dampening materials instead of sound-reflective materials.

195

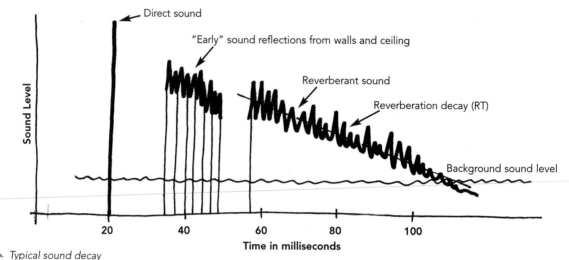

Direct sound

"Early" sound reflections from walls and ceiling

Reverberant sound

Reverberation decay (RT)

Background sound level

Sound Level

Time in milliseconds

▲ *Typical sound decay pattern for worship spaces.*

▶ *The interaction between architectural surfaces and the sound field in a room.*

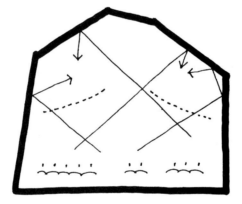

Reverberant sound energy interacts with the overall envelop of the space

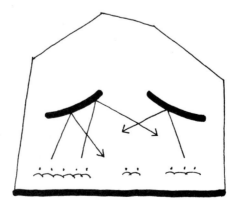

"Early" sound energy interacts with nearby architectural surfaces

Architectural consideration
Hard, impervious, sound-reflecting surfaces.

How to get a "live" environment
Provide hard, impervious room finish surfaces for floor, walls, and/or ceilings. Typically, sound-reflective building construction materials include:

- Concrete
- Plaster
- Wood
- Gypsum board
- Glass

The thickness and mass of a material are important, in addition to its surface finish. Thin, lightweight materials (i.e. ½ in. gypsum board, ¼ in. glass, ⅜ in. wood, etc.) will absorb mid- to low-frequency sound energy via resonance, especially if there is trapped airspace directly behind the material.

Soft, fibrous materials absorb sound. Their efficiency is dependent on their thickness, porosity (airflow), and back up support (mounting). Typical sound-absorbing materials that absorb sound energy and reduce liveness include:

- Carpet
- Acoustical tile
- Curtains
- Glass or mineral fiber products

A diffuse environment

Definition
Provides sound that is smooth, "velvety," and aurally comfortable—not "harsh" or "boomy."

Acoustical criteria
Multiple, uniform reflections of sound energy within 80 milliseconds of generating the initial sound.

Architectural consideration
Shaped, angular, patterned, textured, interior surfaces.

How to get a "diffuse" environment

- Provide hard, impervious room finish surfaces.

- Provide highly irregular surface textures (i.e., not large, flat, and planar).

- Distribute sound reflecting and absorbing materials (if they exist) judiciously throughout the space of concern.

Typical shapes, textures, and modulations that diffuse and scatter sound include:

- Convex curves
- Chevrons
- Ribs
- Irregular splays

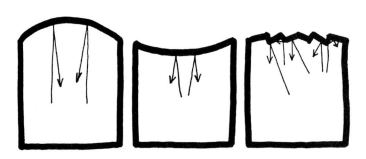

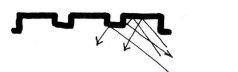

▼ Acoustical shaping of architectural surfaces can diffuse and scatter sound energy.

Imagination and a good design sense are necessary to satisfactorily coordinate and integrate sound diffusion into the architectural aesthetics of a space.

Sound diffusion is frequency sensitive. Surface modulations of 12 in. and less diffuse high-frequency sound energy. Surface modulations of 12 in.–4 ft diffuse mid-frequency sound energy. Diffusion of low-frequency sound energy requires surface modulations greater than 4 ft.

A loud environment

Definition
Provides sound at a sufficient pressure level so that the listener does not have to strain to hear well.

Acoustical criteria
Sound pressure level (Lp) = 85 dBA

Architectural consideration
Thick, hard, massive, sound-reflective interior finishes.

How to get a "loud" environment

- Use hard, impervious, massive room finish surfaces.
- Provide close-in surfaces near the origin of sound and the listeners.
- Minimize the room volume.

Note: Be careful: Reducing room volume can also reduce reverberation. A careful balance, appropriate to the intended criteria, must be achieved.

A spacious environment

Definition
Provides sound that envelops the listeners and increases their perception of spaciousness.

Acoustical criteria
- Lateral energy fraction (LL) = 0/–3

- Lateral energy fraction is defined as the ratio of sound energy that arrives at a listener from outside the immediate frontal direction.

Architectural consideration
Sound-reflective surfaces located close to and along the sides of a space that capture sound energy and redirect it to the listeners from a lateral (sideways) direction.

How to get a "spacious" environment

- Provide reflecting surfaces that will direct sound energy toward the listeners, predominantly from the sides, creating a multidirectional effect.
- Carefully balance the amount of sound directed toward the audience from the front (mono) versus the amount from the sides (stereo). Large overhead panels or clouds alone would direct sound energy frontally.
- Provide enough volume for sound energy to envelope the listener.
- Provide the ingredients for a live, diffuse, loud environment, as previously noted.

A uniform environment

Definition
Provides sound that is distributed evenly throughout a space (audience seating areas) without hot or dead spots.

Acoustical criteria
Sound pressure level (Lp) = ±2 dB throughout the audible frequency range.

Architectural consideration
Properly located and shaped wall and ceiling surfaces to direct sound energy evenly to all seating areas.

How to get a "uniform" environment

- Carefully locate and shape room boundary surfaces, especially near the origin of sound, to distribute sound energy evenly throughout the listening/seating area.
- Avoid severe imbalances of room finish materials (e.g., a highly efficient, large area of sound-absorbing material on one side of a room, and a highly sound reflective surface on the opposite side of a symmetrical room).
- For sound systems, orient loudspeakers to direct sound energy evenly to all listeners/seating areas. The proper type and height of loudspeakers is important to avoid overpowering the front rows and underpowering the rear rows.

Clear, powerful, amplified sound

Definition

Electroacoustic sound and clear, unencumbered listening conditions for performers, audience, and technicians. Special requirements for older people (e.g., with loss of high frequency hearing) and diverse ethnic cultures (e.g., with language difficulty) must be considered.

Acoustical criteria

Same as many other criteria mentioned earlier.

Architectural consideration

Provide adequate space and coordinate the integration of the required systems components (loudspeakers, projectors, etc.) in their proper locations.

How to get a clear, powerful, amplified sound

- Strive for improved, high-quality audio.
- Ensuring good acoustic qualities in a space (i.e., through its size, shape, and room finish treatments) will help to achieve a high degree of clarity and intelligibility from a sound system, because the two are directly related.
- Use state-of-the-art, professional-quality audio equipment that is reliable and durable and offers peak performance.

Audio systems typically include:
- Speech amplification/reinforcement
- Playback of recorded material
- Sound monitoring
- Production paging and monitoring
- Technical communications
- Recording
- Broadcasting
- Sound effects
- Teleconferencing

Systems design should provide for maximum flexibility, portability, and/or future installation where costs prohibit complete initial installation.

Because humans have two ears, one on each side of the head, they are more sensitive to distinguishing sound in the horizontal plane (left and right) and less sensitive to sound in the vertical plane. Therefore, to obtain directional realism for a live talker, it is best to locate speech reinforcement loudspeakers above rather than to the sides.

ARCHITECTURAL (SPACE AND AESTHETIC) CONSIDERATIONS FOR AUDIO

A complete functioning audio system consists of loudspeakers, microphones, amplifiers, wiring, equipment racks, and many other electronic components. Often, the focus of attention is solely on the loudspeakers because they are highly visible.

Loudspeakers

Loudspeakers must be accommodated in the main worship space. Because the critical relationship between the loudspeakers and the auditors is a direct line of sight, there is an aesthetic issue. Typically, the larger the space, the larger the loudspeakers or the more of them are required to provide uniform coverage of the seated congregation. Attempting to make the loudspeakers disappear visually is unrealistic.

Technical performance must dominate. To make the loudspeakers inconspicuous is a formidable challenge, involving close coordination of the interior design of the worship space. Under specific conditions (usually dictated by the architecture of the space in question), each loudspeaker system may be appropriate on its own or in combinations. The more common loudspeaker types include the following:

- Single, center loudspeaker cluster: provides directional realism and good coverage; can be large and visually dominant
- Multiple (right-center-left) loudspeaker clusters: high power, broad range; very large and visually dominant
- Line array loudspeakers: often easy to integrate with worship architecture; provides high clarity and focused sound coverage

- Distributed overhead ceiling loudspeakers: limited-power handling capability for large spaces; lacks directional realism
- Pew back loudspeakers: small, unobtrusive; good for speech quality in a reverberant space; limited frequency and power-handling capability

Control Room

Audio system electronics have to be housed in equipment racks in a sound control equipment room. An equipment rack is approximately 24" × 24" in plan and 7 ft in height. It is not uncommon for control rooms to house many equipment racks: one or two for small systems, four to eight for large systems. Clearance of 3 ft should be provided at the front of each rack for operation, and 3 ft of clearance at the back of the rack for installation, maintenance, and service. The location of each piece of equipment in the rack is important from a technical and operational standpoint. Gauges and operating lights must be visible and easy for the operator to reach.

Operator's Position

A sound control operator's position should not be confused with the sound equipment room, although the two should be located close to each other. The person who operates the sound system should be in the same space as the auditors, not in a separate room, disengaged from the main worship space. Direct line of sight to the main loudspeakers is mandatory; line of sight to the congregants (pastor, priest, lecturers, etc.) and musicians, as well as most of the ceiling and wall surfaces within the room, is desirable.

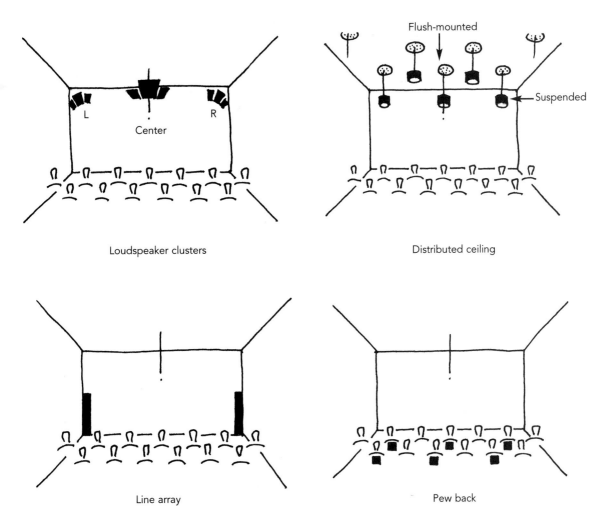

Loudspeaker clusters

Distributed ceiling

Line array

Pew back

▲ *Loudspeaker types.*

The sound system operator requires a console to control individual microphones and to process and mix the resulting combined sound signals before sending them to the loudspeakers via the output of the mixer. Although most of the support equipment can be in a remote sound control room, some electronic equipment, usually located in small, half-height racks located under the console and counter, must be close to the operator. The sound control operator's position can take up the equivalent depth of approximately three rows of seating, and sometimes a width equivalent to four to six seats (approximately 100 sq ft).

Provisions for Disabled Persons

The main provisions for persons with hearing disabilities are signing, closed captions, and assisted listening systems. Some worship facilities offer signing as a ministry for at least one or more of their

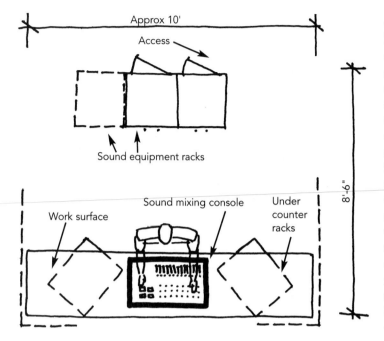

Approx 10'

Access

Sound equipment racks

8'-6"

Work surface

Sound mixing console

Under counter racks

▲ *Sound control operator's position.*

work properly, IR requires an unencumbered direct line of sight between the receiver and the emitter. The system is relatively expensive, has a limited range of coverage, and is prone to potential dead spots. An RF system is not subject to interference from nearby or stray frequencies and can work even outside the walls of the worship space that it is monitoring. It has become the system of choice for most designers of worship space systems because it can also be used for overflow spaces and for others who may want to monitor a service from a remote space within the building. For any assisted listening system, the primary maintenance procedures are replacing batteries and sanitizing the earpieces, which must be carefully followed. For either system, the minimum number of headsets that should be provided is 4 percent of the total capacity of the worship space. Assisted listening systems can have multiple channels and can be used to accommodate multiple languages.

services. Signing utilizes an individual (or more than one person, taking turns) skilled in sign language to visually transcribe the spoken word and songs to members of the congregation who have hearing difficulties. Signers are ususually located at the front and to the side of the worship space.

Closed captions are textual transcriptions (or translations, if multilingual), superimposed on a projection screen or special signage board, of the spoken word and songs.

An assisted listening system is an electronic system, typically using a headset, that serves as an aid to those whose hearing is impaired. The two most popular types of assisted listening systems are infrared (IR) and radio frequency (RF) systems. An infrared system typically has the receiver built into the headset. To

AUDIOVISUAL CONSIDERATIONS

All worshipers must have a direct line of sight to any projected images. This includes congregants and musicians. The size and location of a projected image is extremely important. The rule of thumb for determining screen size is that the height of the image must be at least one-eighth times the distance from the image to the farthest viewer (seat); this dimension is one-sixth if small printed content or computer data are to be viewed. The width of the screen is determined by prescribed standard formats based on the source material. The ratio of an image's width to its height is known as its aspect ratio. Typical aspect ratios (W:H) are given in the table at right.

Aspect Ratio

For standard video projections within a worship space that is 80 ft in length, the projection screen surface should be at least 13 ft 6 in. in width and 10 ft in height (W:H = 1.33 × 10; 13.5:10).

The screen must be located high enough that all viewers can see the bottom without any of the projected material being occluded by other audience members, choir, orchestra, or other architecture elements. Viewers must also be able to view the top of a screen without straining vertically. The closest viewers should be no closer than two times the height of the screen.

For very wide spaces, or where the horizontal line of sight is occluded, two screens may be provided, one on each side of the platform, stage, or altar area. Movable, decorated doors can be provided to cover the screens when video projection is not in use.

Projection Screens

Projection screen material can vary, depending on whether the system includes front or rear projection. Front projection materials can be stretched on a frame and permanently mounted or, more typically, electrically operated and retracted on a cylinder, out of sight when not in use. Rear screen projection surfaces typically consist of a fixed, solid, translucent, light-diffusing glass surface.

Because front projection is based on reflected projected light, maximum viewing clarity requires the ambient room light to be extremely dark, which results in high contrast of the projected image.

Rear projection can produce a good viewing image with a higher ambient light level in the main sanctuary space. With the projector located behind a

ASPECT RATIOS		
Format	**W**	**H**
Television and computer display	1.33	1.0
35 mm slides	1.49	1.0
High-definition television (HDTV)	1.78	1.0

fixed, translucent, coated, light-diffusing window surface, the noise from the fan, integral with the projector, does not impact the listening environment for worshipers in the sanctuary. In addition, there is no distracting shadow cast on the screen by those in front of the projected image. Adequate space, typically a separate room, must be provided behind the image for rear screen projection. The depth of the room should be approximately 1.5 times the width of the screen for the best direct projection. Reflective mirror systems are helpful in reducing the depth needed for rear projection, but

▼ *Contemporary multimedia worship spaces often have multiple projection screens and a very sophisticated sound system.*

they make the focusing of the projector more difficult, collect dust, and can add undesirable aberrations resulting from the folded optics and multiple reflection path of the projected image.

EMERGING TRENDS

The emerging trends in acoustics involve the use of electronics for room acoustical analysis. In addition, sophisticated computer-controlled audio system designs are using electronically "steerable" digital directivity control (DDC) line array loudspeakers. These loudspeakers can maintain a high level of focused direct sound in a very reverberant space. The loudspeaker produces a coverage pattern that is extremely narrow vertically and very broad horizontally. When placed on the floor, the loudspeaker's center of acoustic gravity is slightly above seated head height. These loudspeakers are very tall (often 10 ft or 16 ft in height), but narrow and thin (e.g., 12 in. wide and 4 in. deep), making them less visually obtru-

sive than most other types. Some recent experience indicates that the clarity is so good with DDC loudspeakers that the reinforced sound no longer sounds "natural" for a reverberant worship space. At the request of the owners, additional low-frequency energy has been boosted in some systems (via sub-woofer loudspeaker units) to create more "fullness" to increase the perception of reverberation expected in a worship space.

Digital technology is also available to electronically simulate almost any type of acoustical environment. These systems are best used in an acoustically dead environment, where the listener's aural perception can be totally controlled by the electronically enhanced sound system. Full surround sound, reproducing the expected reflected sound energy patterns from nonexistent architectural surfaces, can further enhance the listening environment.

Computer modeling technology is becoming increasingly sophisticated and easier to use. Programs are available that allow a consultant to develop numerous alternative acoustical designs during the design process, so that one will not have to wait until the worship space is built in order to know what it will sound like. Modeling programs are continually being refined. Architectural computer-aided design (CAD) programs are being integrated into acoustical consulting analysis programs. Some programs can be used for room acoustical analysis and sound system design.

Architects, along with structural engineers, will undoubtedly continue to create exciting, imaginative structures with grand, soaring interior spaces for worship. The tendency to use smooth, hard, sound-reflective materials (e.g., concrete, masonry, plaster, and glass) will

▼ *Computer modeling of sound reflections, Cathedral of Our Lady of the Angels, Los Angeles.*

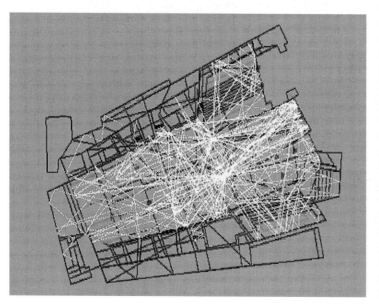

likely continue, resulting in highly reverberant spaces. Herein lies the opportunity for a new set of electro-acoustic solutions. Technological advances can assist the acoustical consultant to analyze and solve the challenges presented by these architectural and structural concepts.

CASE STUDY: CATHEDRAL OF OUR LADY OF THE ANGELS, LOS ANGELES

Acoustical Challenges

The Cathedral of Our Lady of Angels faced several acoustical challenges. The size, shape, and proportions of the cathedral influenced the acoustic quality of the environment within. The 3000 seats on one level automatically set the enclosing walls at a great distance from most of the seating area, making it difficult to get useful reflected sound energy to the center seating areas in a short enough (i.e., within 50 milliseconds) time. Likewise, with the ceiling 70–90 ft above the floor, a very large volume of space was enclosed where the desired early reflected sound energy to the seated occupants was not possible. As frequently occurs on landmark projects, the preestablished architectural constraints provided a set of conditions within which the acoustical consultant had to work. (See the cover image and color plate 1.)

Reverberation Control

Reverberation in the cathedral is a function of its volume and absorption. The 3 million cu ft of volume within the cathedral is enormous. If left untreated, the midfrequency reverberation time would have been in excess of 15 seconds. For a live performing arts facility, where a high degree of reverberation is desirable, 300

cu ft per person is a rule of thumb that has proven successful. Using that same rule of thumb, a volume slightly greater than 1 million cu ft would be adequate for the cathedral. Because of the large volume within the cathedral, the distance from the congregation to the enclosing wall and ceiling surfaces, and the requirement for clear, articulate speech, strategically placed sound-absorbing materials were needed to reduce the midfrequency reverberation time to approximately 3.5 seconds, a compromise between the optimum for speech and the optimum for music. This requirement was confirmed with a computer model auralization study early in the design process. This identified a number of surfaces that caused echo paths and long-delayed reflections that would be acoustically poor if left hard and sound reflective.

▼ *The rear wall of the sanctuary above the baptistery: acoustically transparent and sound diffusing.*

▶ *The proposed choir canopy.*

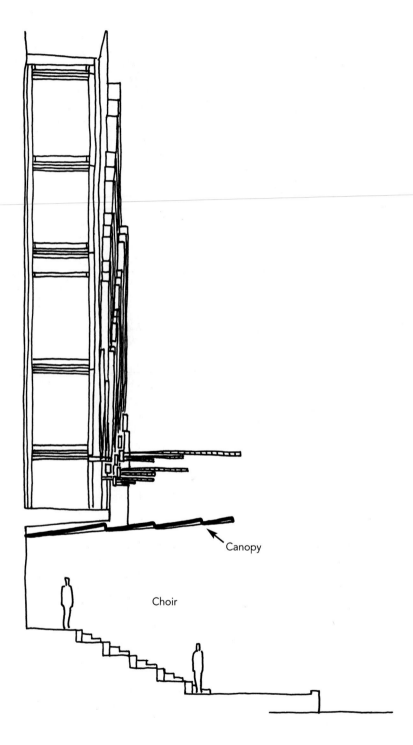

Canopy

Choir

In addition to using sound-absorbing material above a portion of the wood slat ceiling, the concept to use some heavy, dense fabric tapestries depicting the Communion of the Saints along the sidewalls of the Cathedral was developed to minimize undesirable long-delayed sound reflections. In critical locations (e.g., the transepts), large sound-diffusing elements were introduced to help scatter the sound energy being reflected within the sanctuary. These devices allowed the reverberant quality of a cathedral sound to be maintained, while reducing the undesirable long-delayed reflections that reduce speech intelligibility. (See color plates 1 and 4a.)

Some unusual problems

One of the more interesting acoustical solutions to a potentially serious problem involved the rear wall of the sanctuary. Originally, the rear wall was a large, solid concrete surface. If left untreated, this surface would emit very annoying long-delayed echoes to the front seating areas and chancel. The acoustical solution involved opening the rear wall to the baptistery, where sound-absorbing materials were employed. Sound from the sanctuary passes through the rear wall and is absorbed in the baptistery. The remaining slatted rear wall surfaces in the sanctuary are angled to diffuse and scatter any sound energy that impinges on them.

Another acoustical and architectural challenge involved the choir, located immediately below the organ. There were never enough close-in sound-reflecting surfaces surrounding the choir to provide adequate acoustical "envelopment" of sound energy, which is desirable for singers to feel sonically comfortable. An overhead sound-reflecting canopy was

▲ Major traffic arterial alongside the cathedral.

designed to help the ensemble within the choir and to help project the sound of the choir to the congregation. At the time of completion of the cathedral, the canopy had not been installed.

Control of exterior noise was critical. The new cathedral in Los Angeles is located immediately adjacent to the 101 (Hollywood) Freeway. Constant traffic all day, and all night, produces sound levels in excess of 75 dBA at the facade of the building. Where natural daylight coming into the sanctuary was desirable, a double-glazed alabaster and glass curtain wall system was developed to keep exterior traffic noise to a minimum.

Noise and vibration from the building's heating, ventilating, and air-conditioning system were also controlled to maintain a low background sound level, so that worship could occur in a peaceful and tranquil environment, free from the distracting sounds of mechanical equipment.

▶ *Typical distributed overhead loudspeaker concealed in a metal "trumpet" shaped enclosure.*

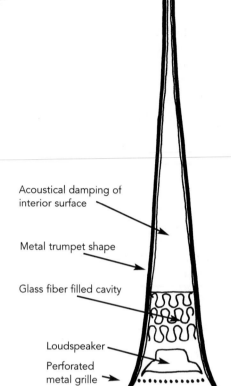

Acoustical damping of interior surface

Metal trumpet shape

Glass fiber filled cavity

Loudspeaker

Perforated metal grille ➤

Sound System

Every conceivable type of sound system available at the time was considered for the cathedral. The aesthetic desire not to have any loudspeakers visible had a significant impact on the final decision. A pew-back loudspeaker system was given high priority by the acoustical consultant; however, the final design solution was a series of distributed, full-range, overhead loudspeakers integrated with the light fixtures. To further disguise the loudspeakers, an extended trumpet shape was developed to house the required volume behind each loudspeaker.

▶ *Distributed overhead loudspeakers concealed in a metal "trumpet" shaped enclosure, integrated with the cathedral lighting system.*

CHAPTER 13
LIGHTING DESIGN

THE ROLE OF LIGHTING IN CREATING SACRED SPACE

The change of sunlight from night to day, the colorful sky of sunrise or sunset, a shaft of light penetrating storm clouds, and the warm embers of a fire are examples of dramatic light experiences. Each of these natural events can produce wonder and awe and evoke further emotional responses.

Historically, light has been a fundamental part of the faith experience, both as a symbolic representation of the beneficial deity and as a literal representation of faith. In various religions, light represents goodness, knowledge, awakening, tolerance, or other attributes of the faithful. Many religions point to light as a benefit from the deity and as a symbol of human goodness.

Lighting design for sacred spaces should inspire reflection and consideration of the human condition. Task illumination should heed the powerful symbolism and emotional power of light.

The Role of the Lighting Designer

Creating a successful lighting approach requires a collaborative design process including a lighting consultant, the architect, and the client, with consideration of both aesthetic and operational objectives.

DESIGN PROCESS

The lighting design process involves three phases: conceptual investigation, detailed design and communications, and construction of the lighting system.

The goal of the conceptual design phase should be to develop solutions to meet a list of lighting objectives. The design team defines the essential properties of light affecting the project in each discipline. Lighting intensity objectives should be reviewed and discussed in conjunction with a calendar of events.

The quality and character of light should be discussed to define the priorities and hierarchy of intensities of illumination and the symbolic design features.

Budget and scheduling objectives should be defined. The lighting designer evaluates these objectives in conjunction with the architect's plans for the building and develops conceptual lighting solutions. The lighting designer presents the solutions as sketch renderings, photos of other lighting installations, models, drawings, or other visuals to describe the intent of the design. The plans at this stage are usually very schematic and may include a rough outline of quantities and preliminary selections of fixtures and control equipment.

Next, a preliminary budget estimate is developed and design objectives and options for different solutions are reviewed.

The design team should prepare a detailed set of design documents after the client and architect have approved the conceptual lighting design approach. These documents should include complete information for purchase and installation of the lighting system, as well as the methods of coordinating the installation of the equipment to integrate it into the architectural and landscape design.

Drawings should include the following:

- Lighting plans, indicating locations and type of equipment, with switch and or dimming controls specifications

- Lighting details to show precise mounting information and any special lighting hardware requirements
- Lighting calculations confirming the lighting intensity (lux) from the specified equipment to verify appropriate lighting for specific events and activities as well as code compliance and conformances with industry-recognized standards
- Architectural reflected ceiling plans, floor plans, elevations, sections, and details, as well as landscape hardscape and softscape plans, indicating the precise locations of light fixtures in relation to the surrounding materials
- Detailed design drawings for custom-made or modified light fixtures, including elevations, sections, plans, and part details
- Specifications defining the materials to be purchased and installed, as well as the quality of execution of the fabrication and installation, as follows:
  - Lighting specifications describing the precise materials to be purchased, including any special features or accessories
  - Lighting dimming control specifications defining the equipment required and the desired control sequence for specific events

Thorough documentation can minimize construction conflicts or errors and assist in controlling cost. The participation of the lighting designer during the construction phase is also important:

- The lighting designer should actively participate in the review and approval process with the contractor and architect to ensure successful construction phase execution.
- The lighting designer should verify all alternatives proposed by the contractor or the construction manager.
- The lighting designer should review, evaluate, and supervise the installation of the equipment as well as the aiming and adjustment of the lighting instruments and controls.

DESIGN CONSIDERATIONS

In addition to the symbolic and emotional qualities of light, illumination issues for a worship space include the light required for:

- Participating in and observing a service
- Reading text of relatively low contrast and small print
- Experiencing reflective or meditative space
- Following safe paths for ingress and egress

Aesthetics and Communication

Lighting should come from light sources that enhance the character of the worship space and help to communicate the sacred ideal.

Light intensity and direction should be controlled to allow a flexible use of the space for activities ranging from meditation to celebration and musical events.

The quantity and quality of light affect both the practical function of the space and the sense of transcendence and meditation. Their objectives are often in conflict, as higher levels of light enable ease of use but are not conducive to meditation.

General Illumination Adequate for Reading

The Illuminating Engineering Society of North America (IESNA) recommended reading task illumination criteria require relatively low illuminance (as measured in footcandles or lux) for various building types, including worship spaces. Because most religious ceremonial reading materials are of low-contrast text, consisting of small to medium print, on gray or textured white paper, a medium to high level of visibility is recommended. This functional quality is best achieved with diffuse light to limit veiling reflections of the light sources on the text surface and to reduce sharp shadows. Because of the higher illuminance required for the population over 45 years of age, higher intensities generally provide the greatest comfort and ease of reading for a wide range of worshipers.

The Illuminating Engineering Society of North America provides a useful recommended range of illuminance objectives. Recommended illuminance targets are summarized in the table on page 212.

These luminance target values are *recommended* ranges. The light directionality and uniformity should be carefully considered in determining the proper light level. Note the impact of room reflectance. Higher room reflectance values associated with light-colored wall, ceiling, and flooring materials permit significantly lower light levels.

Architectural Lighting for Building Surfaces

The range of brightness on the room surfaces affects the perceived comfort and ease of use of any worship space. High-contrast spaces tend be perceived as dra-

▲ *Chapel of St. Ignatius Loyola, founder of the Society of Jesus (the Jesuits), St. Ignatius Church in San Francisco, California. General ambient lighting contributes to the spirituality of the worship space while providing sufficient lighting for reading at the pews. Lighting designer: Francis Krahe & Associates; architect: Brayton + Hughes Design Studio. Photo: Stanford Hughes.*

matic but may hinder basic reading and viewing tasks. Likewise, low-contrast spaces are typically perceived as dull or uninspired but may provide a high degree of comfort for reading and observing the widest range of activities within the space. Good practice includes a design plan for illuminating essential room surfaces to create a balance between contrast and uniformity.

Brightness is the light energy reflected back to a person's eyes from a surface. Brightness (luminance) values can be

RECOMMENDED ILLUMINANCE TARGETS

ROOM SURFACE REFLECTANCE

Area or Activity	Age of Occupants	High (>70%)	Medium (30–70%)	Low (<30%)
			Illuminance in Lux	
Simple orientation for short, temporary visits	Under 40	50	75	75
	40–55	75	75	75
	Over 55	75	75	100
Reading tasks, occasionally performed	Under 40	100	150	150
	40–55	150	150	150
	Over 55	150	150	200
Reading tasks, prolonged but simple	Under 40	200	200	300
	40–55	200	300	300
	Over 55	300	300	300
Reading tasks, prolonged and difficult	Under 40	500	500	750
	40–55	500	750	750
	Over 55	750	750	750
Accent lighting	Emphasis will be percieved when light level is more than three times the reading targets above. As the reading targets increase above 200 lux, accent lighting is less practical.			
Architectural lighting	Approximately 25 percent of the reading target illuminance above.			

objectively measured or calculated. The amount of energy a person sees is dependent on the amount and direction of the light landing on that surface and the characteristics of the surface material (its texture, color, density, etc.), which affect the amount and direction of the light reflected back to the eye. Dark materials absorb light; light-colored materials reflect light. Polished surfaces reflect sharp light-source images; textured or honed surfaces diffuse the source image and scatter light in many directions.

Contrast is the difference between the surface brightness of two adjacent or simultaneously viewed surfaces or objects. We usually view one object or surface as primary and the other as secondary, based on their relative brightness, with our focus on the higher brightness. Our

eyes begin to sense contrast as the brightness ratio exceeds 3:1.

If a space can be described as relatively uniform, then the contrast of surface brightness would be less than 4:1 or 5:1. Uniform brightness is effective for lighting the congregation or areas of multiple uses where a flexible layout of furniture would be desired. Higher contrast is useful to define focus and draw attention from a distance.

Careful study of focal surfaces (surfaces to receive the most light) should consider the appropriate relationship of the building architecture to the celebrant and the congregation. Accent lighting for architectural forms should range from a mid to low level of brightness, with the highest brightness reserved for the liturgical icons. The nave ceiling, walls, choir loft, or organ may present ideal surfaces for accent lighting. However, the design scheme should select one or a few of these components to feature, leaving the others in relatively low light to serve as foils.

Accent Lighting for Liturgical Elements

Light defines a hierarchy of the liturgical components (altar, ambo, ark, bimah, *minbar*, etc.) within the worship space. Prominence is created through contrast, with the highest brightness focused on the most significant components and a descending order of brightness corresponding to their order in the liturgy. Uniform light renders all components equal at long viewing distances (i.e., from the back of the worship space), higher contrast will make the focus easier to see. Extreme contrast (greater than 10:1) should be avoided to prevent fatigue and eye strain. Therefore, there is a relatively limited range of recommended contrast values, from a minimum of 3:1

▲ The high-intensity lighting on the statue of St. Ignatius and the reading desk, in contrast with the lower intensity of the surrounding area, appropriately accentuates these elements. Lighting designer: Francis Krahe & Associates; architect: Brayton + Hughes Design Studio. Photo: Stanford Hughes.

RECOMMENDED CONTRAST RATIOS

ROOM SURFACE REFLECTANCE

Area or Activity	High (>70%)	Medium (30–70%)	Low (<30%)
	Illuminance in Lux		
Leadership position	5	7	9
Supporting clergy	4	6	7
Choir	3	4	4
Congregation	1	1	1
Accent lighting	Emphasis will be percieved when light level is more than three times the reading targets above. As the reading targets increase above 200 lux, accent lighting is less practical.		
Architectural lighting	0.25	0.25	0.25

to a maximum of 10:1. Recommended contrast ratios are summarized in the table on page 213.

The key objectives are to link the congregation and the celebrants or participants and to order the supporting elements within the service. Individual faiths and communities have varying views of the appropriate organizational hierarchy. This ordering should be clearly defined in the design program.

The direction and color quality of light also affects the sense of prominence and visibility. Accent lighting is most effective when directed toward the target object (altar, ambo, etc.), whereby the light is reflected back to the viewer. At the same time, these accent sources should not obscure or diminish the visibility of the celebrant or participant at the direct location. Generally, the most effective accent light is directed toward the target from above, with multiple locations, in front and to the sides above, 30–55 degrees in plan view, and 40–60 degrees vertically. The diagram on page 215 describes this targeting approach.

LIGHT SOURCES

Light is generated by:

- Incandescent lamps
- Halogen lamps
- Fluorescent lamps
- High-intensity discharge lamps
- Light-emitting diodes

Light sources vary by the methods used to generate the light, all of which which affect:

- Size and shape
- Color of light produced
- Lamp life
- Energy consumed
- Heat produced
- Noise level

Incandescent bulbs are the most common and least efficient lamps, and usually most costly to maintain because of their short life. They offer the advantages of warm, accurate color tone with a continuous light spectrum and similarity to the color of light within congregation members' homes. These lamps are easily applied to the worship space and make a connection to the traditional candlelight

▼ A detail of the accented elements shows how the lighting reveals their form. Lighting designer: Francis Krahe & Associates; architect: Brayton + Hughes Design Studio. Photo: Stanford Hughes.

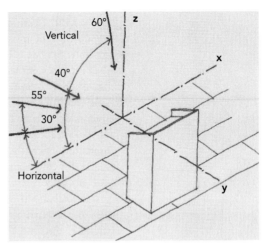

▲ Back light.

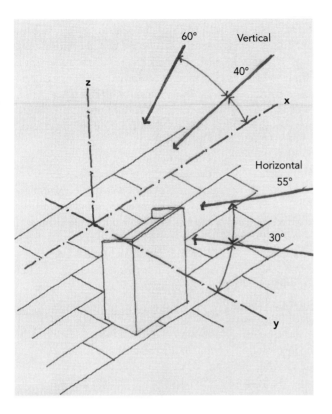

◄ Focal light.

and low-intensity lighting of historical worship spaces. Incandescent lamps last longer with dimming.

Halogen lamps are a more efficient version of incandescent lamps, with extended lamp life and a whiter, cooler color temperature. Halogen lamps are effective for accent and focal lighting because of the precise configuration of the lamp filament and the wide variety of lighting fixtures designed to take advantage of their operating characteristics.

Low-voltage incandescent lamps operate at 5.5, 12, or 24 volts, which increases the current through the lamp filament and produces a brighter source. Low-voltage lamps are also effective for focal lighting at lower ceiling heights. The required

step-down transformer may be a source of noise; electronic transformers are recommended to alleviate this problem.

Fluorescent lamps are more difficult to apply to the worship space because of their whiter color quality and the association with utilitarian facilities, such as offices. They may be dimmed with selective lamp and ballast systems, and as technologies advance, smaller and more flexible systems are becoming available. They are usually combined with indirect light systems and or translucent or colored glass components to soften and alter the color qualities. Fluorescent lamps provide long life and good energy efficiency.

High-intensity discharge (HID) lamps use a mercury or sodium arc tube to create visible light. These lamps are available in a wide range of colors and intensities and generally provide better energy efficiency than incandescent lamps with long lamp life. All HID lamps have a segmented light spectrum, which means that their color is not as consistent as that of daylight or incandescent lamps. This color limitation makes their use in worship spaces difficult, inasmuch as the light does not appear natural. HID lamps also require ballasts, which generate noise and heat. Remote locations are recommended to isolate the sound. At present, HID lamps cannot be effectively dimmed.

Light-emitting diodes (LEDs). A new technology involving the use of light-emitting diodes is developing and shows great promise for very compact, long lived (30,000–100,000 hours), power-efficient light sources. LEDs, utilizing low voltage electronic power supplies, are available in different colors, permitting their use as a decorative element. The electronic power supplies permit sophisticated control. Restricting their use as a functional light source is the fact that a white diode with an incandescent color temperature and high color rendering index (CRI) is yet to be commercially available to the lighting market. It is also difficult to produce high light levels with these sources, practically restricting their use to decorative elements and inclusion in small and special purpose fixtures. LEDs are rapidly being developed, and these restrictions on their use will soon be eliminated.

Chandeliers, Sconces, and Other Decorative Lighting

Ornamental light fixtures create lighted elements, which add scale and detail to large architectural volumes. The location of these light fixtures should be based on the desired light quality, pattern, and intensity. Chandeliers and decorative wall-mounted fixtures may allow placement of light sources at lower elevations and provide an opportunity for lighted detail. The shape and surface detail of a chandelier are good means of conveying a sense of quality.

Chandeliers may be designed to direct light down, up, or in a diffuse, radial pattern. This light distribution pattern is a key to the proper selection or design of a chandelier. Placement of the chandeliers is typically within a 1:2 to a 1:1 ratio of lateral spacing to mounting distance away from the primary illuminated surface (floor or ceiling). Earthquake codes affect the location of chandeliers. Spacing varies according to the light distribution pattern and should be verified with an illuminance calculation based on the actual photometric of the chandelier or by viewing a mock-up.

Chandeliers should also be selected to be in scale with the height and the overall volume of the space. The design detail of chandeliers or decorative lighting elements presents an opportunity to convey the architectural qualities of the building at a very small scale. Translucent materials, metal frames, and other ornamental features should be similar to the building materials, which interact with daylight (such as window frames, door details, trellises, and art panels), so that interaction of the building elements with light is similar by day and by night. (See the figure on page 208.)

Study models and mock-ups are recommended for any custom-designed light fixtures to ensure correct selection of materials and successful fabrication. Testing models will ensure the appropriate illumination levels.

STAGE AND TV LIGHTING FOR BROADCAST TV, CONCERTS, AND OTHER SPECIAL EVENTS

Lighting for broadcast TV and stage performances is a common provision in the design of new worship spaces. Such lighting can accommodate a wide range of performances and activities while integrating the equipment with the architectural design. Use of the worship space for concerts, holiday events, and broadcasts of significant ceremonies is easily achieved with a limited number of strategically placed lighting instruments. The lighting requirements for each of these events are similar, with variations in intensity and color temperature.

The challenge in broadcast illumination is to create depth in the camera view to convey a sense of proportion and scale. Contrast values are increased to create the image of depth.

Broadcast lighting requires high illuminance from the front at the focus (speaker or celebrant), good contrast with the background, fill light from side and rear, and high color temperature sources

Quartz halogen lamps and color-corrected fluorescent lamps are the recommended light sources to provide good color rendering, high light levels (30–100 fc), and angular adjustment (25–55 degrees above horizontal). Advances in camera technology can reduce the level required.

The required illuminance values vary with the type of broadcast equipment. Recommended values are stated in *IESNA's Recommended Practices* as 30–350 fc and a contrast ratio not to exceed 1:25.

Soft, diffuse light is recommended for modeling the celebrants. Hard light with sharp angular shadows is recommended for background surfaces to convey the detail of the setting. Contrast with the background is achieved by the interaction of light with the background color values and the surface pattern. Highly patterned surfaces may present problems for video cameras where fluorescent or other arc tube sources are present. These types of lamps cycle at 60 hertz or higher, and this variation in light wave pattern may interact with the material pattern to create strobe-effect patterns when viewed on camera. Ideal background materials are of uniform color, with medium to low brightness to present a high contrast with the foreground figures.

LANDSCAPE AND EXTERIOR BUILDING LIGHTING

A worship space should be clearly identified at night to define the building as a symbol of the faith community, identify access routes, and provide comfort and security. All exterior lighting should be designed to respect the surrounding community, with clear control to limit off-site illumination and to minimize light projected into the night sky.

Light fixtures should be placed at the primary circulation areas, such as the walkways leading from parking to the gathering space or the sanctuary. The exterior face of the entrance to the worship space should be announced with a comfortable wash of light from above or from decorative light fixtures flanking the entry. The symbolism of the lighted entrance is important to the exterior composition at night and should be a relatively bright area in comparison with the adjacent building and site lighting. This greater brightness helps identify the building entrance and assists in the comfortable transition from the interior to the exterior at night.

Walkways from the sanctuary to a parking area should be illuminated to extend the lighted area to within the parking zone. Outdoor gathering spaces may require illumination for evening events and may serve as a part of this outdoor-lighted space. Landscape lighting and wall wash lighting greatly improve the sense of quality and security. All walkway, pathway, and parking lighting should be shielded to limit the direct view of bright lamps, improve comfort, and limit sky illumination.

Code requirements often dictate a minimum value of light for paths of egress from the worship space to an area of safety on-site or to the public way. These safety values tend to be very bright and may require the addition of accent or landscape lighting to create the appropriate hierarchy of brightness.

The worship space becomes a focal point of the community when lighting is applied to the architectural form at night. Light applied to the façade or steeple can enhance the distant view and create a unique night identity for the sacred space.

ENVIRONMENTAL CONCERNS

Light trespass is unwanted illumination projected from one property to adjacent properties. All lighting within the project site should be shielded and directed down, so that the light falls within the property. Many communities have strict ordinances limiting the amount of light crossing a property line. Good design practice eliminates the possibility of light trespass through a site lighting illuminance study to confirm that the illuminance values are zero at the site perimeter. In addition, all decorative or ornamental lighting on the exterior facade or site should be limited to low-intensity

sources (less than 1000 candelas) and/or be shielded to prevent glare.

Dark Sky regulations are in force in many communities to prevent the illumination of the night sky, which obscures the view of the stars. In urban areas light pollution has overwhelmed the brightness of the stars and made observatories obsolete. To conform to the Dark Sky regulation, all exterior light fixtures should be directed down or shielded to prevent any direct light from going to the atmosphere.

Other environmental concerns with respect to lighting are the disposal of mercury-based arc tubes (which are common to fluorescent, metal halide, and mercury lamps) and sodium arc tubes (high- and low-pressure sodium lamps). For the specified lamps, the most current manufacturing and recycling techniques should be used to limit environmental damage.

MAINTENANCE CONSIDERATIONS

Lighting systems should support ease of maintenance and durability. The selection of lamps should be based on obtaining the longest life sources that meet the performance and quality objectives of the project. The life of a lamp is listed by the lamp manufacturers as the average rated life. Access to the lighting equipment for easy lamp replacement will also determine the type of lamps used. Difficult access to light fixtures may suggest the use of lamps with longer lives to reduce maintenance. The designer must make sure that there is access to all fixtures for relamping. If equipment such as a boom or scissor lift is required, the owners must be clearly informed so that they can buy the equipment or arrange for a rental.

The use of a dimming system will extend the lives of incandescent and halogen lamps substantially. A 10 percent reduction in voltage typically extends incandescent lamp life by 100–200 percent.

Light fixtures should be cleaned regularly (annually at minimum) to prevent light loss due to dust and to maintain their appearance. Group relamping is recommended to allow all lamps to begin their burn-in period simultaneously for consistent color, with clean fixtures. Group relamping also is a more efficient use of labor and scaffolding or stage equipment where access is difficult.

CONTROLS

Worship space design should include the selection of an electronic control system to provide quick adjustments of light intensity to support various events. Electronic controls allow for preset configurations for lighting—on/off or dimming—and other related systems (window shades, screens, audiovisual equipment, etc.) for specific events or services, such as weddings, concerts, normal services, meditation, and so on. A control system also allows for convenient and consistent hours of operation through an integral time clock set to turn lights off in an orderly manner and conserve energy. Control issues include the following:

- For unusual events, a manual override control may be provided. This setting should be used carefully to avoid using custom programming for all events.

- Dimming equipment should be located away from the worship space in a

ventilated, sound-isolated area. Dimmers generate heat and can be noisy.

- Control stations for adjusting light settings should be located with a clear view of the worship space.

- Special event controls systems for concerts or holiday celebrations may require a separate dimmer for temporary supplemental lighting. Space and spare capacity should be considered in the dimmer design.

- A list of day-to-day operations or events can be created to allow preset configurations for typical day or night events.

Other energy-saving systems include motion sensors and photocell controls to turn lights off when no one is present and or when the sun is bright. These control mechanisms can be integrated with the dimmer design.

▲ Nighttime view of the Cathedral of Our Lady of the Angels, Los Angeles. The glow of the internally illuminated nave windows, together with lighting on the facade and bell tower, create a nighttime identity for the Cathedral and make it a prominent landmark after dark. Design architect: Rafael Moneo; executive architect: Leo A Daly; lighting designer: Francis Krahe & Associates. Photo: Julius Shulman and David Glomb.

CHAPTER 14
FURNITURE, FIXTURES, AND ARTWORK

Religious furnishings range from the reading desk, *minbar,* or pulpit for reading and preaching, to the vessels for sanctified water and wine, to the vestments worn by the priests. The furnishings may incorporate artwork, and the building itself is often adorned with artwork in many different media.

Furnishings that include mechanical devices such as water pumps, motors, and controls are classified as equipment and described in Chapter 10.

THE ROLE OF LITURGICAL ART AND FURNISHINGS

Furnishings and artwork are a vital part of the sacred ritual, and they are important in defining the worship space as sacred. Religious images, texts, and artifacts help to signify that a space is dedicated for worship and distinguish it from the everyday world of the profane. Chapter 1 discusses the other ways in which worship spaces are made sacred.

Religious furnishings and artwork have multiple meanings. They are functional objects that are used in ritual, such as the eucharistic table and vessels used in the ritual meal. They are also icons with symbolic value, such as the altar, which for Christians is a symbol of Christ that also, as a symbol of a ritual dining table, reaffirms the identity of the congregation gathered round the table like a family. They may embody the laws of the faith in their design; for example, Roman Catholic instructions require the eucharistic vessels to be gilded on the interior if they are made from a material that can rust. They

refer back to the early beginnings of the religion. For example, the *minbar* refers to the seat from which the prophet Muhammad spoke to the people. Liturgical art and furnishings provide opportunities for teaching, such as the texts that adorn the walls of synagogues and mosques or the stained glass windows of Christian churches. In their beauty, they celebrate the glory of God; their craft shows the faith and dedication of the congregation.

DESIGN AND FABRICATION OF LITURGICAL FURNISHINGS AND ARTWORK

Procuring liturgical art and furnishings is an opportunity to use unique designs that celebrate the congregation and its surrounding community. Although there are many manufacturers of liturgical furnishings who provide catalogs of premanufactured products, their work does not offer this design opportunity and is often of

▼ *Stained glass, Chapel of St. Ignatius, Seattle, Washington. Artist: Doug Hansen; architect: Steven Holl.*

▲ Bronze doors, Cathedral of Our Lady of the Angels, Los Angeles. The 20 ft high inner doors that are opened every day are set in a larger 30 ft high pair of doors. The whole assembly weighs more than 25,000 lb. Manifestations of the Virgin from many cultures, and ancient symbols from different faiths at an appropriate height for touching, are framed by a representation of the tree of life. Artist: Robert Graham; design architect: Rafael Moneo; executive architect: Leo A Daly; liturgical consultant: Rev. Richard S. Vosko. (See also color plate 4b.)

inferior quality to custom-made pieces. There are three different approaches to procuring liturgical art and furnishings.

The architect, working closely with the congregation and its liturgical advisors, may oversee the design of the elements such as stained glass, doors, the baptismal font, the reading desk, or the *minbar* and administer the contract for their fabrication and installation. The advantages of this approach are as follows:

- It ensures that the design of the whole building springs from a single aesthetic vision. (See color plates 14 and 16.)

- It simplifies the process by giving the congregation a single point of responsibility for the design of the entire project.

This process does require the architect to be knowledgeable in the details of the liturgy and the tradition of liturgical art.

The congregation may engage a liturgical designer who designs all the furnishings such as the altar, the font, the *minbar,* the ark, the vessels, and the vestments. The advantages are as follows:

- The liturgical designer is an expert in the field, familiar with the detailed requirements of the liturgy.

- The furnishings will form a unified design, which can be successful, provided the designer is sympathetic to the aesthetic intent of the architecture.

- The liturgical designer provides a third voice in the discussion about design and may help to articulate the concerns of some members of the congregation.

Individual artists and artisans may develop each of the groups of furnishings, such as metalwork, glass, or woodwork, under the supervision of the architect or liturgical art consultant. The advantage is that this approach celebrates the diverse talents of the community's artisans. However, there are some dangers in this approach:

- The risk of creating a visual cacophony

- The substantial commitment of time required of the congregation, the architect, or the liturgical consultant to successfully manage several contracts with diverse artists

The integration of the arts and furnishings procurement into the project schedule is discussed in Chapter 2.

MATERIALS FOR RELIGIOUS ART

Spaces for worship may be adorned with artwork in a wide variety of media:

- Bronze, for sculpture, doors, wall panels, and candleholders
- Stained glass for windows, interior backlit panels, and door lights
- Wood carving for sculpture, furniture, doors, and paneling
- Stone carving for sculpture and lettering
- Painting
- Mosaic
- Tapestry
- Cast plaster, concrete, and resin for sculpture, medallions, and reliefs
- Wrought iron for screens, doors, and candleholders

There are a number of important factors for worship space planners to consider:

- All sculpture should be adequately supported and carefully anchored to guard against theft. In earthquake zones the structural engineer should advise on structural support and attachments to resist seismic forces.
- Stained glass is produced by a variety of techniques. For instance, colored glass is cut into pieces that are held in place by lead cames or copper foil, iron oxide paints may be applied to the glass and fused by firing at high temperature, or these techniques may be used together. Other techniques such as sandblasting, etching, and silk-screening can be combined with traditional craft to create contemporary designs.
- Congregations will want to protect their investment in stained glass against vandalism or accidental damage by covering it with laminated glass or lexan sheets. Care must be taken to allow ventilation between the layers of glass, otherwise the stained glass may be damaged by overheating.
- Tapestries and seasonal draperies must usually be treated with a fire-retardant to meet the code-required flame spread rating for assembly spaces.

CHRISTIAN WORSHIP
The Altar

The altar should be freestanding and should rise directly from the floor of the sanctuary, allowing the celebrants to move freely around it. It should be of an appropriate size in relation to the scale of the building and the number of concelebrants who may be using it. The shape of the altar should reflect the way the congregation is arranged around it. Because most contemporary forms of Christian worship emphasize the congregation gathered around the altar, the altar should be almost square in plan, should not appear to have a front, back, or sides, and should not appear as a counter separating the celebrant from the congregation (Giles 2000, p. 183).

In the Catholic tradition, a church should have a single, fixed altar, made from a solid, dignified, and well-crafted material. "A dignified table of noble proportions and of beautiful materials" (Mauck 1990, p. 82). Ideally, the altar should be of natural stone, because it represents Jesus Christ, the Living Stone (1 Peter 2:4), although wood and other materials may also be used. In the case of

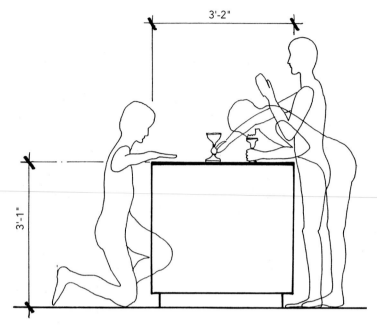

3'-2"

3'-1"

▲ Altar section, showing
desirable heights.

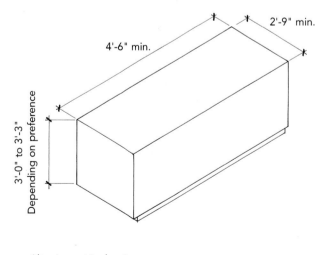

4'-6" min.

2'-9" min.

3'-0" to 3'-3"
Depending on preference

▲ Altar, isometric showing
range of dimensions.

renovated churches, altars that are hard to move and are no longer appropriate to the functioning of the church may be left in place and a new altar consecrated (National Conference of Catholic Bishops 2000b).

The altar must be big enough to hold the book of service and the sacred vessels. Although an appropriate size for a parish church might be 6' × 4', a cathedral altar may be as big as 10' × 8'. The height should be designed for use by a standing celebrant, with the surface 39–40 in. from the floor. Some liturgical designers believe the altar should be lower, to emphasize the Eucharist as a celebratory meal, in which case the book may be supported on a cushion or lectern for ease of reading. The surface of the altar is left as natural material and not decorated, but the base is frequently decorated with religious iconography. (See color plate 4 and the plans on page 39.)

In the Catholic tradition, relics of saints or martyrs may be placed under the altar, in which case a pocket must be left in the floor to allow the relics to be inserted during the consecration. Relics are no longer set into the altar itself (National Council of Catholic Bishops 2000a, p. 15).

The Pulpit, Lectern, or Ambo

The design of the pulpit allows for the reader or preacher to be seen by the congregation, but at the same time it must permit those with disabilities to read and preach. An adjustable-height reading surface allows use by standing readers and those in wheelchairs. The pulpit should be provided with a discrete reading light and microphone. (See the photograph on page 93.)

Seating

Pews have a quality that is distinct from everyday seating; they make clear that the church is not a conference room or a theater but a house of God. They have the following advantages:

- They are exceptionally durable and easy to clean.

- They provide a flexible space for seating that can accommodate families with children, as well as coats and purses.

- They can easily be fitted with kneelers and book racks.

- With modification, pews can accommodate a sloped floor, and they can be upholstered to provide greater comfort and acoustic absorption.

Pews also have certain disadvantages:

- They are immovable and cannot be relocated for different layouts of the assembly or rituals such as baptism and weddings that require more open space around the font and altar, respectively.

- They are usually confined to straight-line layouts, although they can be designed to follow curved plans but at a dramatically increased cost.

Although architects and liturgical designers sometimes develop custom-designed pews, manufacturers can provide good-quality standard pews at a reasonable price. There is also a market in second-hand refurbished pews. Contractors who specialize in pew restoration can provide contacts.

Movable seating, consisting of chairs with upholstered, rush, or wood seats and backs, provides an adjustable layout to accommodate special liturgies or

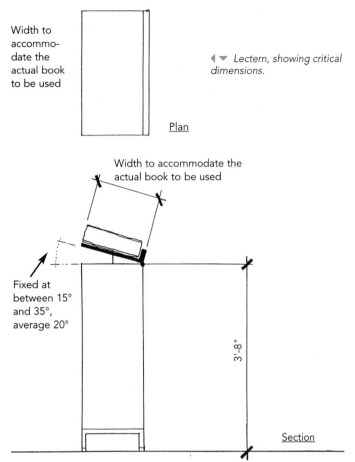

Width to accommodate the actual book to be used

Plan

Lectern, showing critical dimensions.

Width to accommodate the actual book to be used

Fixed at between 15° and 35°, average 20°

3'-8"

Section

changes in the congregation size and may be removed to allow the space to be used for other functions. Chairs are frequently used in conjunction with pews to provide overflow seating and alternate arrangements in open spaces without pews around the font and altar. If specially designed, they can accommodate book racks and kneelers; they should be ganged together to satisfy fire codes. The disadvantages of chairs are that they are easily damaged with use and moving, and they require a flat floor. A storage room is required for chairs that are to be

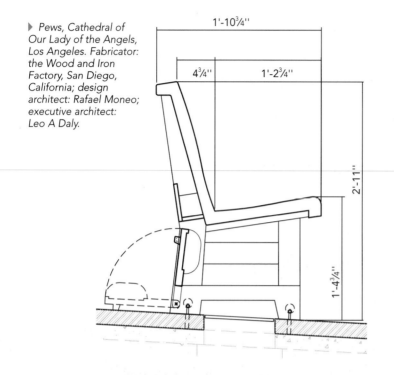

▶ *Pews, Cathedral of Our Lady of the Angels, Los Angeles. Fabricator: the Wood and Iron Factory, San Diego, California; design architect: Rafael Moneo; executive architect: Leo A Daly.*

removed; most contemporary church chairs can be stacked on specially designed carts for efficient transportation.

Ceremonial seating is usually provided in the sanctuary or on the bema for the wardens, elders, priests, or celebrants. In Anglican, Episcopal, and Catholic cathedrals, the archbishop occupies a special seat or *cathedra*. This ceremonial seating is an opportunity for the architects or furniture designers to create furniture similar in color and material but grander in scale than the congregation seating. Plenty of good-quality manufactured ceremonial chairs are also available.

Fixed, theater-style seating provides an efficient and compact layout that adapts well to a curved layout and sloped floor to provide excellent sight lines in large assemblies. The seating is commercially manufactured for theaters and auditoriums and may be modified to provide book racks. Because of the difficulty of attaching kneelers, it is not recommended in churches where the assembly kneels for prayer. Theater-style seating is usually upholstered and provides a similar level of acoustic absorption as a seated person, so the acoustics of the space remain the same regardless of the size of the congregation.

Theater seating is available from manufacturers in a wide range of styles and quality. The manufacturers' in-house designers will generally provide layouts that maximize the seating capacity and take into account fire codes and access for persons with disabilities.

See Chapter 5 for requirements for handicapped access and emergency escape in case of fire.

◀ *Pews, Cathedral of Our Lady of the Angels, Los Angeles. Design architect: Rafael Moneo; executive architect: Leo A Daly.*

◀ Chairs, Notre Dame de la Pentecôte, Paris. When the chairs are spread further apart, the top surface of each chair hinges over to span onto the adjacent chair, creating extra seating for major festivals. Architect: Franck Hammoutène.

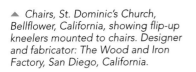

▲ Chairs, St. Dominic's Church, Bellflower, California, showing flip-up kneelers mounted to chairs. Designer and fabricator: The Wood and Iron Factory, San Diego, California.

▲ Celebrant's seating, Cathedral of Our Lady of the Angels, Los Angeles. Designer and fabricator: Jefferson Tortorelli.

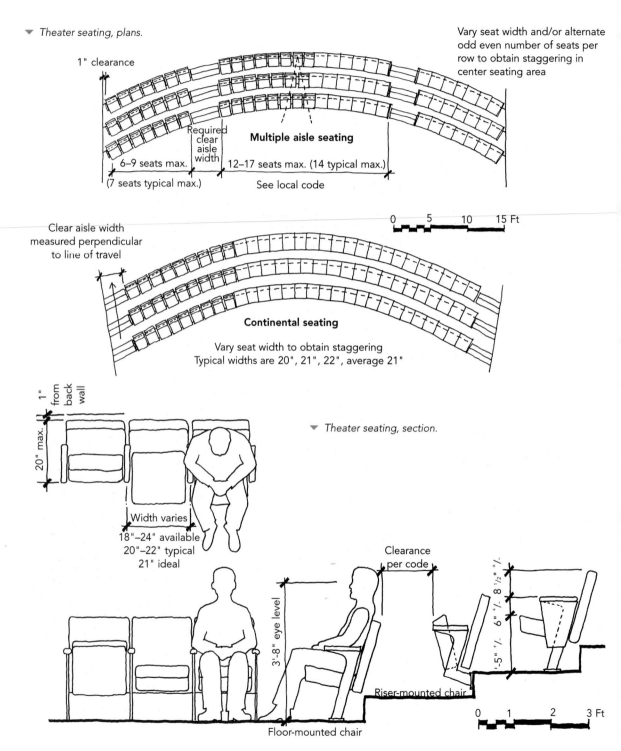

▼ Theater seating, plans.

Vary seat width and/or alternate odd even number of seats per row to obtain staggering in center seating area

1" clearance

Required clear aisle width

Multiple aisle seating

6–9 seats max.
(7 seats typical max.)

12–17 seats max. (14 typical max.)
See local code

0   5   10   15 Ft

Clear aisle width measured perpendicular to line of travel

Continental seating

Vary seat width to obtain staggering
Typical widths are 20", 21", 22", average 21"

1" from back wall

20" max.

▼ Theater seating, section.

Width varies
18"–24" available
20"–22" typical
21" ideal

Clearance per code

8 1/2" +/-
6" +/-
5" +/-

3'-8" eye level

Riser-mounted chair

Floor-mounted chair

0   1   2   3 Ft

Other Furnishings for Catholic Worship

Stations of the Cross. Plaques, mosaic panels, bas-reliefs, or paintings, depicting the events experienced by Jesus on the way to his crucifixion, are arranged in order around the nave or another space, or sometimes on the outside of the building. The practice originated with the desire of pilgrims returning from the Holy Land to be able to repeat their tracing of Jesus' journey to crucifixion along the Via Dolorosa. Members of the congregation may ritually process around the stations to the accompaniment of prayers.

Devotional shrines. Statues, bas-reliefs, or paintings of the patron saints of the congregation may be housed:

- In individual chapels
- In the main worship space or the narthex (entrance foyer)
- Outside in the church precinct

Each shrine inside the building should be provided with a kneeler and a candle rack. Although low-smoke candles are available, shrines need ventilation directly to the outside to remove heat and smoke from burning candles.

The tabernacle. The tabernacle contains the host that has been consecrated in the Eucharist. In contemporary Catholic worship it is conveniently placed for individual devotion in a separate chapel or on a secondary altar in the nave. Locations for the tabernacle are discussed in detail in Chapter 3.

Although the container, or ciborium, in which the host is kept measures only a few inches square, the tabernacle should be scaled to have a presence in the space in which it is housed. Key dimensions are shown in the drawing on page 230.

▲ Devotional shrine with kneeler and candle rack: Cathedral of Our Lady of the Angels, Los Angeles. Liturgical consultant: Rev. Richard S. Vosko.

▼ Tabernacle, Holy Trinity Church, San Pedro, California.

▶ *Tabernacle section, showing dimensions.*

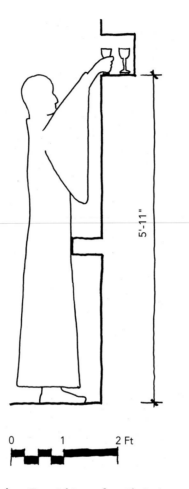

5'-11"

0   1   2 Ft

Other Furnishings for Christian Worship

The following liturgical furnishings will be required for most Christian churches:

- A processional cross
- Sacred vessels for the Eucharist
- Vestments for the priests, deacons, assistants, and, where appropriate, the choir
- Flower vases
- Seasonal hangings

All of these elements should be carefully selected as part of a coordinated design program.

JEWISH WORSHIP
Seating

Synagogue seating differs from seating in other places of worship for two reasons: The services can be very long, and on High Holy Days may last a full day, so the seats must be comfortable. Prayers may be said standing and facing the ark, which may require the congregation to turn sideways. Seating is often provided with a book rest, and in some cases the book rest is hinged to provide more room. Jews are not permitted to carry anything on the Sabbath, so each seat should contain a lockable box for the Hebrew Bible, or Torah, prayer books, and the prayer shawl and bands, the tallith and the tefillin.

These requirements are shown in the drawing on page 231.

The Ark

The ark, or *aron kodesh,* contains copies of the Torah, handwritten on parchment scrolls. Because of the time taken to roll the scroll to the right point for each of the readings in the service, several scrolls are usually kept in the ark. Each scroll is covered with a mantle and adorned with a shield and a pointer. The staves on which the scrolls are rolled are decorated with detachable silver finials, or *rimonim,* with small bells.

The ark should be designed to house at least four scrolls. It is lit internally and fitted with doors that provide security and fire protection when closed between services. The walls around the opening to the ark are decorated with inscriptions in Hebrew and often have tablets representing the Ten Commandments on either side of the opening.

The Bema

The bema accommodates a reading desk, which should be large enough to hold

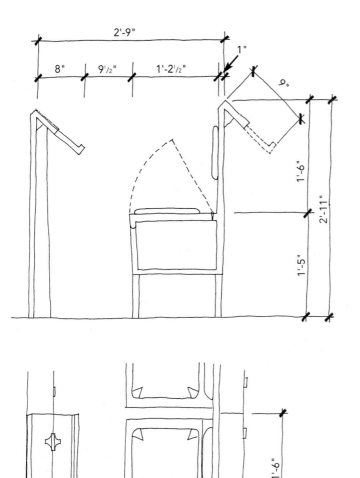

Synagogue seating, showing dimensions.

an open scroll, and seats with boxes for up to four wardens. There must be room for as many as five people to gather on three sides of the reading desk. There should also be room for holding a scroll ready to read and for wrapping one that has just been read. (See the diagram on page 56.)

Seating for the Rabbi and Cantor

A seat and box for the rabbi is provided to one side of the ark, and a seat and box for the cantor, or *chazan,* is provided on the other side.

A pulpit, from which the rabbi preaches, is placed in front of the ark on the centerline of the synagogue.

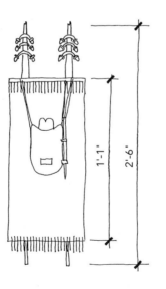

The Chupah

For weddings, the reading desk, seating, and boxes are sometimes moved out of the way so that a wedding canopy, or *chupah,* can be installed on the bema. The rabbi, the wedding couple, and as many members of the family as will fit, stand under the *chupah* during the ceremony.

The Sukkah

During the festival of Sukkoth, when Jews remember the hardship of the flight from Egypt, they are encouraged to take meals in a *sukkah,* or outside shelter. A congregation will frequently install a ceremonial *sukkah* if there is space within the synagogue precinct.

▲ *Ark, Kol Haverim Synagogue, Glastonbury, Connecticut. Architect: Arbonies King Vlock.*

▶ *Torah scrolls.*

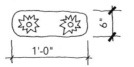

ISLAMIC WORSHIP

Because Muslims pray standing, kneeling, or prostrate, the mosque floor is carpeted, often with a pattern setting up rows oriented toward the *qibla.*

The imam preaches the sermon at the Friday *salat* from a *minbar,* or pulpit, which is a raised platform reached by a flight of steps. Although there is usually a door at the entrance to the steps and a dome or canopy over the platform, the *minbar* may be as simple as a raised platform from which the imam can see all the worshipers.

The representation of human beings is forbidden in Islamic art, but there is a rich tradition of calligraphy and geometric patterning in mosaic, bas-relief, tapestries, and stained glass. The mosque walls are usually adorned with quotations from the Qur'an in a refined and sometimes quite abstract calligraphy. See the illustration on page 9.

HINDU WORSHIP

In Hinduism, sacred sculptures are used as visual metaphors to express the invisible divine deity. Seeing the sculpture gives the worshiper *darshan,* or direct visual communication with the deity, which brings blessings to the worshiper. The deity is also understood to see the worshiper; hence Hindu images often have large eyes to help make this reciprocal vision possible.

Hindu places of worship are filled with paintings and sculpture. A sculpted image of the deity is housed in the *garbagriha,* and the processional route followed by worshipers is lined with the stories of the faith, often carved in bas-relief into the walls. The intensity of the carving rises to a crescendo at the doors of the *garbagriha,* the threshold of the most sacred zone.

▲ Minbar.

Strict rules guide sculptors and painters in the depiction of Hindu deities so that the gods and goddesses will inhabit the carving or painting. Gods take many forms, and their multiplicity is sometimes expressed by multiple arms and heads. (See the photographs on pages 138 and 139.)

233

▶ *Multiarmed Shiva dancing in the skin of the elephant demon that he has slain. Sculpture on the walls of the Hoysaleshvara temple at Halebid in Karnataka, India, 1121 C.E.*

BUDDHIST WORSHIP

Buddhist art serves to support and reinforce the truths of the religion. Because Buddhism teaches transcendence of the physical world, its art tends to be highly stylized.

A key to Buddhism's resilience over its 2500-year history is its ability to adapt to local religious practice, so Buddhist art varies widely in style. It includes both the rich and naturalistic art of India, where Buddhism was born, and the refined and abstract forms of Zen Buddhism in Japan.

Buddhist art includes representations of the Buddha and statues of the *bodhisattvas,* beings who help others in the quest for salvation.

CHAPTER 15

WAYFINDING, GRAPHICS, AND SIGNAGE

For a building complex to be inviting and easy to navigate, the design team must take into account how visitors will find their way to their destinations, a process that is called *wayfinding*. Careful layout of the site plan and the design of the individual buildings can create a natural system of wayfinding where architectural cues such as gateways, porticos, and canopies lead visitors to their destination.

A graphic signage program for a place of worship can supplement this natural wayfinding with directional signs, provide identification for various areas of the complex, and give the visitor information about the religious institution.

WHAT IS WAYFINDING?

Wayfinding is the process of reaching a destination, in either a familiar or an unfamiliar environment. Wayfinding is best described as "spatial problem solving" (Arthur and Passini 1992, p. 25).

The concept of wayfinding grew out of the study of spatial orientation, how human beings locate themselves in space. Spatial orientation relies on the development of a cognitive map, which is a mental picture of the environment, derived from many different viewpoints, that allows people to understand an environment and their position in it.

Going to the top of a tall building and studying a map to understand the layout of an unfamiliar city are examples of cognitive mapping.

There are two distinct forms of wayfinding; one is to use a global spatial understanding of the whole setting, such as the cognitive map. The other method, which does not require a global understanding of the whole environment, is to use linear sequential decision making with the aid of signs or a set of directions. Although people generally have a personal preference for one or the other, most people generally use a combination of the two methods.

How Does Wayfinding Work?

Wayfinding requires a series of processes:

- Perceiving and understanding environmental information: "There is the steeple, that must be the church."

- Decision making: "Let's go down this street, it will take us right to it."

- Execution: Walking or driving in a particular direction.

Research has shown that visitors to a new destination do not plan the entire journey in advance; rather, they work out how to get close to their destination—for example, by maps or directions—and then rely on more specific information that unfolds as they near the destination (Arthur and Passini 1992, p. 27).

These processes are repeated at a series of decision points, which form a hierarchy of wayfinding choices. For example, a visitor going to meet a priest in a large Buddhist temple complex might follow this strategy:

- Find the temple complex.
- Find the entrance to the parking.
- Find the main plaza.
- Find the offices.
- Find the priest's office.

The task of the designer is to make sure that information is clearly available at each decision point so visitors can easily reach their destination.

The Importance of Wayfinding

Wayfinding in religious buildings is important for a number of reasons:

- Visitors are often under stress: they may be coming to seek help, they may be late for a service, or they may be dealing with small children or elderly relatives. To avoid increasing their anxiety, the way to their destination should be clear and easy to find.

- Worship spaces compete with one another, and with other demands of daily life, for the congregation's attendance. To attract new membership, worship spaces must be inviting and easy to navigate. If not, new visitors can easily become frustrated by difficult wayfinding and decide not to return.

- Large numbers of people gather at places of worship. In case of an emergency such as fire, earthquake, or terrorist attack, they need to find their way to safety quickly. Sometimes the main entrance may be blocked, in which case alternate means of egress must be clear and unambiguous.

PRINCIPLES OF WAYFINDING DESIGN

Four elements make up successful wayfinding design:

1. Understanding the visitor's decision-making diagram, which will identify a series of decision points

2. Arranging the functional spaces in the environment in such a way that they are clear and easy to understand

3. Providing architectural information, such as gateways and porches that give visual clues to the visitor

4. Providing graphic information such as maps, directories, and signs, which help the visitor understand the spatial plan and provide directions to specific destinations

Decision Diagram

A decision diagram is a representation of the decisions involved in reaching a destination. The diagram identifies for the designer the decision points at which directional information is required.

For example, in a Buddhist temple complex, the decision points may be the approach to the complex, leaving the parking, in the main plaza, and at the entrance to the offices.

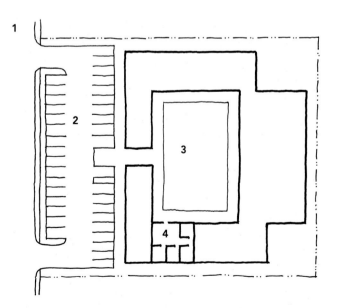

▼ *Plan of Buddhist temple complex, showing the decision points at which wayfinding information is required for successful navigation.*

Spatial Planning

The first task in spatial planning is to identify all the spaces that would be perceived by the visitor as having a common function. For example, offices, whether they are the pastor's office or those of the director of music or the volunteer coordinator, will be easiest to find if they are identified together.

Second, these spaces should be grouped into zones and each zone given its distinctive identity. For example, the child care spaces may be gathered in a separate part of the complex with their own entrance and treated with distinctive materials and colors.

For a visitor to form a clear cognitive map of a setting, it must follow a readily comprehensible pattern. There are a limited number of such patterns, which are the following:

- Linear, which may be an axis or a meandering path
- Focal
- Grid
- Hierarchical focal
- A combination of the preceding patterns

If the setting appears to be the same throughout, it will require another layer of information to make it clearly understood. For example, to provide a sense of direction in a linear plan, it is helpful if it runs up or down hill or between two landmarks, such as the entrance gate and the prayer hall. Grid layouts may run east-west and north-south and may be differentiated by numbered streets and avenues.

Landmarks can identify decision points in homogeneous layouts and help with location and orientation: "Walk down the corridor until you reach the statue of the Virgin, then turn right."

Completely symmetrical plans are confusing, because once inside the building, visitors cannot readily identify which part they are in. The designer should differentiate the various parts by design, materials, or color.

Architectural Information

Most people use architectural cues as well as graphic signs to navigate in the environment. Such cues serve two functions: to indicate a direction to a destination and to mark the destination once it is reached. For example, a dome and minarets signal the presence of a mosque and provide direction across a maze of surrounding streets; they also indicate the presence of the mosque once it is reached. Architectural elements denote their function; for example, porches and

Masjid-i-Shah, Isfahan, Iran, seen across the forecourt. Architectural elements, such as the minaret and the hierarchy of arches, provide the visitor with visual wayfinding cues.

▶ *Linear, focal, grid, and hierarchical plans.*

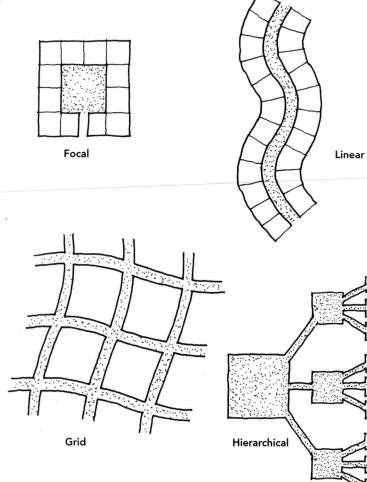

Focal

Linear

Grid

Hierarchical

▶ *Symmetrical plan. Spaces will be hard to distinguish unless marked with décor or iconography.*

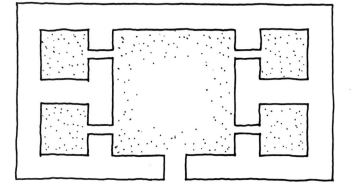

gates designate entrances, stairs and elevators designate vertical movement.

Semiology, the science of signs, stresses the importance of a common language for the meaning of a sign to be understood. For architectural elements to work as signs, they must use a readily understood architectural language. For example, Charles Jencks notes how difficult it is to identify the chapel designed by Mies van der Rohe on the campus of the Illinois Institute of Technology, because its architectural language appears at first glance to be that of the central plant building (Jencks 1977).

Graphic Information

Graphic information in places of worship serves the following functions:

- *Identification.* To identify the complex as a whole, and then identify secondary destinations within the complex, such as meeting rooms, offices, child care centers, etc.

- *Information.* To give general information about the setting, such as the layout of the site, schedules of services, names of religious leaders, etc.

- *Direction.* To provide directional information, generally using signs with arrows

- *Prohibitions and obligations,* such as signs prohibiting smoking or requiring visitors to remove their shoes

- *Code-required signage,* such as fire-exit signs, stair numbers, and bathroom and accessible entrance identification signs

On large projects, a graphic designer should be part of the design team. This design specialist develops a graphics program, which includes laying out the copy for each sign and specifying the sign loca-

tions. The graphic designer prepares design drawings for custom signs, such as monument signs and directories, reviews the contractor's shop drawings, and oversees the final installation. On smaller projects, the architect may specify the locations and copy for the signs, and a signage company with in-house designers prepares shop drawings and fabricates the signs.

▲ *Notre Dame de la Pentecôte, La Defense, Paris. At this busy intersection dominated by freeways and high-rise buildings, this church defines its presence with a powerful sign in the form of a translucent glazed wall. Architect: Franck Hammoutène. Photo: Archipress, artur.*

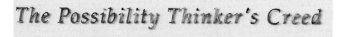

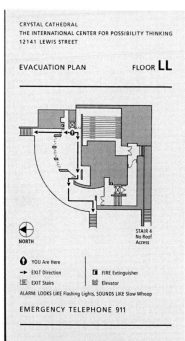

The Possibility Thinker's Creed

When faced
with a mountain
I WILL NOT QUIT !
I will keep on striving
until I climb over,
find a pass through,
tunnel underneath—
or simply stay
and turn the mountain
into a miracle,
with God's help !

▲ Crystal Cathedral,
International Center for
Possibility Thinking, Garden
Grove, California. Architect:
Richard Meier & Partners;
graphics: Follis Design.

CRYSTAL CATHEDRAL
THE INTERNATIONAL CENTER FOR POSSIBILITY THINKING
12141 LEWIS STREET

EVACUATION PLAN   FLOOR **LL**

NORTH

STAIR 4
No Roof
Access

YOU Are Here
EXIT Direction
EXIT Stairs
FIRE Extinguisher
Elevator
ALARM: LOOKS LIKE Flashing Lights, SOUNDS LIKE Slow Whoop

EMERGENCY TELEPHONE 911

IN CASE OF FIRE
USE STAIRS FOR EXIT
DO NOT USE ELEVATOR

▶ Crystal Cathedral,
International Center for
Possibility Thinking, Garden
Grove, California, code-
required signage. Architect:
Richard Meier & Partners;
graphics: Follis Design.

Principles of Graphic Design

The language used on a sign should be simple and unambiguous. The international signs for bathrooms, telephones, and so forth should be used.

The nomenclature should be consistent among the different pieces of graphic information. For example, if the title "Meeting Rooms" is used on the building directory, that area should have the same name on its identification sign and the directional signs.

The lettering should be clearly legible:

- Upper- and lowercase letters should have a height ratio of approximately 4:3.

- Stem thickness should be consistent. Some of the fonts that have good legibility are Helvetica Medium, Paladino Bold, and Frutiger Regular and Bold.

- Lettering size should be appropriate for the viewing distance. Allow 1 in. of letter height for each 50 ft of viewing distance under ideal conditions, or 1½ in. to accommodate people with weaker eyesight.

- Lettering should contrast with the background in both color and brightness. For example, white lettering on a blue background or purple lettering on a white background contrast well, whereas green lettering on a purple background does not have sufficient brightness contrast.

- Signs should be lit or should be located in places where they receive good light from existing sources.

- It helps to have the background of the sign contrast with the surrounding surfaces. Because many building surfaces are light colored, signs with light-colored letters on a dark background are most legible.

- There should not be more than five or six lines of information on a sign if it is to be viewed by a pedestrian, or three lines if it is to be viewed by a motorist.

Designers should bear in mind that visitors to places of worship may have difficulty reading and understanding signs for many reasons:

- They may be sight-impaired. The Americans with Disabilities Act (ADA) now requires the code-required and room identification signage to be written in braille as well as English. Worship spaces should consider expanding the signage for people who are impaired to include talking maps and audible directions.

- They may not speak the language in which the signs are written. A worship space may need signs in several languages to create a climate of welcome and acceptance for different ethnic groups.

- They may be illiterate and have difficulty understanding graphic signs, or they may be mentally disabled and have difficulty with wayfinding. Guides should be on hand to help those having trouble with wayfinding.

- They may be confined to wheelchairs or have difficulty walking and climbing stairs. Designers should make sure that signs are visible from wheelchair height and that they direct the visitor on a path that is accessible.

▲ Typeface showing ¾ ratio of lowercase to uppercase.

| Daycare Center ▶ |
| Parish Offices ▶ |
| Fellowship Hall ▲ |
| Teen Center ▼ |
| Café ◀ |
| Bathrooms ◀ |

▲ A sign with too many lines of type.

Temple Isaiah

Sans-serif bold

Temple Isaiah

Sans-serif italic

◀ The range of appropriate type styles.

Temple Isaiah

Roman

Temple Isaiah

Roman italic

CHAPTER 16

HISTORIC RENOVATION

THE SPECIAL SIGNIFICANCE OF HISTORIC RELIGIOUS BUILDINGS

From the dignified and dramatic spires of urban Renaissance Revival masterpieces to simple clapboard meeting houses, the nation's religious institutions inspire, calm, and ground our communities. Regardless of affiliation, many are shared places in the community, providing vital fabric for the care of those in need. Today's religious institutions often house programs in older buildings that meet human and spiritual needs with programs for families and centers for the arts. The buildings are often visual landmarks, physical reminders of the history of the area and current focal points for today's services. Preservationists use the term "sense of place" to describe the effect that a building from another time period has on today's inhabitants; no building type presents a stronger sense of place than sacred spaces.

Like other historic structures, religious buildings tell the continuing story of America's development, specifically, its history of religious tolerance and pluralism. In this building type, architectural style is not just a reflection of what was in vogue at the moment of construction. These institutions reflect their core values and spiritual beliefs in a variety of physical ways. The Quaker meeting house, for example, with its unpretentious whitewashed walls and simpler furnishings, reflects the philosophy of the Society of Friends.

The practice of worship is made visible in many ways: seating layouts, decoration, and the role of music have their physical manifestations. Historic religious spaces tell the history not only of the denomination but also of the manners and mores of its constituents through the years. Without these physical reminders of the evolution of religious tradition in America, an irreplaceable void will develop in our understanding of ourselves.

Historic sacred places are powerful. They keep us rooted in the community, embodying personal and family history and allowing us to revisit the places of baptism, marriage, and burial even after we have moved elsewhere. They resonate with memory and shared experience. Architecturally, they are often the most imposing and substantial buildings built in a neighborhood. The widespread use of stone and glass, both expensive building materials for much of this country's history, connotes the values of these buildings for their builders. They are not private; they are convening spaces. The resources of many are invested in their design, construction,

All across America, countless religious buildings tell—through their physical form and ornament—an important story about the cultural life, ethnic origins and nationalities of the peoples who have settled here. Taken as a whole, a community's churches, temples, synagogues, and meeting houses, often found within blocks of each other in a single neighborhood, express the living legacy of religious tolerance that first brought settlers to the New World more than three centuries ago.

Indeed, these religious properties are the most important physical evidence of the ethnic, racial and religious pluralism that defines our national character. They are embodiments of America's unique history.

(Cohen and Jaeger 1998)

maintenance, and continued use. As such, they evolve as needs change, liturgies are adapted, congregations shift. But they continue to provide spiritual, communal, and sometimes physical sustenance.

These sacred places are visible anchors, reinforcing the street and providing needed open space in urban areas. They are local examples of fine craftsmanship in woodwork, stone, mosaic, painting, and stained glass.

Many of America's finest architects and artists helped create the nation's sacred spaces: Louis Sullivan, James Renwick, Bernard Maybeck, Cass Gilbert, Frank Lloyd Wright, Bertram Goodhue, and H. H. Richardson. Tiffany Studios, Judson Studios, and other glass artists used their medium to ground the congrega-

tion in religious symbolism, acknowledge donors, and provide an ambience not usually found in other types of structures. Their breathtaking artistic creations produced space for contemplation, set apart from the commercialism that has marked much of American life. Today's historic religious buildings continue to provide that inspiration.

There is remarkable flexibility in these spaces of worship. Historic religious buildings are being adapted in a number of ways to serve today's populations, in both the secular and the religious arenas. The walls tell stories of significant past achievements and are home to new types of services: social services, day care, theater and art, and civic endeavors.

The caretakers of these buildings often deal with complex issues of preservation under extreme adversity. Congregations are small; money for maintenance and capital improvements is tight. Often these stewards must deal with a complex array of technical issues inherent in conservation.

Mid-Twentieth-Century Worship Spaces

Preserving examples of early modern spaces for worship has recently become critical. Many religious buildings from the 1940s through the 1960s are of great historic significance; they illustrate the use of new materials such as steel, glass, and concrete; the use of exposed structure, transparency, and free-flowing space; and floor plans that allow experimentation with new forms of liturgy.

There are particular challenges in the preservation of mid-century worship spaces:

- Relatively inexpensive and sometimes unproven new construction was used

▼ Abbey of St. John, Collegeville, Minnesota. Architect: Marcel Breuer. Photo: Lee Hanley.

for building worship spaces during the rapid growth of communities in the 1950s and 1960s. Further damaged by a lack of maintenance, buildings from this period are often in poor condition, tempting congregations to demolish and replace them.

- Postwar buildings for worship often used what were then innovative materials—reinforced concrete, concrete masonry, and glass curtain wall. Built without the benefit of recent research on longevity, they proved to be vulnerable to attack by water penetration and corrosion. Recently developed techniques for repairing and preserving concrete and metals now allow these buildings to be preserved for the future.

- Religious architecture of the 1950s and 1960s, although significant in its own right, may be stigmatized by its association with a period in history too recent to inspire affection.

Careful evaluation of the historic and architectural significance of these structures, together with outreach and education to the religious leaders and congregations, is important to avoid the potential loss of historic landmarks.

Historic Landscapes

Recent scholarship has emphasized the importance of preserving historic landscapes and the settings that frame buildings. Churchyards and cemeteries in particular are vivid historical documents that tell the story of generations of settlers, not only in the grave markers themselves but also in the trees and ground covers and in the walls, gates, and small-scale features such as curbstones and fence posts.

Historic landscapes and settings require the same level of research, identification of historic and character-defining features, evaluation, and restoration as the buildings themselves.

Types of Historic Preservation
The degree of intervention is defined by the following terms

- *Preservation.* Stabilizing a structure in its existing form by preventing further change or deterioration, which means

▲ *Church of St. Michael and All Angels, Studio City, California, 1962. Architect: A. Quincy Jones. Photo: Larry Frost, A. Quincy Jones Architecture Archive.*

245

the retention of the greatest amount of historic fabric

- *Rehabilitation.* Altering a building for an efficient contemporary use within preservation guidelines

- *Adaptive reuse.* Generally used with rehabilitation to indicate a change in use

- *Restoration.* Returning a building to the appearance it held at a particular defined period in its history by preserving materials from that period and potentially eliminating later construction

Building projects often also include the terms *modernization, renovation, retrofitting,* and *recycling;* these terms are not specific to preservation architecture and are considered too broad to be of use in defining the scope and details of a project.

▼ *A historic landscape: The Walnut Street Cemetery, Brookline, Massachusetts, one of 32 sites documented through the Massachusetts Historic Cemeteries Preservation Initiative, 1999.*

The Role of the Historic Preservation Consultant

Preservation professionals (historic architects, architectural historians, preservation engineers, and conservators) can often assist design architects and owners in determining character-defining features and materials. Although many buildings for worship are architecturally significant and have been recognized by their communities as historic, often their character-defining features and historic elements have not been accurately catalogued. To be authentic, a historic building must contain a significant amount of historic material—the actual bricks, mortar, glass, metal, and wood of its construction.

Preservation professionals also make recommendations for the buildings' continued conservation and maintenance, assist in entitlement and local design and preservation review, and locate sources of funding and incentives for preservation projects.

THE REGULATORY FRAMEWORK

Three regulatory strategies are available to preserve historic structures, sites, and districts. The first is the designation of individual buildings as historic monuments, which can occur at the national, state, or local level.

The second is the designation of a historic district at the federal or local level, which gives municipalities the right to preserve structures in historic districts and to prevent their demolition.

The third strategy is the use of a preservation easement, whereby an owner gives up in perpetuity the rights to develop property or demolish structures in exchange for a charitable donation tax credit. Such easements frequently include maintenance requirements.

Identification of Historic Properties

Four basic criteria are used to identify potential historic properties:

1. Association with events that have made a significant contribution to the broad patterns of our history

2. Association with lives of persons significant in our past

3. Embodiment of the distinctive characteristics of a type, period, or method of construction; or the work of a master; or representing high artistic values either individually or as a unit ("district")

4. The likelihood of yielding information important in prehistory or history

Religious properties qualify for listing if they derive their primary significance from architectural or artistic distinction or historical importance under any of the four criteria listed. All historic resources, regardless of type or size or method of construction, must maintain integrity of location, design, setting, materials, workmanship, feeling, and association as defined by the National Register of Historic Places.

The National Register

The National Register of Historic Places is the nation's compendium of significant physical properties: buildings, structures, sites, districts, and objects. Churches and other religious institutions constitute one building type recognized by the Register as significant to the country's history. The Register and its listings are one of the more visible parts of a national policy of recognizing, preserving, and maintaining historic places, which began with the passage of the An-

tiquities Act in 1906 and was further enhanced by the Historic Sites Acts of 1935, the National Historic Preservation Act of 1966, and the National Environmental Policy Act of 1969, among others. These laws contain the criteria for designation, treatment of historic properties by government agencies, and guidance for public and private stewards in planning for the future of these resources.

The responsibility for identification, nomination, and physical treatment of these resources rests with citizens, state and federal preservation offices, local governments, and Indian tribes. Final evaluation and listing is performed by the Keeper of the National Register, a unit within the National Park Service in the Department of the Interior.

The criteria for inclusion in the National Registry are listed on page 248.

Other Federal Legislation

The Religious Land Use and Institutionalized Persons Act (RLUIPA) was passed by Congress on July 27, 2000, and signed into law by President Clinton on September 22. It provides federal remedies to protect the freedom of religious assemblies and institutions to use their property to fulfill their missions.

Controversy over this law continues in federal and state courts, and its effect on the protection and restoration of religious structures is uncertain at this time. Of particular interest to congregations are the measures that forbid discrimination against religious institutions in planning and zoning.

For example, in the area of adaptive reuse, municipalities that forbid churches to use space in commercial centers, while permitting other forms of assembly such

Criteria for Inclusion in the National Register of Historic Places

The quality of significance in American history, architecture, archeology, engineering, and culture is present in districts, sites, buildings, structures, and objects that possess integrity of location, design, setting, materials, workmanship, feeling, and association, and:

a. That are associated with events that have made a significant contribution to the broad patterns of our history; or

b. That are associated with the lives of persons significant in our past; or

c. That embody the distinctive characteristics of a type, period, or method of construction, or that represent the work of a master, or that possess high artistic values, or that represent a significant and distinguishable entity whose components may lack individual distinction; or

d. That have yielded or may be likely to yield, information important in prehistory or history.

Criteria Considerations

Ordinarily cemeteries, birthplaces, graves of historical figures, properties owned by religious institutions or used for religious purposes, structures that have been moved from their original locations, reconstructed historic buildings, properties primarily commemorative in nature, and properties that have achieved significance within the past 50 years shall not be considered eligible for the National Register. However, such properties will qualify if they are integral parts of districts that do meet the criteria or if they fall within the following categories:

a. A religious property deriving primary significance from architectural or artistic distinction or historical importance; or

b. A building or structure removed from its original location but which is primarily significant for architectural value, or which is the surviving structure most importantly associated with a historic person or event; or

c. A birthplace or grave of a historical figure of outstanding importance if there is no appropriate site or building directly associated with his or her productive life; or

d. A cemetery which derives its primary importance from graves of persons of transcendent importance, from age, from distinctive design features, or from association with historic events; or

e. A reconstructed building when accurately executed in a suitable environment and presented in a dignified manner as part of a restoration master plan, and when no other building or structure with the same association has survived; or

f. A property primarily commemorative in intent if design, age, tradition, or symbolic value has invested it with its own exceptional significance; or

g. A property achieving significance within the past 50 years if it is of exceptional importance.

(http://www.cr.nps.gov/nr/listing.htm)

as movie theaters and bowling alleys, would be in breach of RLUIPA. In the preservation field, local governments may not impose more stringent requirements on religious institutions than they would on other bodies for the preservation of historic buildings.

State and Local Ordinances

In addition to the federal framework, many states protect historic properties through designation and environmental review. An example is the California Environmental Quality Act (CEQA). Similar programs, most with criteria based on the federal criteria, are run by local governments, which enact preservation ordinances. The law is still evolving in the area of designation and regulation of religious properties, with discussion revolving around the free exercise of religion clause of the First Amendment of the Constitution and questions of regulatory taking.

In many areas, local planning ordinances allow the designation of neighborhoods as historic districts and provide local legislation governing their preservation and renovation. Others provide for historic preservation overlay zoning, which is another way of making sure that any building changes or demolitions in a neighborhood are reviewed from a historic point of view. In either case, a historic architectural review board (HARB) reviews development projects within the subject area in addition to the municipal planning, zoning, and building-code agencies.

Evaluating Construction Projects

In addition to establishing designation programs, governments at all levels have provided standards for evaluating the im-

pact of construction projects on historic resources. The most widely used regulatory guidelines are known as the Secretary of the Interior's Standards for the Treatment of Historic Properties with Guidelines for Preserving, Rehabilitating, Restoring, and Reconstructing Historic Buildings.

The standards most commonly used in the conservation of religious structures are the U.S. Department of the Interior (1976) guidelines for rehabilitation, which allow for the continued use, and often encourage additional use, of facilities and their systems.

Building Codes for Historic Buildings

The application of building codes designed for new construction to the rehabilitation of historic buildings complicates the task. A few states, California among them, have developed alternative building codes to meet the needs of historic structures that make it possible to maintain the historic fabric while addressing fire and life safety concerns. Whereas conventional codes may mandate removal of historic material to meet safety requirements, retrofitting of that material under historic codes may allow it to remain in place and continue the building's integrity. In addition to California's State Historical Building Code, other models include the National Building Code, written by Building Officials and Code Administrators (BOCA), and the Uniform Code for Building Conservation, published by the International Conference of Building Officials (ICBO). These codes have developed provisions for rehabilitation that provide levels of safety equivalent to those of new building codes.

The Secretary of the Interior's Guidelines for Rehabilitation and Guidelines for Rehabilitating Historic Buildings

A property shall be used for its historic purpose or placed in a new use that requires minimal change to the defining characteristics of the building and its site and environment.

The historic character of a property shall be maintained and preserved. The removal of historic materials or alteration of features and spaces that characterize a property shall be avoided.

Each property shall be recognized as a physical record of its time, place, and use. Changes that create a false sense of historical development, such as adding conjectural features or architectural elements from other buildings, shall not be undertaken.

Most properties change over time; those changes that have acquired historic significance in their own right shall be retained and preserved.

Distinctive features, finishes, and construction techniques or examples of craftsmanship that characterize a historic property shall be preserved.

Deteriorated historic features shall be repaired rather than replaced. Where the severity of deterioration requires replacement of a distinctive feature, the new feature shall match the old in design, color, texture, and other visual qualities, and where possible, materials. Replacement of missing features shall be substantiated by documentary, physical, or pictorial evidence.

Chemical or physical treatments, such as sandblasting, that cause damage to historic materials shall not be used. The surface cleaning of structures, if appropriate, shall be undertaken using the gentlest means possible.

Significant archaeological resources affected by a project shall be protected and preserved. If such resources must be disturbed, mitigation measures shall be undertaken.

New additions, exterior alterations, or related new construction shall not destroy historic materials that characterize the property. The new work shall be differentiated from the old and shall be compatible with the massing, size, scale, and architectural features to protect the historic integrity of the property and its environment.

New additions and adjacent or related new construction shall be undertaken in such a manner that if removed in the future, the essential form and integrity of the historic property and its environment would be unimpaired.

(U.S. Department of the Interior 1976)

THE PROCESS OF HISTORIC PRESERVATION

The process of historic preservation consists of six steps:

1. Reconnaissance and identification
2. Application for designation
3. Programming and concept planning
4. Construction documents and construction
5. Maintenance
6. Presentation to the visitor

The Reconnaissance Survey to Identify Historic Buildings

The first step in identifying the historic buildings in a community, or owned by an institution, is a complete listing of the buildings, with the following information about each:

- Brief description
- Approximate date of construction
- Integrity, that is, how well the original features are preserved
- Identifying features

Volunteers frequently perform this survey work under the guidance of a preservation professional. The tools generally used for this survey include:

- Large-scale tract maps showing individual properties
- Aerial photographs
- Cameras
- Laptop computers
- Database software with appropriate data entry fields

Some preservation professionals are now using global positioning systems (GPS) to accurately locate historic structures in a geographic information system (GIS).

Such a survey provides a comprehensive database of historic resources and a preservation plan, which can help avert the need for last-minute attempts to save historic buildings. It can also ensure that all the resources have been cataloged and help bring to light little-known structures. The volunteer work associated with the survey also helps to raise public awareness of the significance of historic buildings.

A good example of such a survey is the Prairie Churches Project in North Dakota. The National Trust for Historic Preservation provided training, information, and grants to support a volunteer-led survey of each of the 53 counties of North Dakota. The survey revealed nearly 2000 prairie churches, many of them vacant or in poor condition. The designation of the churches in America's 11 Most Endangered Historic Places for 2001 provided extensive media coverage and helped with fund-raising (National Trust for Historic Preservation 2002).

The Getty Foundation is supporting a comprehensive survey by the City of Los Angeles of all the historic buildings in the city. This survey will include many spaces for worship.

Application and Designation as a Historic Building

Once a reconnaissance survey has identified historically significant structures, a detailed survey is necessary to provide a framework for renovation, whether or not an application is made to the National Register of Historic Places or the local historic building register. The survey, which will require substantial research and the services of a preservation professional, includes the following:

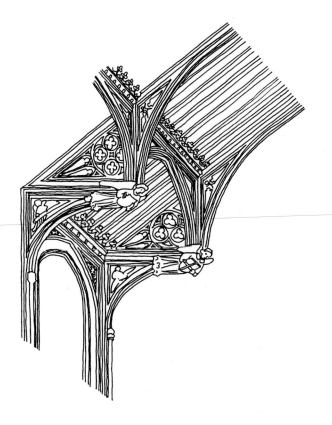

▲ *A character-defining feature: wood roof structure. Blakeney Church, Norfolk, United Kingdom.*

- Historic significance, how the resource meets the criteria for the National Register
- A bibliography of documents and sources consulted in the research

Features, materials, and spaces can be considered significant or character defining if they help to tell the story of the building's use and construction. Not all character-defining materials are decorative; the term also applies to framing, plaster, and other building components. Decorative features (plaster or stone carvings, stained and leaded glass, marble statuary, carved wood molding) are often easiest to identify. Public spaces (sanctuary, altar, vestibules, side chapels, meeting halls) are usually character defining, but private spaces such as offices may contain notable features as well. The identification of such features is the first step in the preservation project and should be closely coordinated with the design phase.

The research process may also identify significant alterations to be considered in the project. These "alterations which have acquired historic significance in their own right" (U.S. Department of the Interior 1976, p. 6) contribute to the building's history but should not be confused with alterations and additions of more modern materials and systems that may do little to illustrate the uses of the building over time.

It is important to include in the survey the building's relationship to its site. The surrounding open space and landscape are often important elements in defining the character of a historic building and require protection along with the structure itself. (See the illustration on page 81.)

- Floor plans and elevations measured and drawn to scale
- Interior and exterior photographs, keyed on the floor plans
- A description of the building, including:
  - Primary construction materials
  - The date of construction of each part of the structure, including subsequent renovations and additions, with the names of architects and builders
  - Historic and present uses of the building
  - Physical condition and integrity
  - Character-defining features, including exterior and interior architecture, artwork, and furnishings

The Advantages and Disadvantages of Designation

For many congregations, the designation of their worship spaces as historic monuments brings both benefits and difficulties.

- The designation will enable a congregation to apply for federal and local grants to support research, documentation, and restoration.

- It also attracts local interest and support and makes the acquisition and demolition of the building for a federal or state redevelopment project more difficult.

- The state and federal Historic Building Codes can be used for repair and renovation, which allow considerable concessions from the energy conservation, structural design, and disabled access requirements of currently applicable building codes.

Conversely:

- Because churches are tax-exempt organizations, there is no tax incentive to historic monument designation, and churches obtain no charitable donation credit by donating easements.

- Historic monument designation imposes restrictions on how maintenance can be performed and limits the changes that can be made to the interior and exterior of the building.

For a congregation with limited funds that must balance its resources between ministry and outreach on one hand and care of its buildings on the other, the higher standards required for historic building maintenance may present an undue burden. For this reason, many religious institutions oppose historic designation of their properties (Diocese of Pittsburgh 2002).

The Program and Concept Plan

With the assistance of an architect experienced in historic preservation, the congregation next develops a preservation and rehabilitation concept plan for the building, furnishings, and artwork. This plan includes preliminary drawings in-dicating which elements of the fabric will be preserved, which removed, and the proposed uses for each of the existing spaces. Particular attention should be paid to housing new equipment such as new heating, ventilating, and air-conditioning (HVAC) units and duct-work, electrical equipment, and fire protection in a manner compatible with the historic fabric.

The decision on how much of the fabric to preserve and how much to remove must be made with great care. A few preservation projects, such as those for buildings associated with great moments in history like the U.S. Declaration of Independence or the Civil War, require the restoration of structures back to their exact state at a particular moment in time. Most buildings, however, are seen as records of development over a period of time.

A worship space is significant as a vessel for histories, a record of patterns of worship and the lives of the congregation. For example, 1960s stained glass windows, stonework, and murals contributed by local artisans in the 1930s, or the elaborately carved confessionals donated at the beginning of the twentieth century, are all records of the congregation's relationship with its place of worship. Much of the fascination of historic buildings is in the layering of information, the poetic juxtaposition of new and old, and the ambiguity and complexity of images that create a sense of mystery and wonder.

253

▲ York Minster, York, United Kingdom. South transept roof replacement. Following the destruction by fire of the eighteenth-century south transept roof, 13 new trusses were fabricated from oak, with the timbers sized to provide a fire-surviving design. Architect: Hinton Brown, Langstone; consulting engineers: Ove Arup & Partners.

Construction Documents and Construction

To avoid damage to the building fabric, an experienced preservation professional should prepare the detailed restoration drawings and specifications. For example:

- To avoid damaging historic masonry, brick walls must be repointed using a lime-mortar mix instead of contemporary cement-sand mortar.

- To maintain the texture of historic woodwork, paint should be carefully removed by hand-scraping or chemical removal, and never by sandblasting.

- To avoid serious deterioration of the structure, walls of unfired adobe masonry should be recoated with mud plaster, not with modern cement plaster.

- Unless properly detailed, the use of modern synthetic waterproofing materials can damage wood structures by sealing in moisture and preventing ventilation.

The architect develops working drawings and specifications as described in Chapter 2, except that the documents also include:

- More extensive drawings and large-scale details of new elements designed to match the old, together with detailed descriptions of historic construction practices if they must be duplicated

- Documentation of existing construction to remain

- Specifications describing the restoration process in detail, including:

  - The contractor's obligation in removing, salvaging, and documenting existing construction

A danger in restoring a place of worship is that these many disparate traces will be erased in the urge to achieve aesthetic homogeneity or to restore the building to a particular moment in time. It is important that the building not be sanitized to a point where, although the original historic building envelope is preserved, its value as a historic record is lost.

The concept plan should include a cost estimate and a budget statement, including anticipated grants. If the project is a national or local historic monument, the concept plan will require review and approval by the regulatory agency.

- The contractor's required level of skill and familiarity with historic restoration
- Particular historic restoration specifications, such as for repointing brickwork, stonework cleaning and restoration, wood stripping and repainting

Because the restoration of historic buildings is a journey into the unknown, much of which cannot be accurately described in drawings, lump sum construction contracts are not appropriate. Unforeseen conditions are encountered continually; the contractor has to negotiate change orders or, if held to a fixed price, has to cut corners and risk sacrificing historic material.

If considerable exploratory removal is required at the start of the project, this work is best performed under a time-and-materials contract. Once the scope of the construction is clearly defined, the work can be performed under a guaranteed maximum price contract. These project delivery methods are described in further detail in Chapter 2.

Maintenance

A historic restoration project is not an isolated event in time; historic buildings continue their lives and require repair and maintenance as they are used. It is critical to their integrity that the same attention to detail and choice of materials be applied in maintenance as it was in restoration. The preservation professional can provide a maintenance program, recommending the frequency of cleaning, repainting, sealing, and repointing, and the materials that should be used. The specifications developed for the historic restoration determine the materials to be used for repairs.

Similarly, alterations and additions are inevitably made over the life of the building. As with the original restoration, it is important not to remove any historic fabric and to ensure that the addition maintains the character-defining features that justified the original preservation. Any alterations should be made under the guidance of a historic preservation architect and the appropriate regulatory authority.

Presentation to the Visitor

An important element of the historic restoration of a worship space is the presentation of the project to the visitor. Guides are often available to help visitors appreciate the work that has been done, and the congregation may prepare a booklet to describe the important features of the project. Such a booklet should describe the main features of the building and their history, the significant details and how they compare with other local structures of the period, and anecdotes from the restoration project itself.

THE SPECIFIC CHALLENGES OF RELIGIOUS HISTORIC BUILDINGS
Accommodating Liturgical Renewal

In most faiths, substantial changes in the liturgy have been made since historic buildings were originally built. In particular, Jewish congregations have sought a greater intimacy and sense of collegiality; some Catholic and Protestant churches have brought the altar into the center of the congregation to increase the feeling of participation.

In some cases, entire spaces have been rendered obsolete. For example, many Jewish congregations no longer have a separate gallery for women, and in

▲ St. John's Cathedral, Milwaukee, Wisconsin. HGA Architects with Rev. Richard S. Vosko renovated this cathedral, parts of which date back to 1853. The altar was brought closer to the congregation, in accordance with the requirements of the Second Vatican Council, and the font relocated to the entry axis. The lighting and colors are updated, and the altar is marked with a corona by Italian sculptor Arnaldo Pomodoro and a crucifix by Giuseppe Maraniello. HGA Architects; liturgical consultant: Rev. Richard S. Vosko. Photo courtesy HGA.

Chapter 3. The following sections discuss how historic religious buildings have been renovated to accommodate changes in liturgy. (See color plates 11–13, 19, and 20.)

Incorporating New Liturgical Furnishings into Historic Architecture

Liturgical renewal requires updated furnishings, which must often be accommodated within a historic structure. The general requirements of liturgical furnishings are discussed in Chapters 3 and 14. Particular considerations for historic buildings include the following:

- The altar, relocated from its historical position against the back wall of the chancel and brought to the center of the congregation. The historic altar can be modified for its new location, or a new altar specially built.

- The ambo or pulpit, which must be made accessible to disabled persons. If the original is not of great significance, renovation provides an opportunity to install a new ambo, accommodating readers either standing or seated in wheelchairs.

- The font, which is often enlarged to provide a pool for full immersion. In some cases the historic font can be reused as a water source in the new pool and for infant baptism and purification (see color plate 11).

- The bema, which in early synagogues was placed in the center of the congregation and within the last hundred years has been located against the back wall, is once again being placed in the center of the congregation. (See color plates 17 and 19.)

Catholic churches the choir is no longer located in a gallery but is instead made a part of the congregation. The admission of women into mosques requires the construction of a separate gallery.

Conversely, the Catholic Church's adoption of the ritual of full-immersion baptism requires a space for the baptismal font with adequate circulation around it and a bathroom close by. The reservation of the Blessed Sacrament, which had previously been located on the altar, now requires a separate space for private prayer.

The requirements of contemporary worship space planning are discussed in

Although some congregations are growing and require enlarged spaces, others are shrinking and demand creative renovation of their spaces to make a smaller congregation feel at home, while providing overflow space for holiday services.

There are a number of important issues to bear in mind when installing new liturgical furnishings:

- The historic pieces often have as much, or even more, significance to the congregation as the building itself. Often decorated with distinctive iconography, they provide a valuable sense of historic continuity and can frequently be reused or modified to suit the new liturgy. A skillful designer can preserve and restore these historic elements while adapting them to contemporary liturgy. For example, a small font that does not provide for contemporary full-immersion baptism can still be used for infant baptism and for members of the congregation to bless themselves if it is incorporated as part of the design of a larger pool.

- It is best to avoid pastiche. Instead of attempting to mimic historic designs, the designer should provide opportunities for contemporary artists and craftspeople to create works that are genuinely of their time.

Adaptive Reuse of Nonreligious Buildings

In some parts of the country, the rapid growth of some religious groups has led them to adapt and reuse commercial buildings such as theaters, industrial buildings, and retail spaces. These buildings present many advantages: long-span structures provide spaces of the right size, and there is usually good access and abundant parking.

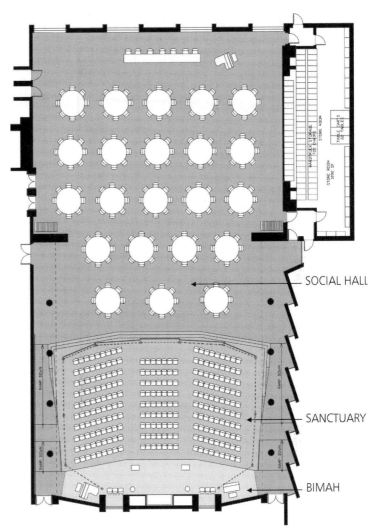

SOCIAL HALL

SANCTUARY

BIMAH

▲ Floor plan for Emanuel Congregation Sanctuary Renovation, Chicago. To reduce the size of this sanctuary to accommodate a reduced congregation while still allowing the entire space to be used for holiday services, Ross Barney + Jankowski designed a demountable curtain structure to enclose the sanctuary. Architect: Ross Barney + Jankowski.

▲ Emanuel Congregation Sanctuary Renovation, Chicago. Architect: Ross Barney + Jankowski. Photo: Steve Hall.

▶ Reflected ceiling plan for Emanuel Congregation Sanctuary Renovation, Chicago. Architect: Ross Barney + Jankowski.

The important factors for a congregation to consider when contemplating the purchase of a building for conversion include the following:

- Are the fire rating and floor loading of the structure appropriate for an assembly building?

- Can the building easily be made accessible to disabled persons?

- Are there adequate exit doors for an assembly building?

- Is there adequate access and parking for automobiles and for fire department vehicles?

As a readily available and inexpensive meeting space, the storefront has become the birthplace of new congregations throughout the United States. Generally located in low-income neighborhoods and converted from retail spaces left vacant, storefronts provide a home for Churches of God, Pentecostal and Baptist churches, Hindu and Buddhist temples, and Islamic mosques. Their location on busy streets provides good visibility, and the facades decorated with dramatic hand-painted signs and iconography identify them as spaces for worship (Vergara 2003). (See color plates 27–30.)

The story of the Masjid Al Falah in Corona, Queens, New York, is one that can be repeated for countless religious communities throughout the United States and Europe. Founded in a rented storefront in a three-story house, its members were subsequently able to purchase a lot across the street on which they built a single-story mosque housing 750 worshipers. They are now planning to add a second story, a dome, and a minaret to the structure (Metcalf 1996).

Protection of Unused Religious Buildings

In some cases, religious institutions with shrinking populations lack the resources to maintain their buildings and frequently allow them to lie empty and fall into disrepair. In the United Kingdom, for example, the Church of England has closed more than 1000 redundant church buildings since 1968, and more than 5000 Protestant chapels were closed between 1940 and 1980.

Historic religious buildings are often significant as landmarks in a community and have an important role in both urban and rural landscapes. Older members of the congregation may also be strongly attached to them and may resist selling and conversion to another denomination or a commercial use.

▼ Stanford Memorial Chapel, Palo Alto, California. Architect: Hardy Holzman Pfeiffer. Photo: Russel Abraham.

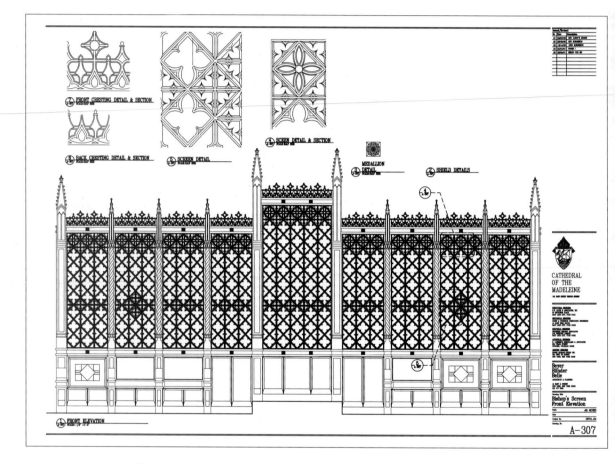

▲ Screen, Cathedral of the
Madeline, Salt Lake City,
Utah. Architect: Beyer,
Blinder, Belle.

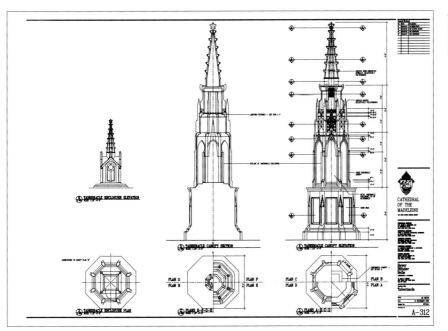

◀ Tabernacle, Cathedral of the Madeline, Salt Lake City, Utah. Architect: Beyer, Blinder, Belle.

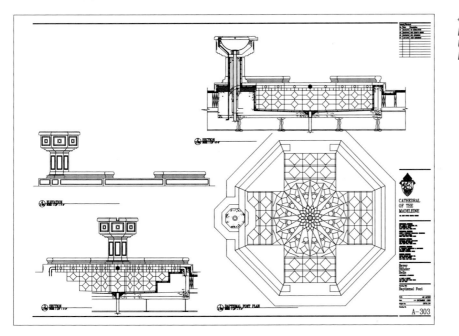

◀ Font, Cathedral of the Madeline, Salt Lake City, Utah. Architect: Beyer, Blinder, Belle.

When these buildings are historic monuments or form part of a historic district, grants are often available for historic preservation and adaptive reuse to other functions.

There are several options for conversion:

- A compatible use, such as a community center, performing arts center, museum, or gallery.

- A use that may preserve the interior but present ethical problems for the congregation selling the building, such as a restaurant or a night club, which may require the community's permission for alcohol and entertainment licenses.

- Uses that preserve the exterior for visual reasons but require extensive remodeling of the interior, such as offices, apartments, and retail stores. The conversion may be built as an independent structure inside the historic shell so that it can be reversed in the future, and it may preserve important detailed elements on the interior such as arches, vaults, door cases, and window frames.

Preservation by Moving

The same advances in technology that have threatened many historic religious buildings have also provided the tools for preserving them by moving them to another site.

Small wood-framed buildings can easily be moved by road, rail, or water. They are frequently cut into pieces to overcome limitations along the route, such as bridges or tunnels, or restrictions posed by the size of the truck or railcar.

Moderately sized masonry buildings can be successfully moved either in one piece or in several pieces, using specially built railcars and temporary tracks. The structures are often stabilized by steel and concrete armatures, and strain gauges monitor their performance during the move. For example, the Church of St. Anne in Warsaw, Poland, was moved out of the path of a road-widening project, and the Church of the Virgin Mary at Most in the Czech Republic was moved 1½ miles away from a coal-mining operation (Fitch 1982, pp. 129–132).

Masonry buildings can also be carefully documented, disassembled, and reassembled in a new location. For example, the Church of St. Mary the Virgin in London, renovated by Sir Christopher Wren and damaged in World War II, was moved to Westminster College in Fulton, Missouri. The stones were individually numbered and located on measured drawings of the facades to facilitate reconstruction (Fitch 1982, pp. 156–157).

▼ Interior view of auditorium, Calvary Church, Thousand Oaks, California. Architect: Gensler. Photo: Greg Epstein.

Provision of Universal Access

No gesture can mar the appearance of a historic building more than a clumsily installed disabled access ramp. With careful thought, however, the design team can incorporate universal access into an existing building without prejudicing the quality of the historic fabric. The detailed requirements for universal access are described in Chapter 5.

SOURCES OF FUNDING FOR HISTORIC RELIGIOUS BUILDINGS

Several private foundations, such as the National Trust for Historic Preservation in the United States and English Heritage in the United Kingdom, have provided grants for surveying historic properties to record them and establish their significance.

Religious buildings are often important landmarks in historic districts. In such cases, funding for restoration and upkeep may be available in the United States in the form of grants from state and local governments, which generally require a quid pro quo whereby historic preservation officials have the right to review preservation design proposals in exchange for funding. In other countries, nongovernmental organizations, such as English Heritage in the United Kingdom, administer historic preservation funds raised by public lottery.

Although religious institutions in the United States and Britain traditionally resisted the challenges to their autonomy demanded by public funding, this attitude is changing with the increasing public awareness of the significance of religious buildings in the urban and rural landscape and their need to comply with legislation concerning historic districts.

Where public funding is not available, congregations may raise money for historic preservation through capital campaigns, loans, and bonds, as described in Chapter 20.

CONCLUSION

Today's congregations are careful stewards of the nation's historic resources, making religious buildings some of the most publicly accessible and used of all historic buildings. Congregations carefully integrate the preservation of historic craftsmanship, materials, and artisanship, the need to maintain a sense of place for their communities, and the provision of sacred spaces for their own worship.

▼ Exterior view from the freeway, Calvary Church, Thousand Oaks, California. Gensler converted an existing industrial building into this church seating 6,000. Architect: Gensler. Photo: Greg Epstein.

CHAPTER 17
INTERNATIONAL CHALLENGES

International projects take many forms, such as the following:

- Buildings overseas for U.S.-based congregations, for example, mission churches and schools in foreign countries

- Projects for overseas organizations in their own countries, such as the Jubilee Church in Rome, designed by American architect Richard Meier

- U.S.-located projects for overseas organizations

The reasons for religious organizations to select international architects and engineers are equally varied:

- The "cachet" of a signature international firm

- A firm's expertise with a particular project type, or access to additional sources of funding

- An organization's experience with a particular design team on domestic projects that may suggest using the same team for international projects

In each case, the architect will encounter challenges in design and professional practice that affect the project's execution.

INTERNATIONAL DIFFERENCES
The Balance between Regionalism and Globalism

International projects are a part of the globalization of culture, and religious organizations have always been in the forefront of this phenomenon. The world religions discussed in this book have brought a universal set of religious and architectural ideas to diverse communities and locales across the globe. For example, the spread of Islam to

Southern Europe from the seventh to the tenth century brought the characteristic forms of the keyhole arch and the use of calligraphy as décor, just as nineteenth- and twentieth-century immigrant communities in Northern Europe and the

▼ *Jubilee Church (Dio Padre Misericordioso), Rome, Italy. Architect: Richard Meier & Partners, New York. Photo: Alan Karchmer, ESTO.*

United States brought the pointed arches and the domes of their native countries to their mosques and theological schools.

At the same time, worship spaces create a balance between universal ideas and forms and the local traditions of religious practice and design. The penetration of a religion into indigenous communities relies on its adaptation to suit local practices, along with its absorption of local aesthetic traditions. For example, as Roman Catholicism spread across Latin America, it absorbed local traditions such as the celebration of the Day of the Dead and the expression of goddess worship in Marian devotion and the dedication to the Virgin of Guadelupe. At the same time, Catholic church architecture replaced its traditional stone building with the adobe construction and brightly colored geometrical ornamentation of the Native American communities it sought to convert.

QUALITY OF PLACE AND CONTEXT

Although worship spaces bring universal forms and ideas to locations all over the world, their design should also respect the topography, landscape, and context of the individual building location and acknowledge the local climate and forces of nature.

Climate and Energy Use

Building design should take advantage of the local climate to improve the comfort of the congregation and minimize energy use. Hot, humid tropical climates and hot, dry deserts; Mediterranean climates; and northern zones—each region demands a different approach to sun control, the use of daylight, building mass, and natural ventilation.

For example, a church in Finland that welcomes the heat of the sun should have a dramatically different design than a church in South Asia or the Persian Gulf, where visitors seek the refreshing cool of deep shade.

Wide porches provide shade and natural ventilation in the hot, humid climate of the Caribbean, whereas massive adobe walls with tiny openings reduce interior temperatures in the hot, dry desert climates of the Middle East.

Available Materials and Methods of Construction

In traditional societies, where the transport of building materials is difficult and costly, regional differences in construction materials define communities. The great religious buildings of history sprang from the confluence of patronage, culture, and fine materials, whether they included the camphor trees that formed the shrines at Ise in Japan, the Pantelic marble of the Greek temples, or the limestone of the cathedrals of the Île de France. Even in a globalized society, with its cornucopia of building materials, the use of local materials creates a building rooted in its site, connects it to the history and craft tradition of a community, and offers a number of practical advantages:

- Local craftspeople are familiar with the materials and their use.

- Compliance with local standards for strength, fire rating, and durability is easy to establish for the benefit of owners and code officials.

- Material delivery times and their impact on construction schedules are minimized.

THE CHALLENGES OF INTERNATIONAL WORK
Economic Systems and Infrastructure

Builders of spaces for worship overseas must confront a wide range of infrastructure and economic conditions. During the planning phase, the project team should investigate whether the following are available:

- Reliable sources of water and electricity at the site

- All-weather roads for transporting building materials and equipment

- A pool of available construction labor

- Reliable communications such as telephone and the Internet

- Accommodations and health care for the project team

Materials and Construction Technology

There are significant differences in construction practices that affect design. For example, in Southern Europe and South America, small workshops fabricate building components such as windows and doors, which offers the designer the freedom to design each individually. In North America, by contrast, construction generally consists of the assembly of standard manufactured components selected from a catalog. Although it offers a much greater range of components, custom design comes at a much higher cost.

Legislation, Building Codes, and Standards

Legislation, particularly in the areas of energy conservation and accessibility for disabled persons, varies dramatically from country to country. Although the International Building Code (IBC) is gaining acceptance worldwide and has formed the basis for many national building codes, differences remain. For example, the European Union has established its own Eurocode and European standards for building materials. Many countries use the American standards for building materials, but quality and rigor of application vary widely.

Professionals planning an international project should carefully research not only the types and levels of approval required, but also the procedures to follow, and whether they need an expeditor to process the approvals.

Design Practice

The roles of architect, engineer, and contractor, and their scopes of service, vary widely from country to country. For example, in Europe and Japan the contractor takes more responsibility for engineering and detailing the design than in the United States. In Britain and the countries that formed the British Commonwealth, the Bill of Quantities is used as the basis of the contractor's bid, rather than the drawings and specifications. Drawing packages take different forms in Europe and the United States, illustrating a different approach to the representation of construction information.

In some countries the architect will be expected to be more of a generalist than in the United States and the United Kingdom—for example, by providing project management, real estate advice, and even financing as part of basic services.

Professionals must understand cultural differences in the relationship between professionals, their clients, and other members of the building team, which can vary widely from country to country. For example, in Spain and Latin American countries, the architect has almost mythic stature, whereas in the United States, architects are seen as members of a project team that includes other design professionals and contractors.

Cultural Differences and Modes of Communication

Successful international work demands sensitivity to cultural differences in the work environment between countries:

- *Language differences.* Being able to speak the language, or at least articulate a greeting and say a few words of appreciation in the native language, is an important gesture of politeness.

- *The approach to time.* In many Asian, Middle Eastern, and Latin American countries, taking time to build relationships is of much greater importance than in the United States, where making decisions and getting on with the job is the primary goal of business encounters.

- *Differences in the perception of personal space and tone of voice.* In some countries, heated debate at close quarters is the norm, whereas others may find this mode of communication rude and invasive.

- *The role of women in business* varies widely from one country to another.

- *The appropriate dress for business* must be gauged by visitors, as well as whether rituals, such as gift giving, are appropriate.

- *Taboos,* such as using the left hand for eating, turning one's back to the host, or showing the soles of one's shoes, must be strictly avoided.

Compensation

For many professionals, getting paid is the greatest challenge of working in a foreign country. The difficulties include:

- Overseas organizations' differing expectations of the design team's services.

- The expectation in some countries that architects and engineers will participate in the project to the extent of linking their fees to the level of fundraising achieved.

- Regulations restricting the export of currency.

- Fluctuating exchange rates.

- Lengthy and bureaucratic payment approvals. Organizations in some countries may insist on holding some payment until the project is complete.

Successful methods used by design firms working overseas include the following:

- Insisting on a substantial retainer in advance, which is credited to the final payment

- Establishing an escrow account held by a neutral third party, from which payments are made as the work progresses

- Insisting on payment in a stable convertible currency, such as U.S. dollars, pounds sterling, or Euros

- Insisting on an irrevocable letter of credit, which is conditional on the delivery of the documents

Security

The construction of worship space in many parts of the world raises security concerns that demand a careful approach to building design. Mosques are firebombed in Northern Europe, Christian churches and schools in Asia are bombed and their priests assassinated, and black churches in the American South are fire-bombed. In many newly industrializing countries (NICs) churches and church schools are targets of violence because they may be:

- Staffed by foreign nationals from a country that opposes terrorists
- Teaching a religion and espousing a culture different from that of the host country
- Seen as taking sides in a civil war
- Perceived as "soft" targets
- Seen by bandits as sources of food or money

Religious institutions in vulnerable situations should conduct a threat assessment using a qualified security consultant. In addition to procedures for the safety of the staff and congregation, a consultant will recommend steps to improve the safety of the buildings, which may include:

- Selecting suburban rather than urban sites
- Securing the perimeter of the property
- Using appropriate materials and design, including providing a "stand-off" distance from public streets, to minimize blast damage

Project teams overseas should carefully watch the political climate in the host country and monitor U.S. State Department foreign travel directives.

Corruption

In many NICs, vague regulations and government staff salaries result in a pattern of corruption. Religious building projects can encounter corrupt practices of government officials at many levels:

- Plan approvals
- Inspections
- Procuring materials
- Obtaining customs approval for imported materials, equipment, and parts

U.S. registered architects should be aware of the Foreign Corrupt Practices Act of 1977, which restricts payments to officials of foreign governments.

Collusion between contractors, whether officially sanctioned or not, will have the effect of raising construction costs. This can be mitigated by opening the project to bidding by foreign contractors, provided they are able to operate legally in the country.

THE INTERNATIONAL DESIGN PROCESS
Selecting the Design Team: The Local Partner

A few countries have reciprocal licensing agreements permitting architects to practice alone in each other's countries. Elsewhere, they must collaborate with local firms that stamp the drawings, help with code approvals, and provide knowledge of local customs and regulations.

Professional Agreements

In many parts of the world, an oral or handshake agreement is considered the normal professional contract. Even so, the scope of work and the expectations of all parties should be clearly spelled out and understood, especially with religious organizations unfamiliar with the building process. Architects should use contracts from their own professional organizations, or their own, attorney-approved contracts, wherever possible.

For projects overseas, architects from Europe and the United States often provide design-development-level drawings, and the local architects and contractors develop the construction documents and details. Methods to help everyone understand exactly what the architect is providing include:

- Providing a complete list of the deliverables at each stage of the project

- Showing examples of the types of material produced on comparable projects

CONCLUSION

Despite the pitfalls, international projects for the design and construction of places of worship offer an extraordinary opportunity for learning and giving. They allow the project team to work alongside people from other cultures and learn about their countries at first hand. They also offer opportunities to give, bringing experience to communities in developing countries. Through internship with the project team, young people of the host country can start on a path of learning that may culminate in their traveling overseas to complete their studies.

CHAPTER 18
OPERATION AND MAINTENANCE

Although religious buildings often have the longest service life of any building type, the funds available for maintenance are sometimes severely limited. As discussed in Chapter 20, running costs are usually covered by the congregation's donations, and in difficult times building maintenance is deferred. Spaces for worship must be designed to survive for periods of time with minimal maintenance.

Religious buildings are rarely large enough to have dedicated building engineers and technical staff. Systems such as heating and cooling, lighting, and sound reinforcement must be simple and straightforward enough for the religious leaders or lay assistants to operate.

MAINTENANCE PROCEDURES
Depending on the size of the religious institution, there are several approaches to building maintenance:

- In a small congregation, volunteers can each take charge of one aspect of the building maintenance, such as cleaning, landscape maintenance, or snow clearing.

- When substantial work needs to be done, volunteers organize workdays for spring cleaning and landscape maintenance.

- Larger congregations may be able to hire a full- or part-time paid administrator or sexton, who takes charge of building maintenance and reports to the stewardship committee.

- In the largest institutions, a facilities management department performs some of the work in-house and contracts out for other services.

There are five keys to a successful maintenance program:
1. Adequate funds must be set aside to cover maintenance, either through an endowment or by setting aside a percentage of the annual operating budget.

2. A maintenance plan should be developed, usually on a five-year cycle, providing a checklist of activities to be performed each month.

3. One individual must take personal responsibility for each task—for example, making sure the boiler is operating correctly in the winter or clearing leaves from the gutters in the fall.

4. Accurate records must be kept of all the maintenance performed so that a new staff member can clearly determine, for example, when the flat roof was last replaced or the emergency generator tested.

5. Staff and volunteers must be trained in the correct maintenance procedures. Irreparable damage can be done, for example, by using abrasive cleaners on metalwork or too much water to mop a wood floor.

OPERATION AND MAINTENANCE IMPACTS ON BUILDING DESIGN
Building Structure
The primary structural elements of a building, such as columns, walls, roof beams, and trusses, should be designed to be visible and easy to inspect for damage. Access panels should be provided for ceiling voids and crawl spaces.

A wood frame building needs to be inspected annually for insect damage and dry rot; concrete and steel frame buildings should be inspected for structural damage after major storms or earthquakes. Masonry structures should be inspected annually for cracking and structural deformation.

Roofs

Worship space roofs should be designed to minimize repairs and maintenance:

- To minimize damage from blocking and overflowing of gutters and downspouts into the building, concealed gutters and downspouts should be avoided; all roofs and gutters should be designed with a minimum $\frac{1}{4}$ in. per ft (2 percent) positive slope.

- To avoid leaks caused by ponding of water and snow buildup, 3 in. in 12 in. minimum pitched roofs should be used instead of flat roofs.

- To avoid leakage at flashings, a minimum 8 in. upstand from the roof surface should be provided at all flashings.

- Maintenance access to all flat roofs should be provided via stairs or fixed ladders.

To avoid leaks and the resulting damage to the building structure, the following maintenance program is recommended:

- Inspect pitched roofs with binoculars every six months and after storms to check for missing tiles or slates.

- Clean gutters and downspouts twice a year; remove leaves, moss, and vegetation.

- Inspect flat roofs twice a year for the condition of the roof covering and flashings and for drainage problems.

Exterior Walls

Exterior walls of worship spaces should be durable and easy to clean. A non-porous wainscot of stone or masonry will help to prevent staining from landscape irrigation and maintenance and from pavement deicing and cleaning.

In urban areas, exterior walls up to 8 ft above grade should be made of materials such as concrete or stone that accept graffiti coating. When graffiti is discovered, the wall must be cleaned and the coating reapplied.

All exterior wall surfaces should be accessible for inspection and maintenance by ladder, rolling scaffold, scissor lift, or boom lift. If there are wall surfaces more than 30 ft above grade that are not accessible by boom lift or from an adjacent roof, tie-offs or davit bases should be provided on the roof above for anchoring equipment for periodic maintenance.

Exterior walls should receive the following annual maintenance:

- Remove ivy and other vegetation.

- Remove birds' nests, maintain bird protection.

- Check vents at the crawl space.

- Check the wall surface for cracking; ascertain and remedy the cause of cracking.

In addition, brick and concrete surfaces will have to be sealed every 5–10 years, and joints recaulked. In cold climates, brick walls have to be repointed approximately every 25 years. Wood and other painted wall surfaces will have to be recoated every 3–5 years.

Windows

Windows require the following regular maintenance:

- Cleaning glass and frames. Stained glass should be cleaned by experts, not with conventional window-washing equipment.

- Checking and lubricating hardware, hinges, and latches.
- Inspecting for breakage and corrosion.
- Replacing deteriorated caulking and glazing compound.

To make maintenance easier:

- Window frames and sills should be made of durable materials, such as bronze or fluoropolymer-coated aluminum, that require minimum maintenance.
- Windows or window walls more than 30 ft above the ground need a system of davits and stages for regular cleaning and glass replacement, unless they are accessible by a truck or trailer-mounted boom lift, as described earlier for exterior walls.

Doors

Over the life of the building, doors and door hardware in worship spaces receive an extraordinary amount of wear. Adhering to the following guidelines will help to avoid failures:

- Only the most durable, institutional-grade hardware should be used.
- Doors should be solid wood core or hollow metal.
- Hardware such as locksets, hinges, and closers should be standardized throughout the building so that a few replacement parts can be stocked.
- Metal kick plates should be provided to protect heavy-use doors.

Interior Walls

Interior walls accumulate dirt from handprints and are susceptible to damage by occupants, furniture, and mainte-

nance equipment. The following measures will help to protect them:

- Plaster and gypsum board surfaces should be protected with a 6 in. high base and a wainscot of durable and easily cleaned material up to 3½ ft high. Suitable materials for wainscots include stone, ceramic tile, terrazzo, and wood paneling.
- Concrete and masonry walls should be sealed to prevent dirt absorption and to allow the surfaces to be cleaned.
- In back-of-the-house areas where chair carts and food trolleys are used, metal corner guards and rails will protect vulnerable wall surfaces and corners.

Floors

Chapter 11 discusses the choice of floor materials for worship spaces and support areas. Floors require regular cleaning, waxing, and polishing. Wood and cork floors also require periodic resealing. Stone floors may need to be rehoned to maintain their coefficient of friction. The following measures help with floor maintenance:

- In Christian and Jewish worship spaces where members of the congregation retain their shoes, design an adequate mat area at each entrance for them to remove grit and dirt from their shoes.
- Use walk-off mats in wet weather to protect the floor from water damage.
- Provide a janitor's closet with a floor sink for storage of cleaning equipment.
- Provide power outlets not more than 100 ft apart for maintenance equipment.

External Maintenance

The landscaped areas of a worship center require maintenance such as:

- Grass cutting
- Weeding and trimming
- Applying fertilizers and pest control
- Inspecting and checking irrigation systems
- Tree surgery

For small projects the maintenance crew can bring their own equipment; for larger buildings a storage shed will be required, with electrical power, water, and drainage, for storage of landscape maintenance equipment. Hose bibs in lockable boxes should be provided around the exterior of the building.

The exterior paving around the worship space will also require maintenance such as:

- Removing snow and leaves from parking lots, walks and steps
- Deicing walks and steps
- Power washing pavement to remove stains
- Reapplying sealer

In snow country, a space should be provided for storing snow removal equipment. The parking lots and walks should be designed with adequate adjacent area for snow storage.

SECURITY AND MAINTENANCE STAFF

On large projects, where there is an in-house security and maintenance staff, the following spaces will be needed:

- In addition to the security desk, a security room for video recording equipment, security equipment, storage, and charging of radios, and a security staff break area
- A maintenance staff office, shop, and storage area
- An area for parking and charging the electric carts used by maintenance and security personnel

The architects should make sure the entire site is quickly accessible by electric cart, using ramps and walkways, so that maintenance and security personnel can rapidly cover the site.

BUILDING SYSTEMS
Lighting

Worship space lighting is generally switched by a lighting control system, which should be simple and straightforward to operate. As described in Chapter 13, a push-button panel will enable the individual presiding over the service to select one of several preset "scenes" before it begins. The brightness of the fixtures in a scene may be adjusted individually to fine-tune the preset scene.

Like other building systems, a lighting system requires regular maintenance, including:

- Cleaning fixtures and lamps to ensure maximum light output
- Inspecting and testing emergency lighting battery packs
- Relamping fixtures according to a lamp life schedule
- Replacing ballasts in high-intensity discharge (HID) and fluorescent fixtures according to schedule

It is the lighting designer's responsibility to ensure that the light fixtures are all accessible for maintenance. The congregation may have to provide equipment for reaching fixtures in tall spaces, including:

- Demountable rolling scaffold that reaches over pews
- Miniature scissor lifts that span over pews and fit through doorways
- Trailer-mounted boom lifts that fit through doorways

Exterior lighting should be accessible from rooftops or by boom lift.

Heating, Ventilating, and Air-Conditioning (HVAC)

HVAC system controls range from an on-off switch and thermostat to a fully computerized building energy management system. In small worship centers it is often the minister, rabbi, or imam who turns on the heating or cooling before services. The system must be straightforward and simple to operate.

HVAC systems need regular access for repair and maintenance, such as:

- Inspecting and testing the boiler(s) each summer
- Replacing filters and cleaning the HVAC units
- Replacing fan belts according to schedule
- Performing scheduled maintenance on package HVAC units, air handlers, and the central plant

Service technicians have to bring toolboxes and bulky parts, such as filters, that cannot easily be carried up ladders to the equipment. Ship's ladder or stairways should be provided to all equip-ment rooms and platforms, and the manufacturer's required working clearance should be provided around equipment.

Audiovisual Systems

Worship space audiovisual (AV) systems range from a simple microphone at the lectern to a performing-arts-level system with a multichannel mixing board and multiple video projectors. Larger congregations may have full-time staff to run the AV system, but in smaller groups it is the presider who turns on and controls the sound system. The system must be very simple to operate, and the volume level should be automatically controlled. To accommodate congregations of varying sizes and minimize the sound reverberation in the space, a push-button panel can be used to select the number of speakers to be energized.

Bell Systems

Bell systems require regular maintenance, including:

- Inspection of ladders and bell platforms
- Checking and repairing bird screens, removing guano and birds' nests
- Checking the bell mechanism and lubricating as required
- Rotating bells a quarter turn to minimize clapper wear

The bells should be accessible for maintenance by means of fixed ladders.

CHAPTER 19
KEY COST FACTORS

Any construction project involves risk for the owner, the architect, and the builder. The more dramatic and innovative the design, the greater the risk. Accurate cost estimating throughout the design phase is an important part of completing the project on budget and minimizing the risk to the owner and the design team.

THE PROCESS OF COST ESTIMATING
The Cost Estimator
Cost estimating services for worship spaces may be provided in a number of ways. The congregation may hire a contractor for preconstruction services, including cost estimating and scheduling. This is typical for the method known as guranteed maximum price (GMP), or CM at Risk delivery method discussed in Chapter 2. To be effective, the contractor should:

- Be brought on while the project is in the schematic design stage
- Be experienced in forecasting costs from schematic drawings, not merely bidding completed documents

The architect may include the services of a professional cost estimator as part of the design team.

The project managers hired by the congregation may provide cost estimating as part of their services.

Whichever method is used, it is critical that cost estimating be explicitly provided during the design phase.

The Cost Plan
The cost plan is a description of all the components that are expected to be part of the building, with an estimate of the cost of each. The cost plan also includes contingencies and estimates of escalation.

Budgets for worship spaces must be developed with a full understanding of the ultimate goal of the client and the architectural team. A budget cost plan is typically developed from early concept design sketches. The cost plan should be presented in a systems format, organized by components of the building such as structure, finishes, and systems. This is a useful format for understanding where the costs are allocated in the building, and it allows costs to be compared with those of similar projects and between stages of design. The cost plan will be compared to the owner's preliminary budget; and the owner, design team, and cost manager will meet to make adjustments to either the budget or the project scope so that the project can proceed into detailed design, with the scope of work and budget in alignment. This is perhaps the most critical stage of project cost development—basic decisions regarding project development are made at this point. If the decisions are flawed, correcting them will likely cost time and money if discovered later in the design process or, even worse, during construction.

Cost Estimating During Design
Once the cost estimator for a project establishes the initial cost plan for construction and the scope of the project is aligned with available funds, the design phase begins in earnest. Throughout the design stage, the cost estimator provides estimates of the final cost of the project. This is a difficult task during the early

COST PLAN FOR A TYPICAL CHURCH PROJECT AT SCHEMATIC DESIGN STAGE	
Construction cost estimate (including contractor's general conditions, overhead, and profit) (See table on page 279.)	$6,011,000
Design contingency (15% at schematic)	601,100
Subtotal	6,612,100
Cost escalation to midpoint of construction (3% per annum for 2 years)	396,726
Subtotal	7,008,826
Construction change order contingency (10%)	700,883
Total building cost	7,709,709
Nonconstruction costs (including contingency) (See table on page 281.)	2,775,495
Total Project Cost	**$10,485,204**

phases of design when there is little detail on the drawings. It is therefore critical that the estimator has experience in preparing estimates from in-progress design documents and, moreover, has prior experience with this building type. A regular dialogue between the design team and the estimator ensures that the intent of the design is reflected in the cost estimates.

Throughout the development of design, the estimates are prepared as a combination of priced, measured items detailed on the drawings and allowances for items not yet shown. The art of estimating requires thoughtful allowances for unknown items, based on past project experience, so that a realistic opinion of cost is presented at all times.

The timing of estimates preparation varies according to the complexity or size of the building and the procurement methods employed. Estimates are usually prepared to coincide with the end of a particular design stage, but the more complex the project, the more regular the estimate reports should be. The cost estimating process becomes much more effective as a cost management and control process when the estimator is providing ongoing advice to the team in regard to costs, reacting promptly to the development of the design.

Cost Estimating for Sustainable Design and Life-Cycle Costing

The design of sustainable buildings, using reusable or recycled materials, and designs that reduce the cost of operating and maintaining the building can have a powerful effect on the environment and significantly reduce the long-term cost of

ST. MATTHEW'S CHURCH RENOVATION DESIGN DEVELOPMENT COST ESTIMATE		
Element	**Total Cost ($)**	**Cost/Sq ft ($)**
Foundations	148,434	6.99
Substructure	274,336	12.91
Superstructure	501,234	23.59
Exterior closure	635,876	29.93
Roofing	147,070	6.92
Interior construction	977,342	46.00
Conveying	110,560	5.20
Mechanical	426,547	20.08
Electrical	386,574	18.20
Equipment	177,110	8.34
Site work	1,114,052	52.44
Direct building cost	4,899,135	230.60
General conditions, overhead, and profit (15%)	734,870	34.59
Total Construction Cost (excluding contingencies and escalation)	**5,634,005**	
Gross floor area	21,245	
Cost per square foot	$265	

operating the facility, but at the expense of a higher initial cost. Life-cycle or whole-life costing is used to determine the cost of a facility over its entire life: the initial capital cost of constructing a building and the ongoing operating and maintenance costs. This is a critical concept, because the cost of operating and maintaining a building over its life will far exceed the initial cost of construction. The most effective solutions result from considering alternative designs and subjecting them to life-cycle costing and sustainability analysis.

Value Engineering

As the detailed design progresses, the cost of the project often rises because some elements are added or become more elaborate. Value engineering is a process often used to bring the project cost back into line. In true value engineering, the project team members propose alternative designs, materials, or means of construction, which are priced and incorporated into the design if appropriate. It ensures the most cost-effective means, both in first cost and maintenance costs, to achieve the congregation's goals for the building.

Cost Management during Construction

Several factors can affect the project cost during construction:

- Unforeseen site conditions, such as bad soil, rock excavation, or hazardous materials underground, can add to the cost.

- Delays that extend the construction period, whether caused by lack of design information, labor or materials difficulties, unusually severe weather, or owner's changes, will increase the construction cost. The contractor incurs a fixed cost every month the project is under way, and if construction time is extended through no fault of the contractor, the contractor will pass this cost on to the owner.

- Lack of design information or errors on the documents, causing the contractor to seek clarification from the architect, will cause delays and added cost.

- Changes made by the owner during construction can also increase costs.

The cost estimator evaluates cost changes requested by the contractor during construction and helps to negotiate a fair adjustment in construction cost.

COST FACTORS
Construction Costs

Worship spaces are generally unique buildings whose features vary considerably. As a result there is no uniform cost benchmarking data available, which presents a challenge in preparing accurate budgets for new worship spaces at an early concept stage. Worship spaces do, however, have certain common features.

They are usually high-volume spaces, with long structural roof spans, and be-cause they have high volumes, they typically have large areas of exterior wall per square foot of floor area. The buildings will have durable, high-cost interior finishes, fixed specialty furnishings, artwork, and specialty lighting. An understanding of these factors is critical in creating a realistic budget at the start.

Indirect Costs

Construction costs cover all items generally included in a general contractor's bid—the "bricks and mortar" of the project. However, construction costs should not be confused with an overall project budget that includes both "hard" construction costs and "soft" costs. Soft (or indirect) costs include all the project-related expenses beyond the actual cost of construction:

- Design fees

- Project management costs

- Allowances for inflation

- Contingencies to cover the cost of unforeseen changes that are likely to occur during the construction phase

- Inspections and testing fees

- The cost of loose furnishings, fixtures, and equipment

- Permits and other fees

- The cost of specialized furnishings and artwork required for a worship building

Indirect costs may also include:

- Land acquisition costs

- Site mitigation costs, such as for hazardous material abatement

- The cost of environmental impact reports

- Legal, financing, and fund-raising costs

ST. MATTHEW'S CHURCH NONCONSTRUCTION BUDGET CHECKLIST

Architect, Engineers, and Consultants (including reimbursible expenses)

Architect
Structural engineer
Mechanical/electrical/plumbing engineer
Landscape architect
Civil engineer
Acoustic/audio consultant
Code/fire life safety consultant
Food service consultant
Lighting consultant
Organ consultant
Security consultant
Voice/data/technology consultant
Waterproofing/roofing consultant
Traffic and parking consultant
Art consultant—liturgical
Cost estimator
Surveyor
Miscellaneous consultants

Subtotal

Testing/inspection
Geotechnical report
Phase I environmental report
Soil inspection
Structural inspection/test
Waterproofing/roofing inspection
Miscellaneous inspection/tests

Subtotal

Administrative expenses
Project management
Project management reimbursement expense
Staff expense
Legal—miscellaneous
Accounting/audit
Additional models/renderings/animations
Photography
Special events expense

Public relations—video
Public meetings
Committee reimbursables
Misc. entertainment
Fund-raising
Archive/files/warranties
Moving expense
Power after permanent connection
Security additional to normal construction security
Insurance—builders' risk/owner's liability/fine arts
Miscellaneous administration expense

Subtotal

Permits/fees/bonds/utilities
Building plan check/permit
City engineer's plan check
County health plan check and permit
Shoring and grading permit
Haul route permit
AQMD/permits
NPDES/water quality permit
Fire hydrant fee
Police facility fee
Sewer facility fee
Grading/shoring bond
Resource management bureau fee
Fire department fees
Planning department fees
Bureau of sanitation fees
Street maintenance bureau fees
Variance fees
Residence tax
Traffic study review
Water connection fees/bonds
Fire service connection fee
Gas company connection fees/bonds
Telephone connection fee
Municipal storm water permit
Miscellaneous permits and fees
Miscellaneous utilities

Subtotal

Total Soft Cost

Furniture, Fixtures, Equipment, and Art
Church adornments—altar, lectern, candle stands, cross
Church FF&E: pews—salvage and refurbish
Pews—new pews
Chairs
Drapes for echo control
Choir seating
Church specialties: devotional
Appliances
Church artwork
Organ—remove/store/move/reinstall (including voicing)
Children's room FF&E
Sound system
Telephone
Security system
Acoustical adjustment of church after opening
Stained glass—remove, refurbish, and reinstall
Childrens playground equipment

Subtotal

Nonconstruction Contingency @ 10%

Land
Land purchase
Closing costs (title, escrow)
Appraisal
Subdivision map/engineering/recording/fees
Miscellaneous expense

Total Land

Total Project Cost

Excluded
– Performance bond
– Trade permits (by subcontractor)
– Finance cost

**CONSTRUCTION COST
BREAKDOWN BY COMPONENT**

Foundations	3%
Substructure	5%
Superstructure	14%
Exterior Closure	13%
Roofing	4%
Interior Construction	18%
Conveying	1%
Mechanical	10%
Electrical	7%
Equipment	2%
Sitework	23%
	100%

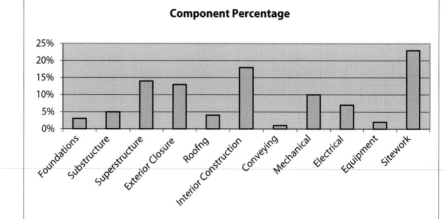

▲ A typical breakdown of religious building costs by components, showing the percentage of the overall construction cost attributable to each component.

Budgeting the soft costs correctly is as important as getting the hard costs right and is not always given enough attention at the early stages. Soft costs are often budgeted simply as a percentage of the budget for construction, based on historical information, and although past project experience may provide useful indicators, no two worship building projects will have the same makeup of soft cost expenses. It is therefore important to research and estimate the actual indirect costs for each project.

Contingencies

Contingencies must be incorporated into the estimating process to protect the budget from unforeseen events and to allow for details that are not yet developed. Inexperienced owners will often try to reduce or eliminate such contingencies; the design team must carefully explain that the contingencies, which include the types listed below, are there for the owner's protection.

Design contingency allowances should be included in each cost estimate report during the design stage to cover elements of the design that just could not be anticipated by the estimator or become necessary increases of scope. At the early stages of design development these may exceed 10 percent of base estimate allowance. The actual contingency amount should vary, based on completeness of the design at the time the estimate is prepared, and should also consider the unique nature of the project. Landmark worship spaces, which may include complex design features, dictate larger than normal contingency allowances. As the design progresses, estimates should include progressively smaller design contingency allowances until they are effectively zero by the time a project is ready for bid.

Types of contingencies

- A construction contingency is included in the project budget to cover inevitable changes during construction.

- An overall project budget contingency covers unexpected increases in any of the budget categories.
- A contingency for inflation is also necessary. Depending on the size of project or the speed of project development, it can often take several years for a project to be realized. The original budget can quickly become out of date without realistic inflation allowances. These should be based on an analysis of current market conditions, along with projections for future inflation.

CONCLUSION

Managing the cost of a worship building project calls for realistic forecasts at all stages of the development. When projects fail to meet their original budget targets, it is usually because wishful thinking came into play at some point in the process. Even the most effective methods of cost management cannot save a project from unrealistic goals. To ensure a successful result, the project team must tackle the financial challenges early and often as the project develops.

CHAPTER 20

SOURCES OF FINANCE

Worship spaces translate into built form the faith and collective will of a congregation. Because religious institutions are supported in most countries by voluntary donations rather than by a compulsory tax, fund-raising is a critical part of religious leadership. To successfully raise and manage the funds for a building project, the religious leaders need vision, leadership, and skilled financial management.

A building project shows that a faith community is growing and changing. It is an investment in the future that will allow the religious institution to expand, update forms of worship, and receive increased donations from an invigorated congregation. It is on the existing members, however, that the that the burden of funding the project generally falls.

SOURCES OF FINANCE

Financing for religious building projects can come from the following sources:

- A capital campaign, which may raise gifts in the following forms:
  Cash.
  Pledges that will be redeemed in cash over a period of years.
  Gifts of stock or real estate that may be converted into cash.
  Gifts of life insurance that convert to cash upon the donor's death.
- Loans, which may be obtained from:
  The institution's central body
  Affiliated financial institutions
  Commercial banks
  Individuals
  (See "Loans and Bonds" later in this chapter for information on securing loans.)

- Bonds, which usually provide a loan at fixed interest for a period of 20 years. They are sold by an underwriter and are purchased by the congregation or outside investors.

FINANCIAL MANAGEMENT

Faith communities differ in their financial management as to how much the laity is involved in budget decisions and the extent to which the central authority controls their spending. For example, the Assemblies of God are financially independent; the preacher manages the church with the help of lay leaders. In the Evangelical Lutheran Church in America, a congregational council administers the day-to-day financial management, but the congregation as a whole votes on the annual budget, capital projects, and the choice of a new pastor. In the Catholic Church, the parish council, or the finance council if the parish is large enough to have a separate committee, makes financial recommendations to the parish priest, who manages the parish and is responsible to the bishop. The bishop, in turn, is responsible to the leadership of the Church in Rome.

THE FUND-RAISING PROCESS
Strategic Planning

Before beginning design or fund-raising, a congregation, with the help of outside professionals, should carefully assess and document its current and future needs in a strategic plan document. A master plan prepared by an architect or planner summarizes these needs in the form of site and building plans, helps to test the potential of the existing facilities, and assesses alternate sites for purchase if additional land is required.

The master plan with preliminary cost information forms the basis of a "Case Statement," a description of the proposed project that a consultant will use for the feasibility study.

The Feasibility Study

To set the budget for the project, the congregation or parish should hire a consultant to perform a fund-raising feasibility study. A number of consultants are available who specialize in surveying the congregation and the community, using the aforementioned Case Statement, to establish a realistic goal for a capital program. The feasibility study also includes an approach to lenders, with an information packet on the religious institution's financial history to determine the institution's borrowing capacity.

When combined with the congregation's other resources, which may include excess real estate that can be sold off and cash in hand, this study enables the congregation to establish a realistic budget for the project.

Preliminary Design and Fund-Raising Presentation Materials

The first step in a successful fund-raising program is for the architect, working with the congregation, to develop a preliminary design that will form the basis for the fund-raising effort. Chapter 2 fully describes this process.

In many cases the community's needs will exceed the currently available funding, in which case a project must be planned in phases. Each phase is designed to stand alone as funding is raised for future phases.

As part of their work, the architects generally prepare a model and colored renderings for use at fund-raising events and in published material. Many congregations are finding that animated computer simulations of the completed project, which can be incorporated into fund-raising videos, are particularly successful.

The preliminary plans and renderings, together with a description of the project, a message from the religious leader, and an appeal for support, form part of a printed "Case for Support." This brochure, which forms the basis of the fund-raising program, should not change substantially throughout the duration of the program. It describes the project for

▼ *Fund-raising brochure, Holy Trinity Church, San Pedro, California. Courtesy of Holy Trinity Parish.*

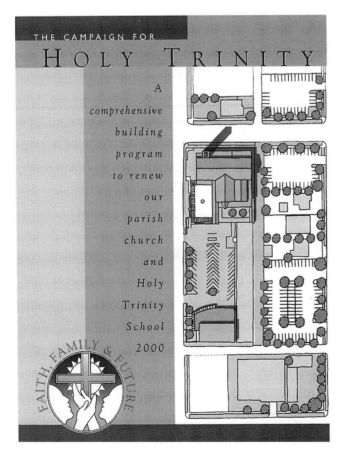

which support is requested and is a form of contract, a promise that the religious leaders make to the donor community, describing the project that will be built with the funds to be raised. The appearance of the brochure is important to convey the quality of the finished project; it is worth hiring a graphic designer to do the layout and printing the brochure on good-quality paper.

The Development Committee

The religious organization forms a de-velopment committee to lead the fund-raising effort. The lay leader of the campaign, who generally chairs the development committee, lends his or her personal stature to the campaign. The leader's reputation in the community gives credibility to the campaign, attracts other donors of equal stature, and gives donors the reassurance that if they give the money, the project will be completed successfully.

The committee is usually composed of individuals who will make leadership gifts and experienced fund-raisers who get the word out to the community. A very large campaign generally has sub-committees devoted to different donor groups. In a smaller campaign, each member of the development committee focuses on a particular area. The main areas of giving include the following:

- Lead donors, whose individual gifts may be 5–10 percent of the overall campaign. Together the lead donors may meet 30 percent of the total goal.
- Major gifts, each of which may be 1–5 percent of the overall program.
- Foundations, whose gifts frequently form a major part of capital programs.
- Individual gifts.

- Corporate gifts. For an urban project of civic importance or a project that has significance in a particular community, corporate giving may be an important part of the program.
- Federal, state, and local grants for historic preservation (see Chapter 16).

In calculating the proportion of the budget met by fund-raising, it is important to include a certain percentage for pledges that will not be redeemed because of donor default. This percentage will vary with the community and the economic climate. It will typically be 0.5–2 percent of the total amount pledged and may be higher during economic recessions.

Fund-Raising Strategies

The fund-raising program may include the following strategies:

- Discussion of the project by religious leaders at regular services
- Mailers to the congregation
- Special meetings of the congregation at which the architect presents the project and the leaders ask for support
- Fund-raising dinners, at which religious leaders and the architect may be on hand to speak about the project.
- Individual meetings, in-home visits, or private dinners with the leaders and key donors
- A public relations campaign that highlights the project in the local print and broadcast media and offers an opportunity for leaders to speak on radio and television and to be quoted in the newspapers
- Signs on the project site announcing the project

For the leaders, a major campaign is a total commitment that may last five years, which means relinquishing or delegating their other professional commitments. They must have the stamina to continue telling the story to each new prospect with vigor and conviction for the duration of the campaign.

Studies have shown that the most successful capital campaigns are those that regard fund-raising as part of the faith community's ministry, rather than a matter of meeting a financial goal. They offer the congregation a genuine opportunity to grow in faith by participating in the ministry and fulfilling the faith community's mission. Successful fund-raising refers to the scriptures and builds on the religious teachings of the faith.

Donor communication

A successful fund-raising program must give donors the feeling that they are part of the project. As well as material recognition in the completed project, they need to feel involved as the project unfolds. There are a number of ways to involve the donors:

- Ceremonies at groundbreaking, topping out, and dedication, at which the donors are acknowledged

- Newsletters describing the progress of the project and acknowledging particular donors

- A website with photographs of the project as it develops and updates on the progress of the capital campaign

- A webcam broadcasting live images of the project under construction over the World Wide Web, which is particularly effective in engaging donors

- E-mail newsletters to keep the congregation informed about the project

Donor recognition

Critical to successful fund-raising is a means of recognizing gifts in the completed project. Although some prefer anonymity, most donors want the part they played to be visible in the completed building. This recognition can take many forms:

- Association of major gifts with a particular item, such as a bell, a tree, a courtyard, or a component of liturgical furnishing such as the lectern or the altar. Most religious groups resist the placement of plaques adjacent to the particular items; instead, the donors can be recognized on a donor wall.

- Recognition of specific gifts on a donor wall, or "tree of giving."

- Recognition of lead donors at ceremonies and dinners, including the giving of special awards to lead donors and fund-raisers.

- The names of other donors can be listed on an honor roll, which may be a book kept in a publicly visible place, or on a computer database accessible from a public terminal.

LOANS AND BONDS

The congregation will generally secure a loan in order to begin construction. Depending on the lender organization, the congregation may need to have 30 percent of the construction cost already in hand. Generally, a congregation arranges for construction financing from the parent body or from a commercial bank, relying on the redemption of pledges and future fund-raising to retire the loan.

Loans

In negotiating a loan, there are a number of questions to keep in mind:

- The loan terms—is the interest rate fixed or variable?
- The amortization period—how soon will the loan need to be repaid?
- What are the lender's conditions, such as limitations on future borrowing?
- What are the prepayment penalties?

Bonds

Bonds constitute a method of financing that has been used by institutions and corporations for centuries, which offers several advantages over bank financing.

- The interest rate is fixed for the full term of the loan, generally 20 years.
- There are fewer restrictions on the institution's activities during the life of the bonds, such as maintaining a certain income, selling additional bonds, or taking out additional financing.
- There are no prepayment penalties.

An added advantage is that members of the congregation can purchase bonds, thus keeping the interest paid on the loan in the community and providing an opportunity for members to give back by forgiving payments on interest or principal.

The origination fee is higher on a bond sale than for a conventional loan, however. If the loan is a short-term bridge or construction loan that will be repaid by redeemed pledges, then conventional bank financing may be preferable.

CONCLUSION

A successful fund-raising and construction campaign not only creates the physical spaces for worship, it also invigorates the congregation, energizes its members' commitment to the faith, and deepens their involvement with the ministry through fund-raising and outreach. But fund-raising does not come to an end with completion of the building project; it is important for a congregation to continue raising money to retire construction loans and create an endowment to cover the building maintenance and running costs.

▲ Donor wall at the Cathedral of Our Lady of the Angels, Los Angeles. Glass artist: Judson Studios.

GLOSSARY

FOR ISLAMIC WORSHIP

Adhan Call to prayer, issued five times a day.

Bab al-sadir Main entrance.

Imam Spiritual leader.

Iwan Gateway at the entrance to the mosque.

Qibla wall The wall that denotes the direction of Mecca.

Masjid Mosque, or place of prostration.

Mihrab Niche in the *qibla* wall from which the *imam* leads the *salat.*

Minaret The tower from which the *muezzin* issues the *adhan.*

Minbar Raised seat from which the *imam* preaches the *khutba* or sermon on Fridays or special occasions.

Muqarnas Vaults.

Sahn Courtyard or transitional area between entrance and prayer hall.

Salat Prayers, which a devout Muslim says daily at dawn, midday, in the afternoon, at sunset, and in the late evening.

Wuzu or Wudu Place for ritual washing of the hands, elbows, faces, feet, and behind the ears before *salat.*

Zawiya A small prayer area found in a larger building complex.

FOR JEWISH WORSHIP

Aron kodesh The Holy Ark, where the *Torah* is kept.

Bema, or Bimah The raised portion of the sanctuary housing the reading desk and seating for the wardens.

Chazan Cantor, the leader of reading, singing, and chanting in some synagogues.

Chupah The wedding canopy erected on the bema or the floor of the sanctuary, under which the bride, groom, and rabbi stand during the ceremony.

Kippah The skullcap worn by Jews during services, and by some Jews at all times. Also known as a *yarmulkah.*

Mechitsah Curtain separating men from women in the synagogue.

Menorah The nine-branched candelabrum used to hold the candles for the festival of Chanukah. Can also refer to the seven-branched candelabrum used in the Temple.

Mikvah Pool for ritual purification used by adults for conversion, or for purification of people and objects.

Ner tamid Eternal light that hangs over the ark.

Rabbi A recognized person knowledgeable of Jewish law, a teacher.

Rimonim Silver finials for the *Torah* scrolls.

Shabbat or Sabbath The most important day of the week, beginning at sundown on Friday and finishing at sundown on Saturday. It is a day for rest and prayer.

Sukkah A temporary shelter used during the festival of Sukkoth to remind Jews of the journey out of Egypt.

Synagogue Meaning "assembly," it is the most widely accepted term for a Jewish house of public prayer, study, and assembly.

Tallith Prayer shawl. A four-cornered garment with fringes.

Tefillin Leather straps and small leather boxes containing passages from the *Torah,* strapped on the forehead and arms for morning prayers on weekdays.

Temple Sometimes used to refer to a *synagogue,* especially in North America. Also the Temple in Jerusalem, destroyed by the Romans in 70 C.E., of which only the Western Wall remains.

Torah The first five books of the Old Testament, handwritten on parchment scrolls.

Yahrzeit A memorial, or anniversary of a death.

FOR CHRISTIAN (INCLUDING ROMAN CATHOLIC) WORSHIP

Alb The white garment used to cover street clothes.

Altar The place of sacrifice in a church or chapel, which represents the table where Jesus shared the last supper with his disciples.

Ambo The place where the scriptures are proclaimed.

Baptistery The place where baptism takes place, the rite of entry into the Christian church.

Basilica A church to which special privileges are attached. It is a title of honor given to various kinds of churches.

Blessed Sacrament The Eucharist, the Body and Blood of Christ, whether at the mass or reserved in a special place in the church.

Campanile Bell tower.

Cantor One who sings, for example, the responsorial psalm, during the liturgy.

Cassock A nonliturgical, full-length, close-fitting robe for use by priests and other clerics under liturgical vestments; usually black for priests, purple for bishops and other prelates, red for cardinals, and white for the pope.

Catechesis Religious instruction and formation for persons preparing for baptism (catechumens) and for the faithful in various stages of spiritual development.

Cathedra The chair in which the bishop sits.

Cathedral The major church in an archdiocese or diocese. It is the seat of the bishop.

Celebrant The one who presides over the assembly and consecrates the Eucharistic Sacrament.

Celebrant's chair The place where the celebrant sits. It expresses his office of presiding over the assembly and of leading the prayer of those present.

Chalice The cup used to hold the wine.

Chancel See *Sanctuary.*

Chapel An alcove in a large church, or a separate building dedicated to a special use.

Chasuble The vestment worn over the alb by priests, bishops, and the pope when celebrating the mass.

Ciborium A vessel used to hold the consecrated bread for the distribution of communion.

Church Either a building used for worship, or a community of Christians.

Communion The Sacrament of the Lord's Supper, the consecrated bread and wine.

Concelebrants Those priests and bishops who join the celebrant in celebrating the mass.

Crucifix A model of the cross with a figure of Jesus on it.

Dalmatic The vestment a deacon wears over the alb on solemn occasions.

Devotional See *Shrine.*

Eucharist The Sacrament of the Lord's Supper.

Font The receptacle for the water used in baptism.

Gifts The bread and wine to be used in celebration of the Eucharist.

Incense Incense (material used to produce a fragrant odor when burned) is used as a symbol of the church's offering and prayer ascending to God.

Lectern The reading desk from which the Gospel is proclaimed. See also *ambo.* In some churches the Gospel and the sermon are proclaimed from the ambo or pulpit, located on the left side of the sanctu-ary (looking from the congre-gation), whereas the epistle is read from the lectern.

Liturgical colors Colors used in vestments and altar coverings to denote special times in the church. Green is used in ordinary times, red denotes feasts of martyrs or the Holy Spirit, purple denotes penitential times, and white is used for joyful occasions including Christmas, Easter, and some saints' days.

Mass The form of liturgy used in the celebration of the Eucharist.

Ministers of communion Those who assist in the distribution of communion.

Miter A headdress worn at some liturgical functions by bishops, abbots, and, in certain cases, other ecclesiastics.

Monastery An autonomous community house of a religious order, which may or may not be a monastic order. The term is used more specifically to refer to a com-munity house of men or women religious in which they lead a contemplative life separate from the world.

Monstrance A vessel, usually of gold or silver, in which the consecrated host is exposed.

Narthex The foyer or entryway of the church.

Nave The part of the church where the congregation gathers for worship.

Pastor A priest in charge of a parish or congregation. He is responsible for admin-istering the sacraments, instructing the congregation in the doctrine of the church, and providing other services to the people of the parish.

Paten The plate used to hold the bread or Host.

Preacher The person who delivers the sermon, a talk given in church on a spiritual or moral theme.

Prie-dieu A detached prayer desk or kneeler, sometimes with a shelf for books.

Priest An ordained member of the clergy who can administer the sacraments of the Church.

Reader One who is called upon to proclaim the scriptures during the Liturgy of the Word.

Relics The physical remains and effects of saints, which are considered worthy of veneration and may be incorporated into the altar.

Reredos A carved or painted wall behind the altar.

Sacrament An outward sign of something special and holy. Roman Catholics, Orthodox Catholics, Episcopalians, and Anglicans have seven sacraments: Baptism, Eucharist, Confirmation, Holy Orders, Reconciliation, Anointing of the Sick, and Marriage. Most Protestant churches recognize only the first two of these.

Sanctuary The part of the church where the altar is located. In Protestant churches the word is sometimes used to signify the entire worship space.

Shrine Erected to encourage private devotions to a saint, a shrine usually contains a picture, statue, or other religious feature capable of inspiring devotion. Also known as a *devotional.*

Stations of the Cross Also known as the Way of the Cross, this devotion to the suffering of Jesus consists of prayers and meditations on 14 occurrences experienced by Jesus on the way to his crucifixion. Each of these occurrences is represented by a painting or sculpture. The devotion can be done individually or in groups, with one person leading the prayers and moving from cross to cross.

Stole The vestment worn around the neck by all ordained ministers. For priests, bishops, and the pope, it hangs down in front (under the chasuble); deacons wear it over the left shoulder, crossed and fastened at the right side.

Surplice A loose, flowing vestment of white fabric with wide sleeves. For some functions it is interchangeable with an alb.

Tabernacle Place in the church where the Eucharist is reserved.

Vestment The vesture that ministers wear.

BIBLIOGRAPHY AND REFERENCES

Acoustical Society of America. 1985. *Acoustics for Worship Spaces*. New York: Springer-Verlag.

Adler, David, ed. 1999. *Metric Handbook Planning and Design Data*. 2d ed. London: Architectural Press.

Alexander, Christopher. 1977. *A Pattern Language: Towns, Buildings, Construction*. New York: Oxford Univ. Press.

Allen, Edward. 1998. *Fundamentals of Building Construction: Materials and Methods*. 3d ed. New York: John Wiley & Sons.

American Institute of Architects. 2001. *Handbook of Professional Practice*. 13th ed. New York: John Wiley & Sons.

American Society of Heating Refrigeration and Air Conditioning Engineers. 1992. *ASHRAE Standard 55-1992: Thermal Environmental Conditions for Human Occupancy*. Atlanta, Ga.: Ashrae.

———. 2001. *ASHRAE Standard 62-2001: Ventilation for Acceptable Indoor Air Quality*. Atlanta, Ga.: Ashrae.

Architecture and Building Commission of the Roman Catholic Diocese of Albany (N.Y.). 1985. *Maintenance Manual: A Program for Inspection and Seasonal Maintenance of Religious Properties*.

Artemis, B. 1994. *The Art of the Structural Engineer*. London: Artemis Ltd.

Arthur, Paul, and Romedi Passini. 1992. *Wayfinding: People, Signs, and Architecture*. New York: McGraw-Hill.

BAPS (Bochansanwasi Shri Akshar Purushottam Swaminarayan Sanstha). 2003. www.swaminarayan-baps.org.uk.

Barrie, Thomas. 1996. *Spiritual Path, Sacred Place*. Boston: Shambhala Publications.

Beha, Ann. 2001. "Designing for Congregations, a Primer for Architects." *Faith and Form: Journal of the Interfaith Forum on Religion, Art and Architecture* 34 (no. 2).

Bokser, Baruch M. 1985. "Approaching Sacred Space." *Harvard Theological Review* 78, (nos. 3–4): 270–299.

Breffny, Brian de. 1978. *The Synagogue*. New York: Macmillan.

Brundtland Commission. 1987. *Our Common Future: World Commission on Environment and Development*. Geneva, Switzerland: G.H. Brundtland.

Bullock, Orin M., Jr. 1983. *The Restoration Manual: An Illustrated Guide to the Preservation and Restoration of Old Buildings*. New York: Van Nostrand Reinhold.

Buntrock, Dana. 2002. *Japanese Architecture as a Collaborative Process*. London: Spon Press.

Cantacuzino, Sherban. 1989. *Re-Architecture*. New York: Abbeville Press.

Cavanaugh, William J., and Joseph A. Wilkes. 1999. *Architectural Acoustics: Principals and Practice*. New York: John Wiley & Sons.

Charles M. Salter Associates, Inc. 1998. *Acoustics: Architecture, Engineering, The Environment.* San Francisco: William Stout Publishers.

Ching, Francis D. K., and Steven R. Winkel. 2003. *Building Codes Illustrated: A Guide to Understanding the 2000 International Building Code.* New York: John Wiley & Sons.

Church of England. *Calendar of Care.* www.churchcare.co.uk/cal_start.php4.

Coalition on the Environment and Jewish Life (COEJL). www.coejl.org.

Cohen, Diane, and A. Robert Jaeger. 1998. *Sacred Places At Risk.* Philadelphia, Pa.: Partners for Sacred Places.

Cole, W. Owen. 1981. *Five Religions in the Twentieth Century.* London: Hulton Educational Publishers.

Conrad, Richard T., and Steven R. Winkel. 1998. *Design Guide to the 1997 Uniform Building Code.* New York: John Wiley & Sons.

The Construction Industry: Issues and Strategies in Developing Countries. 1984. Washington, D.C.: The World Bank.

Cram, Ralph Adams. 1905. *Impressions of Japanese Architecture.* New York: Baker & Taylor. Reprint, New York: Dover Publications, 1966.

Crosbie, Michael. 1999. *Architecture for the Gods.* Victoria, Australia: Images Publishers.

———. 2003. *Architecture for the Gods II.* Victoria, Australia: Images Publishers.

Davies, J. G. 1982. *Temples, Churches and Mosques.* England: Basil Blackwell.

Debuyst, Frederic. 1968. *Modern Architecture and Christian Celebration.* Ecumenical Studies in Worship 18. Richmond, Va.: John Knox Press.

Diocese of Pittsburgh. 2002. *Working Together for Historic Preservation: An Alternative to Forced Designation.* www.diopitt.org/historic_preservation.htm.

Eliade, Mircea. 1987. *The Sacred and the Profane: The Nature of Religion.* Trans. Willard R. Trask. New York: Harcourt Brace.

Encyclopedia of Architectural Technology. 2002. Chichester, U.K.: Wiley Academic.

Evans, Robin. 1995. *The Projective Cast: Architecture and Its Three Geometries.* Cambridge, Mass.: MIT Press.

Feilden, Bernard M. 2003. *The Conservation of Historic Buildings.* 3d ed. London: Architectural Press.

Fitch, James Marston. 1982. *Curatorial Management of the Built World.* New York: McGraw-Hill.

The Four Noble Truths. See, for example, www.thebigview.com/buddhism/fourtruths.html.

Fujiki, Takao. 1997. *Religious Facilities: New Concepts in Architecture and Design.* Tokyo: Meisei Publishers.

The Gemara. www.coejl.org.

Giles, Richard. 2000. *Repitching the Tent.* Collegeville, Minn.: Liturgical Press.

Goldsmith, Selwyn. 1967. *Designing for the Disabled.* London: RIBA Publications.

Hammond, Peter. 1961. *Liturgy and Architecture.* New York: Columbia Univ. Press.

Heathote, Edwin, and Iona Spens. 1997. *Church Builders of the Twentieth Century.* New York: John Wiley & Sons.

Hogue, Dean R., Charles Zech, Patrick McNamara, and Michael J. Donohue. 1996. *Money Matters: Personal Giving in American Churches.* Louisville, Ky.: Westminster John Knox Press.

Holod, Renata, and Hasan-Uddin Khan. 1997. *The Contemporary Mosque.* New York: Rizzoli.

Humphrey, Caroline, and Piers Vitebsky. 1997. *Sacred Architecture.* Boston, Mass.: Little, Brown.

Japan Access. *Architecture: A Harmonious Coexistence of Tradition and Innovation.* www.japan-emb.org.sg/JapanAccess/kenchiku.htm.

Jeavons, Thomas H., and Rebekah Burch Basinger. 2000. *Growing Givers' Hearts: The Ministry of Fundraising.* San Francisco: Jossey-Bass.

Jencks, Charles. 1977. *The Language of Postmodern Architecture.* New York: Rizzoli.

Kaufman, David. 1999. *Shul with a Pool: The "Synagogue-Center" in American Jewish History.* Brandeis Series in American Jewish History, Culture, and Life. Hanover, N.H.: Press of New England.

Kavanagh, Aidan. 1978. *The Shape of Baptism: The Rite of Christian Initiation.* New York: Pueblo Publishing.

Khalidi, Omar. 2000. *Contemporary American Religion.* Vol. 2. New York: Macmillan Reference.

Kramrisch, Stella. 1946. *The Hindu Temple.* Calcutta, India: Univ. of Calcutta.

The Law of Lo Tash'chit. www.coejl.org/learn/je_berman.shtml.

Le Corbusier. 1957. *The Chapel at Ronchamp.* New York: Frederick A. Praeger.

"Lighting for Houses of Worship." 1991. Illuminating Engineering Society of North America (IESNA). New York: IESNA, RP-25.

Lynch, Kevin, and Gary Hack. 1990. *Site Planning.* 3d ed. Cambridge, Mass.: MIT Press.

Macdonald, Susan, ed. 2001. *Preserving Post-War Heritage: The Care and Conservation of Mid-Twentieth Century Architecture.* Shaftsbury, Dorset, U.K.: Donhead Publishing for English Heritage.

Matics, K. I. 1992. *Introduction to the Thai Temple.* Bangkok: White Lotus Co.

Mauck, Marchita. 1990. *Shaping a House for the Church.* Chicago: Liturgy Training Publications.

———. 1995. *Places for Worship: A Guide to Building and Renovating.* Collegeville, Minn.: Liturgical Press.

McCormick, Susan, and Steve Swanson. 2000. "A Continuing Legacy: The Westlake Bible Church." *Faith and Form* 33 (no. 3).

Meek, H. A. 1995. *The Synagogue.* London: Phaidon Press.

Metcalf, Barbara Daly, ed. 1996. *Making Muslim Space in North America and Europe.* Berkeley: University of California Press.

Michell, George. 1988. *The Hindu Temple.* Chicago: Univ. of Chicago Press.

Millet, Marietta S. 1996. *Light Revealing Architecture.* New York: Van Nostrand Reinhold.

Mills, Edward D. 1956. *The Modern Church.* New York: Praeger.

National Conference of Catholic Bishops/United States Catholic Conference, Committee on the Liturgy. 2000a. *Built of Living Stones: Art, Architecture and Worship.* www.nccbuscc.org/liturgy/livingstones.htm.

———. 2000b. *The 2000 Revision of the Institutio Generalis Missalis Romani.* www.usccb.org/liturgy/current/revmissalisromanien.htm.

National Fire Protection Association. 2001. *National Electrical Code 2002.* Albany, N.Y.: Delmar Publishers.

National Trust for Historic Preservation, North Dakota Office. 2002. www.nthp.org/state_and_local/activities/2002/northdakota.html.

Nishi, Kazuo, and Kazuo Hozumi. 1996. *What Is Japanese Architecture?* New York: Kodansha International.

Parent, Mary Neighbor. 1985. *The Roof in Japanese Buddhist Architecture.* New York: Weatherhill.

Passini, Romedi. 1992. *Wayfinding in Architecture.* New York: John Wiley & Sons.

Pearce, David. 1989. *Conservation Today.* London: Routledge.

Pugin, Augustus Welby. 1841. *The True Principles of Pointed or Christian Architecture.* London: John Weale.

Rudin, Andrew. 1990. *A Primer on Maintenance: Ten Steps to Good Stewardship.* Melrose Park, Pa.: Interfaith Coalition on Energy.

Schwarz, Rudolf. 1958. *The Church Incarnate: The Sacred Function of Christian Architecture.* Trans. Cynthia Harris. Chicago: Regnery Press.

Serageldin, Ismail. 1996. *Architecture of the Contemporary Mosque.* London: Academy Editions.

Shopsin, William C. 1986. *Restoring Old Buildings for Contemporary Uses: An American Sourcebook for Architects and Preservationists.* New York: Whitney Library of Design.

Snyder, Mark, and Gil Clary. 1991. "A Functional Analysis of Volunteerism." In M. S. Clark, ed., *Review of Personality and Social Psychology.* Thousand Oaks, Calif.: Sage Publications.

Soloveitchik, Rabbi Joseph, Rabbi Samson Raphael Hirsch, and Meir Loeb Ben Jehiel Michael. www.coejl.org.

Sovick, E. A. 1973. *Architecture for Worship.* Minneapolis, Minn.: Angsburg Publishing.

Steele, James, and Ismail Seralgeldin. 1996. *The Architecture of the Contemporary Mosque.* New York: John Wiley & Sons.

Stephens, Rev. Rod. 2001. Presentation at Catholic Worship Conference, Los Angeles (author's notes).

Suzuki, Kakichi. 1980. *Early Buddhist Architecture in Japan.* Tokyo: Kodansha International and Shibundo.

Tyler, Norman. 1999. *Historic Preservation: Introduction to Its History, Principles, and Practice.* 2d ed. New York: W. W. Norton.

U.S. Conference of Catholic Bishops. 1999. *Glossary of Church Terms,* Washington, D.C.: Office of Communications United States Conference of Catholic Bishops.

U.S. Department of the Interior, National Park Service, Preservation Assistance Division. 1976. *The Secretary of the Interior's Guidelines for Rehabilitation and Guidelines for Rehabilitating Historic Buildings.* Washington, D.C. (rev. 1983 and 1990).

U.S. Green Building Council. *LEED-NC Reference Guide.* www.usgbc.org/ LEED/Online_Reference_Guide.asp.

Vergara, Camilo Jose. 2003. "The Storefront Churches of South Los Angeles." *Los Angeles Times,* 12 January.

von Simson, Otto. 1988. *The Gothic Cathedral.* Princeton, N.J.: Princeton Univ. Pres..

Vosko, Rev. Richard S. 1988. Seminar on designing the worship space of the future, Leo A Daly, Los Angeles (author's notes).

Wetherill, Ewart A. 1995. *Concise Encyclopedia of Preaching.* William H. Willimon and Richard Lischer, eds. Westminster, U.K.: John Knox Press.

Wetherill, Ewart A. 1996. "Acoustics for Worship." *The American Organist,* August.

———. 1997. "Hidden Sounds." *American Guild of Organists,* April.

White, James F., and Susan J. White. 1988. *Church Architecture: Building and Renovating for Christian Worship.* Nashville, Tenn.: Abingdon Press.

Wigoder, Geoffrey. 1986. *The Story of the Synagogue.* New York: Harper & Row.

Yun, Venerable Master Hsing. *Buddhism and Architecture.* Building Connections, pamphlet no. 34. www.blia.org/english/publications/booklet/pages/34.html

INDEX

INDEX